JOURNEYS WITH SOUL

*Adventures and Cures
That Came True*

JOHN HERLIHY

Journeys with Soul

Adventures and Cures
That Came True

SOPHIA PERENNIS

SAN RAFAEL, CA

First published in the USA
by Sophia Perennis
© John Herlihy 2008

Series editor: James R. Wetmore

For information, address:
Sophia Perennis, P.O. Box 151011
San Rafael, CA 94915
sophiaperennis.com

Library of Congress Cataloging-in-Publication Data

Herlihy, John.
Journeys with soul: adventures and cures
that came true / by John Herlihy.—1st ed.

p. cm.
ISBN 978-1-59731-090-1 (pbk: alk. paper)
1. Religions. 2. Spiritual life. 3. Spirituality.
4. Spiritual healing. 5. Healing—Religious aspects. I. Title.
BL80.3.H48 2008
200.9—dc22   2008042627

CONTENTS

Dedication

PREFACE

THE GREAT STONE FACE

When will I come and see the face of God?
(Psalm 42:3)

JOURNEYING BEGINS in the infancy of childhood imagination. Children happily build castles in the sand and fly through the air on imaginary magic carpets with all the ease of clouds moving through the heavens. A bouncing ball can become a source of wonder and a firefly illuminating the darkness of a summer night contains all the mystery of the universe with its flashing, phosphorescent glow. They carry in their pockets dried autumn leaves, shining pebbles, and perhaps a rabbit's foot as the valuables on offer by the world. They delight in the sight of a farmer's scarecrow and their hearts feel terror at the face of a pumpkin illuminated by well-placed candles in its eyes, nose, and mouth. Their flights of fantasy and their incredible sympathies with the unseen specters of their imagination lay waste to all the counterfeit ambitions of humanity and pull away the false mask of the world.

Regrettably, we do not take with us from our youth the sense of mystery and wonder that enlivens the fleeting hours of childhood with their innocent perceptions. To make matters worse, this is not an era in which legends are born, and the legends that we have preserved from antiquity no longer thrill us with their mysterious tales of dragons, knights, and vanishing cities. The Golden Fleece has lost its luster and the silvery waters of the Nile and the Ganges have turned an inglorious muddy brown that belie the glorious ancestry of these sacred rivers. The Arc of the Covenant and Holy Grail are vestiges of a lost era whose quest does not speak directly to the modern soul. Atlantis now lies at the bottom of the sea as a myth that was never made true and the ghosts of Minchu Pichu are but airy clouds passing through the ancient ruins of a lost civilization without care or interest for the ruins below. Is there still a road to Damascus to stir the worldly-wise cauldron of our hearts or set our souls in tune with the vibration of those celestial harmonies, a road whose journey has the power to reduce our pretensions to ashes and lend wings to our holy desires? Is there not some thimble still ample enough to preserve the paucity of our sacred desires as a legacy for future generations, who will need to enter the inner sanctum of their own temples to unveil the secrets of the ancients and who will need guidance concerning the whereabouts of their own holy of holies?

As a child, I turned to books to extend my horizons and take me into worlds that I couldn't go on my own. I wanted nothing more than to charge boldly into the promise of the unknown, across savage seas, deep into the jungle where Tarzan roamed freely with the animals. Fairy tales held a special delight because they made the improbable believable and contained within their simple similitudes the secrets of the abiding truths that children instinctively value. Between a book's covers and embedded within the words strewn across the page like talisman's of the imagination lay the winter garden of the selfish giant, the encaged bird that sang from the heart to gain its freedom. The lost city of Shangri-la reappeared from the mists of time, and the hidden treasures of King Solomon's mines would forever remain beyond the reach of avaricious humanity. I knew that one day I would venture forth in search of the answer to a question that lay just below the surface of my consciousness, a question that would need answering if I were ever to resolve the enigma that lay reflected within the well of my imagination.

Within each of us, there is a sacred center—call it a well, a bridge, and a hidden cave—that harbors the secret of one's inborn destiny, the well to view the reflection of heaven, the bridge to cross between visible and invisible worlds, and the cave to meditate upon and internalize the knowledge of the world as the wisdom of the ages. I remember an experience from childhood that had a lasting impression on my native, childhood mind that may well have been the catalyst that put me inside the bottle of my fertile imagination and cast me adrift across the tumultuous sea of life in search of the Holy Grail, the source of some inner Nile, the lost tribe of Israel or the enchanted garden where myth becomes a narrative for truth and the illusions of the world become the signposts of a higher reality.

When we were children, even though the family didn't have much money, my parents made every effort to bring us to places of natural beauty within reach of our home just outside of Boston as a way to escape the dull routine of everyday life. Every summer, the family of seven would pile into the old broken down ranch wagon, distinctive enough with its wooden-framed sides, to make our way up into the White Mountains for our little jaunt into the wilds of New Hampshire. For us children, these vacation trips had the makings of an adventure that would lead us to the edge of frenzy and set our hearts on fire. My parents had meticulously set aside enough money during the wintertime for these summer excursions and therefore had enough money to afford a couple of nights in one of the local motels featured along the country roadside. We walked the gorge at Franconia Notch and sat in canoes on one of the lakes in the shadow of the White Mountains, although why they were called "white" was never resolved in my childish mind.

I mustn't have been more than six or seven years old at an age when the mind is ripe for making distinct impressions that endure, like a seal in hot wax, and that forever leave behind their indelible mark. My mother sent my fantasy aground on a shore of expectation with the promise that we were about to see "the old man of the mountain". It set my heart afire and I could think of nothing else, imagining to myself what it could possibly mean. "Who is the old man of the mountain," I asked my mother, and she replied, "it is a great stone face that will come alive and smile down upon those who believe."

It was late in the day. The sun was going down, casting the mountains on the left side of the road in silhouette against a bountiful summer sunset, ablaze with a rainbow of fiery colors. It was the perfect moment to witness the magic of an illusion, when my mother whispered reverently that the "old man" was about to come into view. "Look to the side of that mountain crag over there," she intoned reverently, "and you will see his noble face." True to her promise, after looking so hard that my eyes hurt, the grand countenance of what appeared to be an "old man" hung in profile at the edge of one of the protruding cliffs. Carved within the rough stones as though by the hand of the Divinity, it was suddenly relatively easy to discern the profile of the grand patriarch with a flowing mane of hair perched on the side of the cliff and overlooking a vast landscape. This was obviously the work of Nature formed on the precipice of a mountain by some immense rocks which were thrown together and weathered in such a way that, when viewed from a particular angle and at the proper distance, bore the uncanny features of a human face.

It was our happy lot to see this illusion a number of times in our travels through the White Mountains over several summers, and I never tired of gazing upon that mysterious visage whose tranquil gaze looked contentedly out across the broad expanse of the mountains and valleys clear to the horizon, as though all the world were at the mercy of his glance. I remember thinking in my childish imagination how much I wished that the face of the old man would turn its head and cast its benevolent smile down upon my expectant heart, but I soon realized it was not meant to be and rested content with the sublime profile of the man whose image seemed to cast its gaze from the depths of a deep warm heart, a heart that embraced all of mankind with its affections and still had room for more. "One day you may see the full face of the old man," my mother chided, "so you better make sure you are ready to meet his gaze."

It was a prophecy that would take root in my imagination to grow into a desire to search the world for the benevolent smile of the old man in every cloud, rock, and ragged hilltop. Would I be man enough to meet his gaze with equanimity and insight? My sensibility was such that in gazing at the horizon of my own world, I felt impelled to search for the mythical land of beyond, to explore every cave, to cross every bridge, to look deep down into every well for a reflection of that mysterious face that would set my heart free with the serene gaze of its divinity and benevolent smile close at hand to show me the way.

In this particular volume, we have gathered together a number of fugitive tales of unexpected encounters and cures that might have remained objects of fantasy if they had not slipped through the envelope of time and come true. Certainly with reference to people and places, I never envisioned in my wildest childhood dreams that I would find solitude and spiritual in-dwelling in the monasteries of Mount Athos or experience the supreme silence of an ancient Buddhist monastery amid the arid mountains of Ladakh, mountains that in the drama of their immensity lay like sleeping behemoths, under the roof of Heaven and in a world in which time and all its affairs are excluded from this rarefied setting. In a world of false promises and faded hopes, who could have predicted that I would find friendship and love not from the near shores of my own country, but in the wild landscape of a tribal culture in Northern Pakistan where a Pathan family would take me into the arms of its warm embrace and sit me down at the hearth of their sacred sympathies.

In an era of undiagnosed diseases that escape the scrutiny of modern medical inquiry and chronic illness with no hope for recovery, blessed is the person who can seek out and find, amid the palm groves of the Keralan countryside and in a village kampong in the jungles of Malaysia, not only the promise of a cure, but its living reality, a cure that embodies the traditional knowledge and ancient wisdoms that originate in sacred scripture and that still uses those scriptures as a means of recovery and well being. Finally, as the alpha of the earthly journey and the omega of the spiritual quest, I had the good fortune to embody all my spiritual hopes and aspirations in the physical journey to Medinah and Makkah, a pilgrimage that brought me not only to the beloved tomb of the Prophet Mohammed, upon him blessings and peace, but also to the very center of Islam, the focal point of billions of hearts and the point of departure heavenward on our journey of spiritual ascent.

In my wayward dreams of travel, I wanted to ply through oceans and trek through deserts scooping up the grand world of nature into my arms for safekeeping like the fairy-tale giants of my story books. The Pacific, the Gobi, and the Himalayas all inspired me with their grandeur, their majesty and their ineffable mystery of magnitude and presence, portending a secret that I wanted to explore and contain within myself as an experience that once achieved no one could take away. Travel was an escape into the ancient history of humanity and the events they lived through as evidence to their success and failure. In my imagination during history class, I had roamed the Roman Forum, climbed the Greek Acropolis, and stood in awe at the gates of Thermopylae; but was never able to capture their essence or true meaning from the dusty pages of my school primer. At best, I was left with a hollow feeling that could not be filled through pictures and words until I saw these things in person and filled my mind, heart, and soul with their message of the former grandeur of now vanished worlds.

Although the journeys described in this volume cut across a number of diverse counties including India, Malaysia, Pakistan and Saudi Arabia, and while they represent a variety of experiences, they have one thing in common that binds them together in the spirit in which they were written, namely SOUL. If I could put it another way, it is as if I had stepped inside a bottle like a message encased in glass to be sent off by some invisible hand across the broad expanse of the vast ocean in readiness for the vicissitudes that may come my way; but in anticipation of some unique encounter or cure that may break open the encasement of the message to reveal the inner wonders of an experience come true. Whether visiting the mountainous regions of the Karakorum in Northern Pakistan or making the ritual circumambulation around the sanctified ground of the Kaaba within the Grand Mosque at Makkah, one becomes a pilgrim soul in search of the holy land within one's own being. Through a variety of sacred encounters that touch the body, mind, and heart with the wand of spirituality and well-being, I trekked through the deserts of Arabia and the jungles of the Far East to meet up with unique people in exotic places that have the power to touch the pilgrim soul in us all.

In my quest for travel that had meaning and journeys that would broaden my horizons, I was following a call that must be obeyed, like the mystic draw of the lodestone when its magnetic potency summons iron. I hoped to find the open face of the "old man" that is inscribed in all the wonders of Nature, from the majestic mountain ranges where I originally saw the great stone face in profile, to the grand deserts of the earth with their parch, ascetic quality and their stark message of the sacred woven into the face of its undulating sands. Would I have to visit the great Sphinx in order to hear in person the whisper of its eternal sigh? Would I ultimately discover the benevolent face of the old man amid the rocks and boulders thrown down by the Divinity on some distant mountain cliff? The answer lies somewhere between the illusions of the world and the promises of a reality that weaves its expression of unity into the golden thread of life's tapestry, in order to disclose the mystery we have been in search of all along, but never had the presence of mind to witness firsthand: "Wherever you turn, there is the Face of God." (Quran 2:115)

1

IN THE SHADOW
OF MOUNT ATHOS

ALONE AND ON FOOT IN AN
ANCIENT MEDIEVAL LAND

NEARLY 40 years have now passed since one sunny, summer morning in Northern Greece when I eagerly climbed into a small fishing boat on my way to visit the sacred enclave of Mount Athos. As I trace my own footprints back into the ever receding and distant past before they completely disappear, I recall that the sunlight passed through the dry clarity of the air with a knife-like sharpness unique to the Mediterranean area. The sea was wild in the wind; the light reflected off the water with an insistence that was blinding. Some unknown impulse from deep within had brought me to that point, in spite of myself. Perhaps it was the same force that brought color to the sky, reflected light in the water, and entered my mind through the sensors of my youthful vision.

The rugged peninsula is celebrated as a monastic enclosure with twenty ancient monasteries tucked into the cliffs on the coast of the Aegean or perched like soaring eagles on top of a rocky promontory overlooking the landscape below. These monastic sanctuaries of meditation and spiritual rigor date back a thousand years where history and arcane accounts of the area have receded into the darkness of the past and can no longer be reclaimed. I cannot hide the fact that I was forty years younger in my early 20s back in the late 60s when the youth of the time were called "flower children" and the era itself was called the "beat generation" who seemed to follow

some inner drum that not everyone was privy to. What I was looking for then was what I am still looking for now, still searching, still
seeking for the "eye of certainty" that leaves no doubt and that
makes no mistakes, the eye of wisdom and enlightenment that leads
like a torch along the way to one's chosen destination. Over the
years, I have noticed that I sometimes hear an inner voice that
makes no audible sound but that tells me what I need to know. If
fact, we all have such a voice; whether we listen to it and trust its
inner guidance is another question. Fortunately, I have had the
good sense to listen to what my intuitions tell me, a tendency that I
attribute to the no-nonsense attitude my mother had toward life
and its mysteries.

I had been living and working as an English teacher in Continen-
tal Europe for several years gaining what working experience I
could as a young, naïve, and inexperienced professional. One benefit of teaching is that it offered me long leisurely summers off with
plenty of free time and ample places to visit within the historic and
carefree Europe of that era. I was young and adventurous and took
it upon myself to drive up and down the length and breadth of the
Continent, enchanted with the ease with which I floated across borders into strange lands and ancient realms that I had only read
about in history books. I was intrigued by the mystery and tension
of border crossings, undoubtedly learned from watching 1940s film
noir movies, where one had to prove one's identity and pass inspection by the border officials. I visited the lush vineyards in France
and took in the unique island of Mont St. Michele with the amazing
rush of its tidal waters. I roamed the rugged coastline of Brittany
and shivered in its frigid Atlantic waters. The wine tasting chateaus
of the Loire Valley and the Bier Gardens of Bavaria held little attrac-
tion for me, having about as much substance and allure as the
frothy suds floating across the surface of the dark brew on offer in
those dark and musty beer cellars so full of shallow camaraderie
and false cheer.

I had been living in Europe for a year and had the summer free to
explore places of my own choosing. A chance encounter with a fellow traveler the summer of '68 brought the alluring name of Athos
to my ears. I soon found out that Athos was none other than the

holy mountain of Athos, a lonely and secluded wilderness that still existed in the upper reaches of Northern Greece with the great mountain chain of Athos running down the length of the peninsula like the spine of the land's rugged body.[1] It is in fact a well preserved holy monastic enclosure that dates back beyond the Middle Ages into the Dark Ages of Europe, a peninsula in Northern Greece that has survived the onslaught of natural storms, the ravages of war and the turmoil of political conflict down through the ages. The Holy Mountain has been the center of Orthodox Christian monasticism for the past millennium. Its recorded history spans the millennium, while apocryphal legend introduces Mary, the mother of Jesus, to the area much earlier than that. In engravings of the Mount, the monks display the image of the Holy Virgin high above the crest of Athos as its celestial patroness and protectress.

According to the apocryphal account, the ship she was traveling on with St. John the Evangelist was blown off course arriving in sight of the wooded mountain ridge. The Virgin gazed at the high peak, saying: "This mountain is holy ground. Let it now be my portion. Here let me remain."[2] The first clear account of the beginnings of monastic life on Athos commences with the story of the 8/9th-century monk, St. Peter the Athonite, who spent fifty years in a cave which still exists at the edge of the cliff near the Great Lavra monastery. St. Peter is a prime example of a solitary monk in combat against hostile forces. The next step was the development of a *lavra* or colony of hermits, founded by St. Euthymios of Salonica, a spiritual guide born in 823 who attracted others by his personality and the force of his ascetic reputation resulting in a small colony of ascetics.

By the end of the ninth century, many hermits had gathered in the area and followed a monk named Andreas, the first hesychast[3]

---

1. "Mount Athos" is the name of the peak which rises 2,033 meters out of the sea at the southernmost point of the northernmost peninsula of Halkidiki in Macedonia, Greece. The entire peninsula is referred to as Athos; officially, however, its Greek name is *Aghion Oros*: the Holy Mountain.

2. Philip Sherrard, *Athos the Holy Mountain* (Woodstock, NY: The Overlook Press, 1982), p12.

3. Hesychasm, meaning stillness, rest, quiet, silence, is a tradition of prayer in Eastern Orthodox Christianity practiced by the hesychast.

who held what later became the important position of *protos* or primate of Athos. The Great Lavra itself was founded in the middle of the tenth century by St. Athanasios. Born in Trebizon, a Turkish town on the Black Sea of wealthy parents, he was brought up in Constantinople where he came to know Nikephoros Phokas, a Byzantine general who eventually became emperor and was known as the "White Death of the Saracens" because he drove them out of the Western Mediterranean. It was the plunder of this campaign that went toward the building of the Great Lavra. History bears out the fact that the Virgin must truly be a fervid protectress of the sacred enclosure. Basil I issued an imperial charter to the monks in AD 883 that prevented his military from interfering with the rites and devotional practices of the monks on the holy mountain. An edict by Emperor Constantine issued in the year AD 1060 forbade all females from entering the peninsula, including females of all species of animals except cats that apparently help control the rat population. Curiously, during the Second World War, Hitler never invaded the area and left the monks to themselves.

When I heard that visitors could go there under certain conditions after having obtained the appropriate documents, I knew in my heart that I wanted to go there; I had to go there. This was an opportunity that I could not pass up, my first stop on the road to the vanishing lands passing out of sight beyond the edge of memory, beyond the horizon of my world and beyond the hem of the known world. First, I had to fulfill the obligations of an abiding bureaucracy. This was the era of the Regime of the Colonels, a military junta established in Greece in 1967. The military government of that time wanted to maintain control over who came and went to such places as Athos, a remote enclave of austerity and devotional practices by the reclusive monks, but they were not completely beyond the long arm of the government who controlled all those who entered the peninsula. I made my way to the American Consulate in Thessaloniki where I needed to secure a letter of permission from the US authorities. In those days, US Consulates were breezy villas surrounded by gardens and palm trees rather than military blockades with traffic busters. I remember a pleasant and helpful first officer who took an interest in my inquiry after I told him I was a high school teacher trying to enrich my summer holidays by going to a place like Athos that I could tell my students about. He gave me a quizzical smile, but signed and stamped my letter with an official seal after telling me apologetically that the monks feared vagrants and thieves invading the serenity of the area with their evil intentions.

At the Ministry of Foreign Affairs, a severe-looking women, and undoubtedly very unhappy one I remember thinking at the time, sat behind an oversized wooden desk in an otherwise empty room, but for the adornment of a few unrecognizable flags. She ordered me to sit down in a chair in front of the desk as if I were a prisoner in the dock awaiting sentencing. An overhead fan stirred the stagnant air and cast ominous moving shadows across the desk and wooden floor. I was young and inexperienced, and as I sat there looking at her, my heart rose up somewhere near my throat as she examined my documents. Finally, her penetrating eyes landed on my solemn, youthful face like a probing dart as my heart beat wildly, although I knew not why exactly, except that I had heard fearsome stories about the Colonels and their ways with the local population stirring an undercurrent of resentment and anger among the carefree and fun-loving Greeks.

"Why you go Athos," she asked a little too loudly, as though wanting to make an unpleasant accusation of some kind.

"I have read about the thousand year old monasteries on the peninsula and would like to visit them," I stammered, attempting to sound like a budding history buff worthy of the name. "I want to spend my time usefully here in Greece and see its culture and history." I had sense enough to realize that she would not understand that my heart was on fire and my soul was in search of something that I myself could not identify, but was willing to look for all the same.

"Nothing useful for Athos," she snorted, adding "nothing but bedbugs and old monks." She signaled for an aid with a flourish of careless fingers. "If that what you want, that what you get." With a few abrupt hand signals, she had the necessary letter of introduction drawn up which she ceremoniously signed and sealed with an official stamp. "Much luck," she finally said, handing over the letter to me with the hint of a smile creasing her sad face. I bowed slightly and thank her for facilitating my visit to the holy mountain.

I made my way expectantly to the small fishing village called Oranopoulos, which means the city of Heaven, the last stop-off point before entering the secluded area where the monks lived in their remote monasteries. As I approached the town, I took note that the landscape was becoming increasingly more mountainous, rough and inaccessible. Twenty miles before the village, the road abruptly ended. My little Fiat 500 complained, but managed to struggle down the sinuous path to this last bastion of modern civilization. I passed by other smaller villages or clusters of huts snuggled next to the emerging foothills. In the narrow fields within the valleys, I took note of entire families at work, the children frolicking around the legs of the oxen and work horses, or alternatively teasing and chasing the goats feeding on the grass nearby. The glistening Aegean Sea lay off to my right, noble waters that served as the birthplace of two ancient civilizations[1] and later witnessed the rise of the city-states of Athens and Sparta. On this day, with a couple of old men weaving fishing nets by the shore, the waters shone with all the pristine purity and innocence of an age-old Golden Era resurrected once again in a flashback of time to strike my imagination as if by some magic wand.

It didn't take long to arrange for a fishing boat that would take me to a small port of entry called Dafni along the coast of the peninsula. From there I made my way on foot to the central village of Karyes, said to have been built by Constantine the Great. Situated in a forest of walnut and hazel in the middle of the peninsula, this village represents the administrative center of the area at an altitude of 370 meters and home to the representatives of the monasteries. In a small unpretentious building off the main square, I presented my "letter of introduction" to one of the officials presiding within the building. With no Greek of my part and little English on his, there wasn't much of a ceremony; yet his inquiring smile was welcoming and with graceful hand gestures and one or two words of English, he opened my way to visit and explore anywhere along the length of

---

1. The Minoans of Crete and the Mycenean civilization of the Peleponnese, site of the original democracies. Plato described the Greeks living around the Aegean "like frogs around a pond".

the peninsula. I understood that I would be welcomed to stay at any of the monasteries and would be taken care of from the time of my arrival to departure. I thanked him and made my way out into the brilliant sunlight.

* * *

As I look back in time through the prism of my nostalgic imagination, I marvel at my willingness—indeed my boldness—to embrace the exotic and the unknown, as though these were challenges of my inexperienced soul that I needed to overcome, not to prove anything to myself; but rather to rise above myself and the limits that my nature and condition in life had allotted me. I remember feeling the ominous quality of apprehension and vague regret as I made my solitary way down a pathway into the forested mountains beyond the edge of the settlement. Once inside the stately limbs of those grand trees towering high above me, loneliness crept over me that felt like a cloak a size too small. They say that one can feel a sense of powerful loneliness in a crowd of strangers; however, nothing can quite compare to the feeling of supreme solitude amid a forest of trees with only the solitary path leading forward to some unknown destination tracing a message of purpose and promise amid these ancient hills. I had been told that it was impossible to get lost if that was any comfort. The sea coast was not far off to my right; in fact I could hear the resounding sound of the surf recreating in my mind the tumult of the Aegean not far away. The path itself was like a corded necklace with the 1,000 year old monasteries strung along the way like cultured pearls inviting the pilgrim wanderer to partake of their mystery and fascination.

As I made my way along the narrow pathway through the forest, I began to shed my latent fears and absorb the wild ambiance these stately trees created as they cast their subtle spell across the face of the peninsula. The heart of the forest inspires reverence and awe. As in a cathedral, there is something that speaks directly to the inner soul. It radiates its character of primeval wilderness almost as a physical presence and conveys its feeling of wild inviolability to all who enter its confines. One walks softly and subdued within the general calm of its sublime depths, as if in some vast hall that has been pervaded by the deepest sanctities and solemnities given evidence within Nature. Every tree seems to have a spiritual quality; every branch and leaf reaches upward towards the heavens as if upholding the sky with their praise of God. These age old patriarchs never cease their worship and praise, but are forever conscious of the Divinity within the confines of their own sacred nature. Would that we could emulate the tree and exhibit the same unfailing integrity and fortitude in our own nature in today's modern, fast-paced world?

Trees are the silent sentinels of the earth. People are born, live and die, but trees watch over the earth through the millennia and contribute to the harmonies of the natural order with their calm and stately repose. Cultures may fade into oblivion and entire civilizations may crumble and die without disturbing their magnificent nobility and self containment. Barring accidents or the machinations of humankind, they give every appearance of being immortal. In order to die a natural death, a tree needs an abundance of time and nature holds no surprises for them that they cannot bear. Perhaps that is why the wanton destruction of the great forests of the world seems so evil and so unnatural. Some trees were in their prime when Christ walked the earth. No other thing in nature has looked down upon the passing of the centuries with such detachment as these regal monarchs of the great primeval forests. The forests themselves are a remarkable study in self containment and splendor. The silence of a forest can be deafening; countless trees are gathered together as a forest unity in mute splendor, like a great, collective spirit.

In walking through the grandeur of a forest wood, I felt myself shedding the turmoil of my days and observing the stately pines with the natural eye of the chip monk and the owl. The residue of some melancholy heartbreak has come and gone; the frustration and failure of my routine efforts no longer find firm ground; the anger, jealousy and other petty miseries that punctuate the days of a life disappear with some passing wind. The rays of light find their way through the branches and leaves to cast their warm glow onto the forest floor like a torch from heaven. Their photons have passed millions of miles to make their presence felt within the human mind. The trees of the forest stand tall and lend something of their calm, ennobling grace. Through their act of giving, they become a part of me and I become a part of them, a living, walking, breathing tree, a pillar of strength, standing tall, rooted to the earth, but immortal because of a vision they convey that leads far above along the pathways to the stars.

In pursuit of the quest to make my way on foot across the peninsula visiting whatever monasteries I came across, I made my way with determination through this primeval wood. The paths that link the monasteries were actually a main feature of the area. In those days, the paths were for the monks as well as the random visitors such as myself. Many of them were beautifully cobbled, clean and fairly well maintained. Some were signposted, stating the number of kilometers to the next destination or the number of walking hours. There were even wayside fountains or drinking places, often nearby some wayside shrine. Nowadays, Athos is full of roads linking monasteries. What this form of modernization has robbed from the experience is the true sense of pilgrimage while on a spiritual quest that comes from making one's way on foot. I was not simply on a mission to get to one shrine or another, nor to visit these ancient monasteries as objects of curiosity. This sacred adventure was a deliberate attempt to give myself up to the conditions of the journey itself rather than arrival at some ultimate destination, not in the habitual conditions of comfort and safety that we are usually accustomed to as tourists and modern-day travelers. Subconsciously, I wanted to break from this kind of servitude and set out on my quest into the unknown, not only on a journey into the interior of the forest and the forbidden sanctum of the peninsula, but on a journey into the center of the self as a true seeker of experience that harbors within its folds a revelation. Within this perspective, walking on one's own two feet became an essential part of the experience.

There is nothing so honest and effortful as the experience of making tracks in the earth, traversing great distances, and arriving at some unique destination on one's own steam, especially in this day of jet age travel and business class convenience when the world passes us by and we take no notice of it. On such a journey, one's own feet actually tread the earth from which we are made. The five senses are alive to the revealing messages of nature, marveling at the beauty of the natural forest, the sound of the insects and birds, the bold shafts of light that filter their elegant rays through the density of the forest like swords of light, the timeless vistas of the surrounding sea with its generous display of color and light. The inner meaning of an experience becomes made up of cells in a thriving honeycomb of wonder and imagination, creating an inner edifice that becomes a permanent remembrance of something deeply felt that has touched the membrane of a deeper self, awakening us from the deadening and soporific routines of our day that entrench us within the crude sensations of the outer world only, rather than lifting us up and away through the wisdom of higher level seeing, listening, tasting, smelling and touching or being touched by that sacred mystery which brings us into our own true selves and reveals the best of our true nature. One of the monks has written on the power of perception in using the physical senses for something more than ordinary seeing, smelling and listening to the world around us.

> I say not that man (Adam) should not have used his senses, for not in vain was he clothed in the body; but I say that he should not have dissipated himself in sensory things. He should not, abandoning intelligible beauty, have fastened upon sensory things.... Yet this is what he did. And because he used the senses wrongly, and marveled at sensory beauty, thinking its fruit beautiful to the sight, and good to taste, and eating of it, he abandoned the enjoyment of intelligible things. Therefore the just Judge, judging him unworthy of what he scorned, of, that is, the contemplation of God and of all beings, deprived him of Himself and of immaterial realities, and made darkness His hidden place."[1]

Of course, we are humans struggling to come to terms with higher consciousness within the modern setting and not birds in

---

1. From "The Theoretikon of the Blessed Theodore", in the *Philokalia* (Athens 1893), quoted in *The Holy Mountain of Athos*, op. cit., p151.

flight or butterflies alighting from blossom to bloom in search of nectar for the hive. I was searching for nectar of another sort to fill the inward cavern of the heart with heartfelt and revelatory experience, including the weariness of extensive trekking, the hardship of traversing the dense shrub lands and hills. But all the while, through the effort and loneliness emerge a prayer to fulfill one's purpose in making the pilgrim journey in the first place with fortitude and perseverance. Slowly, an inner change begins to make itself known, a new rhythm begins to grow beyond the sound of my own footfalls; a deeper harmony manifests itself that matches the serene movement of the clouds passing with detachment across the crest of the mountains and the rhythmic texture of the arching trees bending in prostration to the force of the wind.

Here, at least for a time that has perhaps long since vanished in reality, the dragon of the modern world has had no true entry. It was as thought I had stepped into a fishing boat with a few monks returning to the Mount, my heart aflutter in this strange environment like the flapping wings of the seagulls that encircle the boat. Through some miracle of time travel, it felt like I had alighted like a nervous dragonfly onto the dock of some ancient medieval world. It was as thought I had slipped through an invisible crack in the modern world to find myself in another dimension altogether of sun and forest and grand medieval monasteries that looked like huge castles or well fortified citadels of yore strewn across the mountains and coastal shore by giants from another age. On one level, I felt like some alien being thrust onto the shores of a remote island; but on another level, I felt close to finding some inner hearth in the sight of those towering monuments, perched on those rocky crags like bald eagles watching detachedly over the life passing below them and yet beckoning the wayward pilgrim with the message of some mysterious promise awaiting the interested traveler who might pass through this ancient realm in search of a truth that will satisfy all desire.

All of the monasteries are modeled along the same pattern, given the nature of the terrain and the history through which these edifices were constructed and evolved into living communities. The architecture of each of the twenty monasteries reflects a certain basic pattern which has carefully been modified depending on the topography of the land, certainly in the instances when the monastic enclosures were built atop the cliff of some rocky headland such as the Grand Lavra, founded by St. Athanasios in the tenth century, at the outermost lip of the peninsula overlooking the board sweep of the Aegean. The typical monastery found on Athos was essentially a walled fortress, with a four-sided rectangular court with a main church, the *katholikon*, in the center with various chapels and other essential buildings such as library and refectory well positioned about the inner courtyard as space allowed. Many of the monasteries, in keeping with their image of being impregnable bastions, had massive walls and a strategically placed tower. Interestingly enough, as the buildings rise toward the heavens, often from broad-based foundations struck into the rocky crest of the mountain, the windows become larger, the top rows even have wooden balconies projecting from the stone structure and supported by wooden buttresses that provided magnificent, indeed awe-inspiring views of the surrounding area, including both rugged mountainside and placid seas.

* * *

I will not attempt to name, number or describe, as in some timetabled travelogue, the exact places I visited or the program I followed. What interests me to remember and what may interest readers to hear described are the collective remembrance and the evocative quality of this uncommon experience, since that is what I remember now in hindsight, forty years down the road of my life. The monastery Dionysiou is built on a huge perpendicular mass of rock overlooking the steep forbidding coastline of the peninsula with jagged rocky cliffs cascading straight down into the sea; the monastery Stavronikita stands at the edge of a small rocky headland giving the appearance of a kind of lighthouse floating above the nearby sea. The gardens below the monastery of Simonopetra wind hundreds of feet down the slope toward the sea. Each of the monasteries has its own unique ambiance and sacred presence as it blends within the natural setting of the mountain. Another monastery lies hidden in the midst of tall trees growing at the foot of a sloping, dense hillside. Above and beyond rises the towering peak of Athos itself, looking brave and bold and almost human against the celestial blue of the heavens. My trek through the forest brought me past various *skete*, a small monastic village composed of a number of cottages. I saw a *hesychasterion* or hermitage on a remote cliff high above the sea that is virtually inaccessible where a true solitary lives amid this sublime solitude.

My pilgrim experience found its flowering in a visit in this wonderful monastery at the end of the Athos peninsula, the prototype of all the monasteries in these medieval environs. As I approach its impressive gate giving entrance to the grand monastery that resembles to my inexperienced eye a monolithic Turkish structure, I take note of the towering peak of Athos in the distance, as though the 1,000 year monastery still stands under the patronage of its watchful gaze throughout a long and varied history. The gate upon closer inspection is actually a four-pillared portico that covers a domed verandah where I image the monks sitting in the early evening watching the creeping shadows descend in a darkness that matches the silence of the night, the passage of day to night being an event worthy of notice in places such as this, out in the wild natural order with no sign of civilization creeping around the edges of the mind and heart. I also sit down, fairly exhausted after my day long trek through the forest and over the jagged foothills of the area surrounding the Mount, wondering what will happen next as I take note of a couple of stately cypresses bending slightly in a gentle wind amid a sea of rugged olive trees, but feeling confident that I will soon be in good hands. It is still hot and on the waves of heat float the intoxicating scent of crimson oleanders that spill down from the roof of the verandah.

No doubt, the porter, who resides in a kind of lodge abreast of the double doors, framed with plates of iron, has heard the rustle of my sandals and my weary sighs, or perhaps he is on the lookout for wayward travelers who come knocking expectantly at these massive iron-clad doors. Whatever the case may be, he greets me with a nod of the head and the hint of a smile through a small aperture in his flowing, white, patriarchal beard. It's the eyes that are penetrating and clear. After uttering a somber greeting in Greek from beneath his bowed head, he leads me affectionately by the arm with one hand, while the click of his beads make their way through the fingers of his other hand. We pass down through the narrow passage of this ancient gateway, up a small slope until we pass through another smaller door that gives issue beyond the inner wall into the courtyard of the monastery, a narrow rectangle that I later learned was about 400 feet long and 150 feet wide. Around the courtyard and rising heavenward run the rows of cells making up the honeycomb of the old wooden-galleried buildings. The porter leads me with some determination into one of these buildings and shows me into a sparsely furnished guest room where he indicates that I should leave my backpack. He then takes me to a main reception room where he gestures graciously for me to sit and wait. After a few minutes, he returns and there is a solemn kindness in his offer of the traditional tray of refreshment, including the well known Greek ouzo, Turkish delight with its distinctive taste of pistachio nut sprinkled with powered sugar, and black Greek coffee in a miniature cup, followed by a glass of fresh cool water that I imagine has made its joyous way down from the holy mountain into the well of the age-old monastery. I drank down the draft like the waters of the first primordial spring, its sparkling freshness enervating me anew with its untouched pristine energy.

All is quiet now. The grand silence of the evening is interrupted by the murmur of the Aegean surf whispering its perennial secrets into the nooks and crannies of the rugged shore. The harmonious echoes of the monks chanting the sacred psalms of Vespers in the nearby chapel recalls to me a far distant memory of a time in primary school when I too sang the mesmerizing verses of Gregorian chant as a member of the boy's choir. Even at that young age, I was taken in by its sobering melodies and mellifluous rhythms, reflecting a more traditional era in time when such sacred music could be composed and chanted as though by heavenly choirs. In this setting, these simple, haunting melodies reach deep down into some inner well to draw, like fresh mountain water, the sweet memory of some long forgotten dream or deeper presence that lies within us, a witness if you will, of all that is sacred and dear to our conscious selves. Finally, it is the responsibility of a punctual monk to intone the evening bell that makes its way through the corridors of rooms and cells announcing the evening meal and summoning the monks to table.

In the center of the rectangular courtyard I find everyone making their way to the refectory for their evening meal. As I follow and mingle with them, in my naïve youth discreetly trying to blend in, I am politely ushered inside by a charitable monk and guided to a place to sit down at a long table made of marble slabs on seats of solid stone covered with a piece of wood. This monastic eatery is cruciform in shape and as I gaze about waiting for the food to be brought, I notice that the walls are covered with wall paintings, with scenes of the last Judgment, the terrestrial paradise, the Last Supper, together with portraitures of Athonite monks. At the end of the transept, I see the Tree of Jesse[1] and the death of Athanasios, the founder of the monastery. The walls and ceiling, which is arched and painted with colored baskets of fruit, are darkened by the smoke left behind by candles burning down through the centuries. The food that I was served along with the other monks was simple and honest fare, a thick, homemade soup with soft noodles and a piece of farmer's bread hard enough to crack a tooth, but temptingly softened in the thick broth. The meal itself had a ritualistic quality about it. A reader stood solemnly at a lectern and read psalms from some leather-bound manuscript like a grand patriarch, the words tripping off his tongue with sober resonance. At certain moments during the reading, the monks sipped at their soup, while at other times they drank red wine from small metal goblets.

That evening, before returning to my allotted guestroom, I step out onto a nearby corner balcony to rest my weary bones and attempt to absorb something of the mysterious and serene ambiance that hovered about the place, half expecting the ethereal spirits of monks past to float by on the way to some netherworld. I had noticed that balconies are common enough in many of the monasteries, hanging from the heights of the outer walls like damsels in

---

1. Jesse is the grandson of Ruth and the father of David. From the 11th century, the Tree of Jesse has been portrayed in wood carvings, manuscripts, stained glass windows and wall paintings. Jesse is usually portrayed recumbent with a tree rising from his body.

distress, and commanded magnificent views across the waters clinging as they were to the sheer walls of the towering structures. I
noted they are often used by the monks who sit quietly together and
talk with one another. As I sit there alone on a wooden bench surrounding the porch, fenced in by a rot-iron grill on all sides,
through which I can see the gentle movement of the dark, nighttime waters of the Aegean far below the cliff, I begin to reflect on
this amazing experience. This is a night touched by the late summer
moon climbing out of the sea with its fiery orange light, glistening
in triumph in its agelessness and spreading across the earth its wild
freedom to inspire the mind and set the heart aglow. Now that night
has fallen and silence reigns, the soul of the monastery seems to
hover in the air like a spectral ghost as it wafts its way through the
open places of the buildings like a gentle probing mist. The light of
the moon cuts across the expanse of sea like a scimitar cutting its
way through black velvet, creating a laser beam of light from the
horizon to my slippered feet as I sit there gazing reflectively beyond
the horizon of my own imagination.

There hovers in the backcloth of my mind an unexpected awakening that may never fully see the light of day unless I help it nurture and grow. I think of what I have seen since my arrival,
including a variety of somber, indrawn monks with their beards
and rounded caps and flowing black cassocks, the medieval monastic stone citadels still surviving like crowns of glory from another
era, the natural beauties that provide the setting for these ancient
buildings and enhance the spirit of the monks and recluses, all artifacts of another time and place that are still here to inspire people
who live within this environment with a spiritual message that transcends time and the passing of generations. There is a spark in every
one of us that needs only to ignite the flint of some inspiration
within nature to awaken the dormant witness within us of something greater than ourselves, to feel the sudden inrush of some
experience vaster than ourselves coming as though through a crack
from another world and another self, an experience that echoes the
natural cadences of rhythm and nature whose harmonies trace their
origin back to God. Why shouldn't thoughts and impressions that
are strange and beautiful and true resonate their harmonies within

the firmament of the human soul so that we can participate in the sublime messages of nature when they shine their wonder down upon us? As I sat on the balcony absorbing the subtle ambiance of the night, I was beginning to realize that nature's beauty and peace will shine its mercy down upon those who are receptive to its natural call and will flow into their aspiring soul just as naturally as sunshine flows into trees.

That evening, I laid down to rest in the austere guestroom, painted stark white and furnished with a broad divan and an iron bedstead with a pillow and clean, white sheet. Along the wall opposite the bed was an olive wood writing table and chair standing on a flagstone floor. It has been a dry, hot day with an intense sun; but now a cool breeze wafted through the open window and spread its benevolence upon the bed and tabletop as I drifted away into the well earned treasure of untroubled slumber. But before I do, I think how little in our routine day do we sufficiently address ourselves to the clues and signals that life has to offer us in terms not only of life's implicit mystery, but also in terms of its hidden disclosure of what God wants us to know. Our intentions and meager efforts, our shallow imagination and our empty satisfactions, our hollow words and our feeble aspirations will all go unsung across the generations because they are unworthy of our true attentions and unfit as the stuff of our heart's desires. Few men and women ever perceive the great mysteries of life on their own; they need to rely on the largeness of their mind and wisdom of their senses to perceive the archetypes of a grander order fall down into the symbolic images of nature and humankind, filling the everyday forms of life with otherworldly, spiritual meaning. We cannot escape the world, except occasionally, as I have done on this monastic pilgrimage; not many people even want to these days and prefer to live out their time benumbed by the attractions of this world bereft of their inner meaning. In this rarefied environment, however, I was able to take leave of the mundane world, to receive the wondrous perceptions and noble dignity conveyed through a hole in the fabric of our experience that leads us on an inward journey made complete by its wisdom and blessing, in order to balance the outward one we make through life with its insistent quality and its implicit mystery. That evening in the shadow of Mount Athos was such a moment that summarized the entire pilgrimage, matching the sublime beauty of nature, the traditional history of the area, and the spirit of the surroundings with the awakening of my own consciousness to achieve possibilities of a higher order of magnitude and to touch a greater truth that lies beyond my own limited horizon.

* * *

My permit to roam the peninsula and visit the monasteries gave me one final day to absorb the wonders of this Athonite setting before I must once again set off from the rugged shore in a fishing boat that passes by the Grand Lavra in the late afternoon. My adventure through this medieval setting begins in the central rectangular courtyard I had entered yesterday at sunset. Opposite the refectory stands the church, built by St. Athanasios who founded the Grand Lavra monastery (*Megisti Lavra*). Upon entering, I must pass through two huge cypress trees, one of them allegedly planted by St. Athanasios himself, which rises majestically from a protective stone ring. The church itself has a faded red color with a broad cupola rising from the center of the edifice and matched by two side cupolas. I enter through magnificent wooden Turkish doors that seem to guard the entrance to the church with their stately presence. Inside the church, there is a somber hush that complements the overwhelming scent of incense and burning candles. Grand paintings dating from the 16th century cover the inner walls of the vestibule. Once inside, there are two chapels layered in darkening shadows, with only the faint hint of the light of day shining through the stained glass windows. In one of these chapels, lying between four pillars of marble, is the tomb of St. Athanasios covered with the offerings of pious pilgrims. The other chapel is that of St. Nicholas. Inside the nave of the church there are towering portraits of two great soldier-emperors of Constantinople, Nikephoros Phokas and John Tzimisces, the monastery's original benefactors, each of them crowned and wearing imperial robes.

Back outside in the courtyard, I notice an amazing structure between the two cypresses and connected to the church by an archway. It is a monolithic *phile*, or covered font, with a solid dome upheld by an open ring of pillars in the Turkish style. Inside the dome are paintings once again dating from the 16th century, representing the baptism of Christ. Amid a company of surrounding angels, the figure of Christ with a dove over his head is immersed in the cleansing waters of the River Jordan. Below this spectacular inner dome resides the fountain, consisting of a huge monolithic basin, eight feet in diameter and extremely old. Bronze tubing rises from within the font in the form of water-spouting beasts, surmounted by an eagle with outstretched wings. At the base of the fountain, two stone dogs show their ancient Oriental faces in a perpetual smile. I spend time describing these things because it fascinated me to think that people from more traditional eras were able to express their inner visions in such an subtle manner, leaving behind legacies of art and culture and architecture that remind us of the breadth and depth of their desire to give expression to the way they understood their world.

The life of the modern-day monk is set within the ancient Orthodox surroundings of the monastery, surrounded by vineyards and fruit-trees, olive trees and vegetables gardens that the monks themselves tend and cultivate, with the eternal sea spread below their windows and balconies like an exotic Oriental fan. Today the routine of the monks is still much like the life described by an 18th century Athonite monk, Konstantinos Daponte, in a passage that recreates something of the joy and self containment that are the innate blessing of the monastic order. He writes:

> And I had a small axe and I cleared pine-trees, olive, holm-oaks, and I chopped them up. And sometimes I planted olives, sometimes pears, or apples, or almost-trees, or vegetables, leeks and garlic, and I rejoiced in the soil as the worldly man in money. I found myself in a garden of graces, in a true paradise of delight. And sometimes I went down to the sea and gathered limpets, shells, crabs, and sometimes prawn, and in these I rejoiced more than in courtly banquets of lords and ladies. I was all gratefulness to the Lord, and my heart was full of unspeakable delight. The place was full of fragrance, the trees

gave out their odours, birds flew round about, singing while one chanted, and the ground was covered with various flowers and lilies, delighting the eye and ear and filling one with gladness. . . . Hearing, sight, touch, smell all offered thanks to God. You tire of the cell? Go out for a walk, strolling through the solitude's loveliness. Go to the spring, or to the seashore with its beauty. Go to the caves, to the cells of ancient ascetics, divine palaces, repeating always as you go the "Kyrie Eleison" so that you do not stop the flow of mercy. You see the mountain? The plain? Wonder at the creator's wisdom and power. . . . You see some beast? Do not fear — it will not harm you. . . . You see your terrible enemy, the devil? Do not be troubled: show him your cross. Your walk is over? Return to your cell, take your work-tool, or your papers. You tire of that? Take your spade up. You tire of the spade? Take again your axe. You tire of that? Take up your chaplet. The chaplet feeds the heart with joy. It is the hour for prayer. Embrace it eagerly, speak a while with God, with unspeakable joy, with such delight and honour as the Angels."[1]

I have seen these monks go about their business, maintaining the basic routines of both spiritual and earthly life, through prayer, the recitation of the offices of Matins in the morning, obligatory attendance at Vespers in the evening as monks have done down through the ages. Every aspect of their daily rituals contains meaning by virtue of their symbolic significance. Everything they do from work, to prayer, to eating, to communing with the other monks contains a sense of something that transcends themselves and the world they live in. Beyond its archaic quality with thousand year old monasteries and a way of life searching for fulfillment in work and contemplation and silence, they do not ask for anything more in life than to be able to slip through its cracks to reveal another side of reality. There is an unreal quality to their world

---

1. See Konstantinos Daponte, *The Garden of Graces* (Athens 1880), quoted in *Athos the Holy Mountain,* Philip Sherrard (Woodstock, NY: The Overlook Press, 1985) p145.

especially during this post-modern era; but as in the world of
childhood, it is a world that cannot lie. The moment they enter the
Athonic realm, they are entering a world that abides by spiritual
practices and rhythms of life that are the legacy of the ages and that
follow a tradition that is still integral and whole, linking them with
the most profound realities of the spiritual world. It is this world
that still hovers over the peninsula like an abiding presence, an
eternal mist if you will, protecting all those who enter its confines. I
felt both honored and humbled to be among such company.

Ultimately, the quintessential prayer ritual the Eastern Orthodox
Church has to offer is the practice of the Jesus Prayer,[1] alternatively
known as the inner prayer of the heart." This prayer is a well-known
and well-practised spiritual method that goes under the name of
Hesychasm, which comes from the Greek word *hesychia*, meaning
"tranquility". St. Paul admonished the Thessalonians to "pray without ceasing," and this is at the heart of the remembrance of the Jesus
Prayer. The tradition of *hesychasm* was a traditional expression of
stillness or repose. The practice of the Jesus Prayer has been well
documented in the 19th century classic of Russian spirituality called
The Way of the Pilgrim. The pilgrim travels far and wide to learn
how to pray without ceasing. He finally meets a *staretz*, a man of
advanced spirituality. The prayer "that doesn't stop" is the prayer of
Jesus, he is told, a prayer that is formed with the lips, but lies well
placed in the heart in order to nurture the inner spirit. Through its
contemplative repetition, it literally brings the person into the presence of Jesus, at all times and in all places, amounting to a kind of
Western mantra in terms of its practice and its possibilities. "I grew
so accustomed to my prayer," writes the anonymous author of *The
Way of the Pilgrim*, "that when I stopped for a single moment I felt,
so to speak, as though something were missing, as though I had lost

---

1. The monastic centers in Russia and the Balkan countries had eminent mas-
ters, called *geron* in Greek and *staretz* in Russian. The "Elder" Zosima, in Dosto-
evsky's *Brothers Karamazov*, is a fanciful portrait of such a master. While Mont
Athos is the most famous center where these methods were practised, they are also
traced back to the Desert Fathers in Egypt and other parts of the Christian East.
The Jesus Prayer reads as follows in Latin: *Domine Jesu Christe Fili Dei miserere
nobis*, in English "Lord Jesus Christ, Son of God, have mercy on me."

something. The very moment I started the prayer again, it went on easily and joyously."[1] As in many other religious forms of contemplation and invocation, what is crucial is the invocation of the holy name of Jesus as a means initially to serve as a purification of the mind followed by a purification of the heart with the "cleansing fire" of the Divinity.

My sojourn in this rarefied setting was all too short; but looking back in retrospect now and with forty years of hindsight to support my fading remembrance, I can honestly say that this brief spiritual interlude had a profound effect on me, leaving behind a subconscious desire to probe deeper than the surface experiences that life had to offer, superficial experiences that amounted to little more than smoky white breath on a chill winter morning. When seeds are planted and sewn into the earth, they sometimes take considerable time to develop firm roots; but once these rootlets take their sinuous hold, they can grow into an unexpected awakening we would never have consciously discovered on our own. The initial force of spiritual emotions makes itself known in small doses so as not to overwhelm the simple and inexperienced soul with their miraculous wonder. These higher emotions are but fragments of an experience that become the colored stones of an elaborate mosaic that when bounded together make up an individual life. It has taken 40 years to forge these words on the page as footsteps into the past. No subsequent trip I have taken, whether it be into the jungles of Malaysia where I learned the mysteries of the traditional cure, or into the broad valleys of the Himalayas where I learned about the simplicity of the Buddha nature, can approximate the virgin quality of this brief sojourn in the shadow of the holy mountain of Athos. It was my first journey with soul, a journey into the unknown as though I were on a search for some unspoken treasure, a journey that one must make alone. It was a journey in which something is left behind that you could afford to loose, in order to take something with you that you could not afford to leave behind; the true price of wisdom being this recognition that the non-vital can be

---

1. *The Way of a Pilgrim*, tr. by R.M. French (San Francisco: Harper & Row Co, 1991), pp 33–34.

gladly abandoned for the absolutely essential, when it presents itself.

I took leave of the holy mountain late one afternoon as anonymously as I came. The fishing boat arrived on schedule to pick me up along with several monks and another traveler on their way back to the mainland. The sun has already fallen behind the mountain creating a silhouette of Athos, behind which the burning sun cast a halo of light around its stark peak. As we leave the shore and float out into the depths of the agitated waters, the great "ark of Byzantium" as the monks themselves call Mount Athos, continues to float on through these sublime waters as the last bastion of a traditional bygone era, an anachronism that will not die until the final few monks depart from this world and there is no one to take their place. Soon it will be dark and I will be in Thessaloniki. The day is coming upon Vespers, the hour for prayer, and my heart is filled "with unspeakable joy, with such delight and honour as the angels." Ahead lie many years of travel and discovery as I explore my childhood dreams of flying carpets and secret caves; but no future trip will have the pristine quality of this first journey with soul, alone and on foot on the holy mountain of Athos.

2

UNDER THE ROOF OF HEAVEN

JOURNEY THROUGH THE
SILENT PLACES OF LADAKH

LADAKH CANNOT BE UNDERSTOOD with the mind alone; it can only be visited as a body, mind, and soul experience of a remote land from a more traditional age. The mountains, the heavens, the broad expanse of valleys and flowing rivers all speak of high and sacred mysteries, and imprint themselves on the mind like the woodcuts of one's first primer, primitive, ancient, and mythic. The true spirit of this experience sinks deep into the well of the traveler's soul to reveal a natural awe that awakens a sense of transcendence and contains an intimation of higher worlds. The country cannot be thought through, reasoned or measured in terms of size, shape, or population figures, although it undoubtedly lies far above the lapping shores of the Indian Ocean and just under the roof of heaven. Its physical presence contains a special stature like the natural wonders that create its otherworldly mystique. The force of its experience strikes the traveler in the same way that a bell creates a resounding note when struck. The area strikes a resounding cord within the bell of one's being that resonates with purity and truth that is hard to come by in today's modern, frantic world. Ladakh has a gift to give. The unsuspecting traveler needs to explore the silent places of its mountainous terrain and its ancient, traditional sites in order to uncover what that gift might be.

In planning any trip to a far away destination, some secret desire lies within us in search of fulfillment. Whether it be the lure of a virgin landscape to lift the spirit of the weary traveler, the hush of a distant horizon promising some untold, bold adventure, or the mysterious spell of the legendary Shangri-la as *ultima thule* to every traveler's fondest dream, we seek to escape from ourselves and the mundane turmoil of our lives for a few weeks a year in order to enter the realm of some never-never land where our dreams may come true. Indeed, I had two weeks available one summer and wanted to be "taken away" to that far distant land where the sun forever shines and where the mountains glow through the mist. Where might that be but on the rising plateau of the grand Himalayas surrounded by magnificent snow-covered mountain peaks in the land of the eternal snows, with the promise of the lost valley of Shangri-la nestled somewhere in the mist as a testament to the myth of a living Eden, less a physical place, perhaps, and more a vision of enlightened consciousness where peace and harmony might reign supreme.

I once made an unexpected journey through the silent places of Ladakh, a province of Northern India nestled between the scenic Kashmir in the West and the Tibetan plateau in the East, an area that echoes the broad silence of distant ages in the presence of its natural wonders and ancient artifacts. I roamed through the broad valley of the Indus River that creates a brush stroke of lush farmland on either of its banks amid the vast stretches of this brown and desolate moonscape, the imposing snow-clad mountain peaks reaching to carve the meaning of their mystery on Heaven's walls, and the ancient monasteries perched atop a mountain crag like a watchful eagle witnessing the passing of centuries. An eerie silence pervades the landscape, offering the promise of an alternative and unique experience to the hustle and bustle that we have grown accustomed to in all the major metropolises of the world.

After flying into New Delhi early one morning, a city bedecked with a steel grey, murky sky that hovered over the land as a ghostly cloud cover pregnant with the monsoon rains soon to break out across the land, I quickly transferred to the domestic side of the airport to catch my flight to Leh, capital city of Ladakh deep within the heart of the Himalayas. Not a half hour into the flight, I knew I was entering another world. Not far below lay the immensity of the

snow-capped mountains, flagrantly defying the mid-July temperatures as they glistened in the intensity of the early morning sun. The
mountains themselves recalled all the power and force of a herd of
sleeping buffalo you would not want to awaken, lest they overcome
you with the force of their presence and latent spirit. The captain
suddenly announced a safety warning to fasten seat belts for the
"special descent" into the valley of Leh. The plane immediately
made a rapid descent creating the sinking sensation of a fast moving
elevator. The small Boeing 737 veered around a broad mountain
pass and headed down into the narrow valley that housed the miniaturized town of Leh in the distance. This is a one chance, last
chance descent with no margin for error as the plane enters the cul-
de-sac of the valley below. Within minutes we were gliding down
the airport tarmac of the world's highest airfield at 11,500 feet after
that breathtaking descent into the narrow valley beyond the horizon of this world.

As soon as I left the cabin of the aircraft, I was assaulted by a
number of sensations: the surprising lack of oxygen that immediately gripped the body, the spectacular ring of mountains that
encircled the airport, the clarity of the air and light that conveyed a
sparkling quality seldom experienced in big cities and, finally, that
broad, blue sky as it must have been freshly painted at the dawn of
creation by the Hand of the Creator. Indeed as I climbed into the
airport bus that was to take us into the small terminal, I was already
suffering from a breathlessness that a 30% lack of oxygen will pro-
duce and my heart was aflutter and beating wildly in its demand for
more oxygen. Still, I calmed myself by gazing serenely upon the
grand scene of mountains and valleys that surrounded me and the
crackling quality of the air and light that filled my senses with their
sublime purity, as though the crisp air and shadow-edged light had
been touched by the wand that created the first day, full of revelation and edge. This was the real thing, true mountains and a real
blue sky interrupted only by the occasional puff cloud seemingly
glued to the sky to counterbalance the broad monotony of that brilliant blue heaven, and making the smog and cloud-covered entry
into Delhi but a pale remembrance to the grandeur of this magnificent landscape.

The bus ride into town gives testament to the brave new world that I had just had the privilege of flying into. The town itself was nestled amid the sleeping forces of those grand mountains, as though these peaks and troughs had been thrown down at random to please a divine wisdom that was not to be fathomed. The early morning air brought out the local inhabitants all dressed in their distinctive traditional attire. The shops and houses line the side of the road as in all cities, but they also cascade down the side of the hills and cliffs that make their way beyond the end of the street. It is the faces of the people, however, that immediately strike my imagination as worthy of note. There was much variation in their features, some being markedly Mongolian with thick folds surrounding the slit eyes, while others could have passed without difficulty for Europeans, descendents, some say, of the army of Alexander the Great when he passed through this area. Many of these faces are dark and deeply lined by the intensity of the elements of sun and wind at this great altitude, as thought the forces of nature had engraved their own hardship and experience onto the faces of the local inhabitants. Yet by way of compensation, I also note an aura of strength and presence that one doesn't usually see in Western faces that must endure the hardships of pollution and stress that is the mainstay of Western society. These faces appear solemn and sober as opposed to the twisted, painted and depressed faces that you see on your way to the Mall. These faces are determined and full of purpose, as though the life they live in close proximity with the natural environment has left its mark on their broad visages to the extent that their faces reflect the spirit and nobility of the mountains they live among. If anything, these faces have the mark of eternity about them; there is a natural sanctity and spirituality within the flesh and bones that gives the people walking down the street nobility and purpose as they go about their business.

The aging jeep climbs the steep hill and turns a sharp corner to reveal the grand archway through which all and sundry enter the town. It is painted in the Buddhist fashion, full of color, light, and symbolic meaning, this traditional artistic proclamation leaving no doubt as to the orientation of the inhabitants of the town, for this is a deeply Buddhist community with clear allegiance in terms of guidance and direction in life coming from the dictates of Lord Buddha. Beyond the gate and central to the entrance of the town stands the grandiose prayer wheel, a round disk housed within a small protective structure whose handles are there for the passersby to turn the wheel and activate the prayer cycle. Upon the prayer wheel are mantras and prayer epithets etched upon plate brass. Setting the wheel in motion sets in motion the aspirations and holy sentiments of the wheel, to be sent into the pervading atmosphere to dispel evil spirits and sent forth sacred energy in the elements. My guide, driver and I breeze past this traditional archway reflective of a higher spirituality, setting a special tone as we enter the town. We move past the shops selling pashmina shawls and Kashmiri hand-woven carpets. The handcrafts hang randomly from windows and awnings giving the impression of an abundance of hand craft and art work that is stunning to behold and inviting to explore and buy. A short distance away and perched at the edge of the Namgyal hill overlooking the town lies the ancient palace of Leh, much smaller but resembling the Potala in Lhasa, built in the 17th century and now a captivating architectural ruin creating a feeling of history and lore as a fitting backdrop to the town.

However, this is no extended metropolis and soon enough, we turn down a side street narrow enough for one car with small streamlets running along either side of the dusty road. Even the driver and guide had trouble finding the small country inn that I had reserved on the Internet. It was tucked away anonymously about a mile outside of town, a sturdy structure of two floors that looked quaint and inviting. I am greeted with smiles and bedecked with three silk scarves over my head as tradition dictates. "We give you the best room in hotel," the obliging attendant tells me with deferential politeness. "You have two-sided view of mountains from corner room," he beams and indeed, I quickly take in the spotless chamber complete with fresh towels and TV. The glistening mountains shine in upon me like a living postcard from two sides of the room. I can look upon these images of snow-capped peaks and rugged cliffs and ponder their eternal message of stability and strength, now that I have arrived on the first leg of what promises to be a very interesting journey.

* * *

Ladakh is a land of ancient artifacts and spiritual remembrance, whether it be through the wonders of its natural beauty or the miraculous spiritual heritage that still represents a living tradition in today's anti-traditional and materialistic world. The people seem to live in this natural environment of river and mountain with the same acceptance that they adjust themselves to a thirty percent reduction in oxygen at this altitude of over 11,000 feet. To the unaccustomed eye of the traveler such as myself, this is a primordial landscape, untouched and wild and achingly beautiful. My parched sensibility drinks in this draught of natural beauty like nectar of the gods. Scattered through the landscape are the spiritual vestiges of a traditional past in the form of stupas spread dramatically across the sweeping plain and prayer flags and prayer wheels by the side of the road. They stand as silent sentinels of some ancient memory that bears kindling and they amply fulfill their function by simply being where they are, sending the spirit of the mantras written upon the flags and wheels into the blowing wind.

I am on tour through this primordial never-never land and hope to visit some of the more spectacular monasteries and gompas that are sprinkled throughout the province as a testament to a strong and enduring traditional spirituality that continues to intrude itself into the modern world in these remote places. I awake after my day of mandatory rest required to acclimate myself to the exigencies of the altitude, ready for my first foray into the wilds of the Indus Valley and the architectural treasures that it provides sanctuary for. Fortified with cornflakes and warm milk and a glass of the Ladakh traditional tea, with my stomach rumblings now subdued and headache nearly gone, my guide and I, together with the ever silent and faithful local driver, make our way down the east side of the mighty and swift-moving Indus River, intense rays of the high-altitude sun streaming in through the window of the jeep and settling on my face and arms with a ferocious intensity; but no matter. No sensible person of my pale complexion ever travels without sun block in this day and age.

Our ultimate destination is the renowned Hemis Monetary situated about 50 kilometers from the capital at Leh on the opposite side of the Indus River (Singge Tsangpo); but on these roads and with this traffic, including all manner of bicycles, motor cycles, trucks and wandering water buffalo, it takes well over an hour to make our way. Along the way, the guide suddenly shouts through the wind and roar of the Jeep, "There's the Shey Castle and Monastery. We will stop here first and visit the grounds before making our way further to Hemis." Indeed, off in the distance, perched atop a rocky cliff off to the left, I have my first glimpse of one of the many monasteries that adorn the arid landscape of Ladakh. Its ancient aura of power and grandeur dominate the vista of this magnificent landscape. It could be a sleeping dragon full of latent energy and primitive power. Its very image summons the respect of the ages and invites questions such as how and when and why. The castle was built by the first king of Ladakh, Lachen Palgyigon. Within its walls stands a sacred copper-gilt statue of Lord Buddha, three stories in height, renown as one of its kind and build in 1633 by Deldan Namgyal in memory of his father King Singge Namgyal. Not far beyond lies Thiksey Monastery situated yet again on top of a hill and founded over 500 years ago. There are over 80 monks in residence and the monastery itself houses many sacred shrines and precious objects. At this point, lunch time is fast approaching. The guide suggests that we stop to enjoy the picnic that the hotel has prepared for us. We walk through a small roadside restaurant and out again into the back garden where we spread out our lunch of bread, boiled eggs, boiled potato, crackers and a candy bar washed down with mango juice as we sat at an outside table under the shape of a spreading tree. "We will have to pay something for the use of the table," the guide apologetically tells me. "How much?" I ask, frowning theatrically in good humor. "About a dollar," he tells me. I think we can handle that.

Another lengthy drive finally brings us into the vicinity of the Hemis Monastery. First, we cross the mighty Indus River, muddy brown and fast moving in agitation as it makes its way west and then south where it passes through the length of Pakistan before emptying into the Arabian Sea. The road is narrow and windy and we move through a parade of stupas on either side of the road as we approach the great edifice of the monastery together with its cascading buildings and cells tucked deep into the inner recesses of the parched and rugged mountains. Hemis is the largest and most famous of all the monasteries in Ladakh, founded 350 years ago by Stagsang Raschen, invited to Ladakh by King Singge Namgyal. He was a Lama who had traveled all over India and Kashmir and who was known to have received a vision of all eighty mahasiddhas and who later realized the "rainbow body". Within the monastery, we view the copper-gilt statue of Lord Buddha, various stupas made of gold and silver, sacred thankas and many other precious objects, including sacred books housed within the walls of the temple precinct. On the other side of the mountain beyond the monastery lies a sacred hermitage founded by the great Gyalwa Kotsang where his meditation cave can be seen. His footprint and handprint are on the rock within the cave. As much as I would have liked to visit this sacred place, I simply didn't have the stamina or wherewithal to make the climb deeper and higher into the rugged terrain because of the threat of more altitude sickness. My guide told me that he once visited the place and found two Englishman there. They had been there for several months and had grown long hair and beards and according to him looked very wild.

Many of these monasteries still maintain the tradition of holding elaborate ancient festivals that are well-attended by the local inhabitants from miles around. Providentially, the festival of Hemis Tsechu was held on the day that we visited the monastery. We parked the Jeep at the base of the hill and wandered up with the rest of the crowd to find our place within the central courtyard of the monastery. Shortly after 9:00 am, with a huge crowd of locals and a few foreign tourists jammed into the confines of the courtyard, the grand festival began in all its true spectacle. In one corner of the courtyard sat the musicians with their drums and horns and cymbals, playing that distinctive ancient Buddhist music that we have become familiar with through movies such as "The Last Emperor" and "Seven Years in Tibet." The serene monks sat in their red robes and meditatively played on their instruments as though the melodies they construed were emanations of their own soul in harmony with the other players. Particularly notable was the droning of the horns, deep and rich and vibrant, and whose unearthly sound seemed to echo across

the vast silent spaces of the mountains only to return as some animate specter giving voice to the deepest emotions of humanity, or
was it my stimulated imagination thinking that the earth itself was
giving voice to some preternatural sound coming from the abyss of
some netherworld within the earth. Beyond this eerie, preternatural
sound lay the symbolic sight of the monks dressed in elaborate regalia and donning hand-painted face masks that made these humble
individuals larger than life and somehow spectacular. They
descended the central staircase from an upper story of the building
into the courtyard which was itself bedecked with a central prayer
flag flapping its divine remembrance into the morning wind, and
entered the courtyard in a slow motion dance that obviously had
balance and symmetry as a central message of the choreography.
The great painted face masks displayed every emotion from happiness to despair and conveyed a larger than life quality in their projection toward the onlookers. As for the spectators, such as myself and
the other foreigners, we were spellbound by this magnificent display
of color and costume and tradition. Of course, we didn't realize what
it all meant for the locals; but as colorful drama embodied in sound
and dance and light, it resurrected feelings of wonder and awe, stirring deeply latent feelings of reverence that lie sequestered within
every human being ready to be roused through the force of such
ancient, arcane traditions. These rites and ceremonies would continue for another several days; but my guide signaled me that it was
time to leave, and we made our way through the dense crowds and
eventually took our leave of the premises, making our way once
again down the rugged hills to the waiting vehicle that would take us
back across the river and into town.

On another day, not far from the shadow of the Hemis monastery, we visited an oracle inhabiting a small rustic house by the river.
We had to leave the Jeep and driver behind to make our way over
hills and rocky crags down toward the edge of the swift moving,
muddy river. The turbulent waters of the Indus were not inviting
even if its name was mythical; but the courtyard enclosure in front
of the small mud and yellow brick house was warm and inviting. In
this desolate setting, with the sound of rushing waters invading the
background of my expectant mind, we sat under a verdant tree that

graciously spread its shade over us against the relentless mountain sun. A monk sat with us draped in deep red robes, head shaven, of course, and looking ascetic and boyish at the same time. While chatting with my guide about what to expect from the oracle and giving me some background and guidance, the monk suddenly spoke up. "What a magnificent river," he said. "You speak English," I replied, surprised to learn of this monk's linguistic ability and delighted to have the opportunity of speaking with him. "The Pakistanis call it 'the father of rivers' while the Tibetans call it 'the Lion River.'" "I can see why," I replied and the monk smiled. "Where does it originate," I asked and he told me that it flowed down from the glaciers of Tibet, across Ladakh and the Kashmir and over into Pakistan whence it flows in a southerly direction the entire length of Pakistan to merge into the Arabian Sea in the vicinity of the port city of Karachi.

While I was hoping to gain some insight into the kind of man he was and the kind of routine he might lead in his life as a monk, I quickly noted that he didn't say much about himself and I, for my part, was too reserved to ask directly what being a monk meant to him as we do in the Western style. He did mention the long history of Buddhism in Ladakh, having been brought over from Tibet in the early history of the spread of the religion. While we were talking, an old woman came out of the house dressed in a long black tunic with a red plaid belt holding it together. She had a sprightly air and a deeply lined, darkly tanned and incredibly strong face. She made a couple of comments to the various people around, as though she were looking for something of no consequence. The guide leaned over and whispered in my ear: "That's the oracle." Indeed, I thought, I never would have guessed. She looked like someone's grandmother rummaging around the dust of the courtyard. Closer scrutiny, however, revealed a deeper mystery embedded within the fold of her ancient, parchment face. She had a thick patch of dark black hair pulled back from her forehead and dressed as a single pony tail that resembled more a thick rope than a horse's tail. Her toothless grin was endearing; but somehow belied the potential energy and strength that I was beginning to observe in her every gesture and movement. There was promise here of something much deeper than somebody's grandmother searching for an infant.

After she disappeared within the stone cottage, numbers of people arrived, many of them foreigners who came to attend the oracular session gripping their digital cameras, and replete with all kinds of electronic equipment such as videos hanging down from their necks to capture this rarefied moment in time. Soon, we were all ushered within one of the rooms of the house that resembled some kind of religious shrine, with images of the Buddha on the walls, various mandala paintings with their striking workmanship and hidden messages reaching out to those that gaze upon them. The place smelt of earth and overripe fruit and incense as we all sat cross-legged and expectant on the floor in front of the shrine. The old women I had seen earlier, the oracle, came into the room and knelt down on a carpet in front of a small shrine equipped with the bells, oils, clappers and shawls that she would need in the execution of this ceremony. This was not the same women I had observed earlier in the courtyard. She was now bedecked with colorful traditional garments and an elaborate headdress whose every tassel and peak contained some hidden meaning that I was not privy to; but it didn't matter because it was the effect that mattered. This was now a presence to be reckoned with. When the oracle speaks, people listen.

She then proceeded to chant the ritual Buddhist sutras in Sanskrit with a strong, unwavering high-pitched voice that seemed to pierce the air like a knife. There was no doubting the power and efficacy of these ritual intonations whose reverberations filled the room and undoubtedly moved deep down into the bodies and minds of many of the people there, including myself. I believe in the power of prayer and incantation whatever the particular religious form it may take. In my own case, I have experienced the power of Quranic recitation, when through reading the words and verses a powerful energy is established, first within the body through vibration and resonance, then in the mind through the meaning of the words, and finally down into the very soul of the individual in order to shower the total entity with the higher consciousness and blessing that the sacred texts and ritual ceremony convey. This incredible chanting continued for some time, accompanied systematically with the ringing of a bell with the left hand and the use of a clapper in the right. I have knelt or sat cross-legged for hours on end and chanted Quranic scripture, so I was able to realize the effort and concentration such a discipline required of the woman.

At the end of a lengthy session of chanting, the oracle was ready to receive the petitions of the people. The room was crowded, but suddenly a local Ladakh peasant moved through the crowd and knelt down before the oracle. I later learned that he was complaining of some kind of stomach ailment. I saw the oracle open his tunic and massage his stomach for a time while applying some medicated oils. Whispered remarks could be heard, but I had no idea what was being said. He eventually stood up looking relieved and return back into the anonymity of the crowd. All the while, some of the Westerners were moving about taking pictures, angling for a better video shot, tripping over the people sitting around the room. I questioned the wisdom of this effort, thinking that they were capturing perhaps a moment in time; but were somehow actually missing the true experience of the moment in their frantic effort to seize it forever on celluloid.

Finally, there was a rustle of limbs and a modest, attractive looking middle-aged European woman with shot-cropped hair approached the oracle with a local guide as translator. A hushed silence fell across the room. At first, the women thanked the oracle for listening to her troubles through the voice of the translator; then she began to relate the story of the loss of her 25-year-old son several years ago. He had had an unexpected car accident and was suddenly gone from this world, to where she did not know. This afflicted soul began to sob heavily and I saw her shoulders shaking in heavy convulsions. A deeper silence covered the room as I felt my own emotions rise to the surface subliminally through this women's tragic loss of her son. Without hesitation, the oracle made extensive comments in the local Ladakh language, and through the translator we together with the afflicted mother were all able to learn what the oracle said. She told her that there was a time for tears, for they can be a blessed and purifying gift of the higher powers, but that the time had now passed and further tears would merely be a human indulgence detrimental to her spiritual health and well being. It was time to move on because her son was safe and where he should be. "Where was that?" came the timid question; but the oracle simply replied that it was enough for her to know and experience and enough for us to respect the individual destiny of others. Finally, the oracle advised the woman to move beyond the sorrow and suffering and perform good works and reach out to others with compassion and love. This is what her son would appreciate and this is what would temper a broken heart. Of course, this seemed to be the message that came to me through the crowded room and as a result of the translation. I felt uplifted by the experience and hoped that the woman who had lost her son had begun to find him again through the knowledge that he still existed within the fold of his own unique destiny, somewhere, sometime, but not of this world.

I finally summoned the courage to rise from the floor and seek the advice of the oracle, although I am reluctant to make a public display of myself, much less give voice to my innermost thoughts. Still, this was a rare and unique occasion that I didn't want to let pass by. With a nod to my guide, we rose and knelt in front of this ancient presence. I whispered my comment into the ear of the guide. When my guide translated my words into the Ladakhi language, I detected a faint smile cross her lips, as though a cool breeze had passed us by: "What should I be doing in my life that I am not doing?" I do not like to air my troubles in public, thinking that they have a natural life cycle and will eventually pass on their own. However, I was interested in finding out what more could be done in order to fulfill my destiny here on earth. I could see her rhythmic breathing as she gathered her words: "You can never do enough of what you should be doing. Seek within yourself . . . reach out to others . . . stay on the path. You will find your true destination." The oracle had spoken. We both receded back into the shadows and soon thereafter took our leave of the cottage. Her advice had the quality of an iridescent flame, ephemeral and burning with light.

* * *

Several days into my stay in Ladakh, I was scheduled to travel deeper west on the way to such places as Kargil and the Kashmir, off limits of course because of the perennial unrest in the area. The attendants at the hotel made a great fuss, insisting that I have a solid breakfast to fortify me for the coming journey. I am not sure I knew what they meant, but their engraciating smiles and the promise to keep my room ready for me for the several days that I would be gone endeared them to me. Once out of the protective cocoon of the capital city Leh, we were heading further west deeper into the more impassible mountain ranges of the Himalayas. This area was indeed mountainous desert, with high, rugged and barren mountains bereft of any trees or vegetation. The road followed the course of the Indus River which made its own meandering course through the desolate hills. The mountains rose straight up from the valley floor at nearly right angles. As we drove through the area on hairpin turns and looked down through the car window at a drop hundred of meters below to the muddy, swift-moving river, I took note of the steep cliffs on either side of the narrow valley. This is earthquake country, I thought to myself. The shuddering of the earth in this environment would bring immediate catastrophe to anyone with the misfortune to be a part of this primitive landscape. And yet for all of the rugged topography, the steep drop to the river and potential for land and rock slides, there was an enchantment to this natural setting that was intoxicating to behold.

As a modernite of the metropolises of the world, I was thirsty for the natural beauty and mystique that nature offers the human soul. You could drink it like a draft from which dreams are born. It sets a person thinking of the natural wonders that God has scattered across the earth like tinker toys, but that we hold in awe at their very sight. At several points along the way, I asked the driver to stop and cut the engine. As the voice of the engine flowed away like vapor, a fragile, brooding silence quickly emerged to overwhelm the mind with its deadly suspension of sound. These were the silent places of Ladakh out in the middle of nowhere, but that around every corner was a new vista and a new destination. One of the natural by-products of such natural environments far away from any sign of people and civilization is that deeper thoughts and emotions begin to emerge from some deep well within us, leading to questions that have few true answers. Would I find what I was looking for, I wondered, indeed what was I looking for that would bring me to this moment sitting on the edge of a rocky cliff with the Indus River flowing majestically below my feet amid such fragile and delicate stillness.

In these silent, awesome places, we can keep company with Nature at her own discretion. Nature becomes larger than life itself and we as humans are reduced to the insignificance that we truly are. We become Lilliputian and the spaces in which we find ourselves are gigantic beyond the measures of the earth. The mountains loom above us and the valleys drop below our feet; the sun moves across the heavens casting stark shadows across an indifferent earth like some great inimical and magnificent spirit. In withdrawing from the world and arriving in such far distant, wild and remote regions of the earth, the journeyer feels drawn into some mighty simplification through the experience of these raw manifestations of nature, as though the complexities of the world were reverting back toward their original primordial unity in which all of created nature, including the sun, moon, and stars, become once again powerful symbols of a higher order of magnitude that accompanies higher consciousness. The natural environment was no longer apartment blocks, advertising signs, and networks of highways; but rather mountains, valleys, rivers and streams, the blue sky overhead and the intense sun moving westward, casting ominous shadows across the earth. In such an environment, extraneous considerations disappear. The entire cosmos of experience comes to be an expanse of rugged plain and a solitary trail leading beyond the next bend toward some unknown destination about to be arrived at. As a once in a lifetime journey, I hoarded the drops of this experience, as the life of the world around me beat through me together, with the beating of my own heart.

At one point along the road, we passed through an area called "the magnetic hill," an area that allegedly defies the law of gravity. It is said that when a vehicle is parked in neutral on this magnetic road, it will slide up rather than down the road. As we made our way through this picturesque landscape, we finally came to the confluence of the Indus and Zanskar Rivers. The narrow valley that we had been following along the river suddenly opened into a crossroads of multiple valleys through which the mighty Zanskar River flowed. It was a rude awakening for the Indus which until that point had had free reign of the landscape tracing its sinuous path through the line of least resistance through mountains valleys in search of its terminus in the broad opening of the Arabian Sea. Now this muddy, turgid river met the emerald green placidity of this other great, meandering river, a meeting of mighty forces if there ever was one. It was a sight to behold, these two proud rivers, the one dark and turgid and the other deep green and slow-moving, coming together in a marriage of opposites that from henceforth would make their way together through these sublime mountains.

As it happens, we did know our destination and I had the luxury of a guide, jeep and bottled water to service our needs along the way. We were on our way to a base camp deep in the western mountains of Ladakh on the road to historic Kargil and Kashmir which for the last decade has been off-limits for most travelers because of the sectarian turmoil that continues to plague the region. The promise of a deluxe tent awaited my arrival; but before settling into camp, we made our way off the beaten path into a side road barely worth the name to the village of Alchi that hosted a monastery that was built over 1000 years ago. Unlike many of the other monasteries I visited during my stay in Ladakh, the Alchi monastery distinguished itself by remaining hidden at the tail end of the village. We made our way downhill through the village amid the gurgle of running streams on either side of the road. It was a hot and dusty mid-afternoon after the long drive from Leh and the sound of the rippling streams was refreshing, if not uplifting, amid the ancient ruins of this small village. In turning one final corner, my guide pointed up beyond the wall. "The story goes that the Lama who founded and constructed the monastery placed his walking stick on this spot near the entrance of the gompa he intended to build on his way from Tibet." I looked up and saw a number of crude walking sticks placed along the back of the wall. "I don't understand," I said confused. "You see that tree behind the wall?" my guide asked me. "That's the Lama's cane. It has grown into a tree." And indeed, I now clearly saw a beautiful willow tree rising heavenward that was once the walking stick of the Great Lama Rinchen Zangpo, called the Translator, who 990 years ago build the ancient and still beautiful Alchi monastery tucked mysteriously in the back end of the village Alchi. We visited

the various temples that house ancient traditional mandala paintings, now fading and disintegrating from age and weather. There are
also exquisite wood carvings in the Kashmiri style said according to
the biographies of the famous Lama to have been done by 30 crafts-
man personally brought over from the Kashmir by the Lama
Zangpo who is said to have been responsible for the building of over
100 temples within the province. What extraordinary souls these
people must have been with such industry and vision.

It was now time to take rest and settle down at the base camp
deep within the Himalayan mountain range. We arrived at the
camp around 4:00 in the afternoon where I had arranged to stay in
what was identified in the travel documents as a "deluxe tent". I had
no idea what to expect, but both the tent and the camp grounds met
my every need for reasonable comfort. The camp itself comprised
about thirty well constructed tents together with other facilities,
including a large open-air building used as what the Arabs call a
majlis or social area where people from all over the world could
meet and discuss the wonders of their travel experiences. The tents
were constructed on a waist-high cement base, followed by a tent-
like structure complete with windows and screens for air circulation. Several people could easily stand and walk within the tent.
There were two beds constructed on a cement base and fitted with
comfortable mattresses, duvets and bedding separated by a night
table with a small lamp, in the end a fortuitous arrangement since I
was going to spend a lot of time in that tent over the next day.

That night, I decided to step out into the night for a breath of
fresh air to celebrate the return of my strength. There was a hushed
silence all about as I sat myself down in one of the bamboo chairs in
a nearby garden. The feeling that overcame me as I sat there in the
darkness, however, was much more than the presence of an
unearthly silence. It was as though I had stepped through an open
door into another dimension altogether. This was not the same garden and wicker chair that I had sat in when I first arrived in the light
of day. This was another world entirely and the feeling of deep
silence that hovered at the edge of this experience had an otherworldly quality strong enough to arouse the instincts of the soul. As
I looked up into the night sky, I felt stunned with disbelief. At this

altitude and within this rarefied setting deep within the Himalayan Mountains, the night sky was a brilliant field of myriad stars, enough to take your breath away. There were so many of them in clusters and clouds that they seemed to form pathways to infinity. I have walked through all of the major cities of the world, but have never witnessed such a spectacle before. It reminded me of an enchanting evocation of nature I once encountered in one of Ralph Waldo Emerson's essays. He encourages the 19th-century reader to "look at the stars" and know that God has provided humanity "the perpetual presence of the sublime," through the inspiration of these heavenly bodies. "Seen in the streets of cities, how great they are! If the stars should appear one night in a thousand years, how would men believe and adore; and preserve for many generations the remembrance of the city of God which men have been shown! But every night come out these envoys of beauty, and light the universe with their admonishing smile."[1] Indeed, how true, I thought, as I sat there looking up at the brilliance of this particular night. How we ignore the beauties of nature that we have available to us and how we forget the secret messages that lie hidden within the symbolic signs of nature that surround us every day of our lives. As I sat there gazing upward in contemplation, the stars seemed to shine as specks of light through a blanket of night, permitting the light of heaven to shine through to us mortals below and recalling the words of Genesis referring to the stars as "lights in the firmament of heaven." Here, in the image of the night sky, we have the perpetual image of the "city of God" at our disposal, and yet we very seldom have the time or inclination to take note of the spectacle of this mystery, much less understand the sacred implications of "what is written in the stars." As I made my way back to the tent, I took note of the three-quarter moon that seemed to hang in suspension in all its beauty as it climbed over the horizon of the looming mountains, like the eye of an owl hidden in a tree.

* * *

1. *Selected Essays of Ralph Waldo Emerson*, Larzer Ziff (ed.), New York, Penguin Books, 1982, p207.

The next morning, we made one final foray deeper west on the way to Kargil and the Kashmir, a province that enjoys legendary fame for its carpet weaving. We soon left the main road which was hardly wide enough for two cars. The road we entered followed the snake route of a small tributary stream hardly worth the name that flowed down from some dwindling glacier far beyond those distant peaks. We were on our way first to the Lamayuru Gompa followed by a brief visit to the Rizong Monastery before heading back to the capital city of Leh. Lamayuru, with its medieval village seemingly growing out of the rocky hillside, belongs to the red-hat sect of Buddhism. Ancient legends say that at the time of Sakyamuni (the Historical Buddha) Lamayuru's valley was a clear lake where holy serpents lived. The Bodhisattva Madhyantaka foretold that the lake would be emptied and a monastery built there. In the 11th century an Indian Buddhist scholar named Naropa came to Lamayuru and spent many years meditating in a cave which can still be seen in the Dukhang. The guide led me to the Dukhang, a large building next to a tall prayer flat pole in the central courtyard. The entrance verandah has been recently painted with a colourful depiction of the Guardians of the Four Directions. In the wall on the right side of the Dukhang is a small cave known as Naropa's cave, where he is supposed to have meditated for several years. Each of the many monasteries scattered through Ladakh have incredible histories attached to them, how they were founded and why a particular location was chosen. These were the centers of power and enlightenment down through the ages until the present era where they continue to exist and influence the area as a living spiritual tradition.

From there, we made our way deeper into the mountains to Rizong Gompa, built more recently about 150 years ago by the great Lama Tsultim Nima and famous for its strictness in upholding the Vinaya teaching and for its apricot trees that when in bloom must be a magnificent sight. This gompa lay hidden behind the many folds of the mountains. We followed the narrow mountain road steadily uphill with room enough for one car only. God forbid that anyone should come down from the other direction. A number of stupas lined the way to announce the proximity of the gompa. "There's Rizong in the distance," my guide shouted, and I saw the magnificent monastery tucked into the cul-de-sac of these dense mountain crags, a virtual miracle of construction, built in terraced layers along the ridge of the mountains, gleaming white in the sun like a mountain village. We passed through the gate of the monastery and arrived at an open courtyard full of children at the base of the layered building. This monastery housed a school for young monks; the children were very young indeed running and playing in the courtyard, their red robes flowing in the wind. They were very rough and tumble and not especially monk-like, but then what would one expect from children anywhere. An older boy was holding a young one by his two hands and was swinging him around in circles lifting him completely off the ground. The younger boy draped in his red robes was flapping in the wind like a flag banner, his face lit up with exultation. It is all natural to these people, I thought, the rugged mountains, the monastic traditions that date back centuries, aging monks sequestered in small cells wrapped in meditation, small children going to school and flapping like a flag in the wind. Life goes on in the same spirit that it has for centuries without missing a beat.

We climbed up a back stairway higher and higher into the inner sanctum of the monastery. There are outgrowths of rooms upon rooms, doors leading I know not where. The guide went to find a monk and get a key to the uppermost temple where we spent some time looking at the mandalas painted on the wall full of meanings I cannot fathom, but can appreciate as works of sacred traditional art that are incomparable, rare and unique. Equally rare and unique are the books that at first I didn't recognize as such that lined the walls, until I was told by the guide what they were. The walls contained cubicles that held one volume of the long Tibetan manuscripts, wrapped in rich cloth and placed between two painted wooden slabs to keep the precious contents as perfect as possible. I noticed that there were a few items for sale on a shelf, one of which was a book written by an Englishman who has come to stay at Rizong in the early 60s as a novice monk. Out of curiosity, I bought the book and later read it in the hotel when I returned to Leh, enchanted to have the opportunity of reading about the life of a novice in the famous Rizong monastery that I had personally visited.

Before leaving the sacred precinct, I stepped over to the porch of the temple and gazed reflectively at the panoramic scene before me. As the mountains fell away down the face of the cliffs, I listened to the silence that lay over the land as an abiding presence. The sea has its reflection of the stillest and darkest night; the woods are quiet with hundreds of lesser noises but here was the suspension of sound, except for the occasional bird or movement of the rows of prayer flats flapping in the wind. At first, the silence of the landscape strikes the visitor like a flea in the eye or a splinter under the skin. It feels bothersome, leaving you to wonder where the comforting noises are that we have become accustomed to. You look around and wonder what happened. The silence floats on the wind and whispers into the ear of mysteries unrevealed and narratives unread. The bell of one's sensibilities echoes with the waves of this emptiness clear down the bottomless well of the soul. It is as invisible as the wind and as soundless as the void; a borderless and boundless overlay to the serenity of the valleys and the majesty of the mountains that surround me. I feel shaken and humbled by this unaccustomed silent intruder into my consciousness, as if the noise of the city were a long lost and comforting friend, far from the familiarity of the chaos and cacophony that reminds me I am alive. We have grown accustomed to the turmoil of sound and feel uncomfortable with the silence of the night sky or the hush that hovers over the valleys and mountain peaks. Will I grow as accustomed to the unheard and unseen premonitions of this native landscape in the same way that we grow accustomed to the hush of a church and the lingering scent of incense and feel comforted by their abiding presence?

We began to make our way down the side of the mountain once again, when the guide asked me if I wanted to visit the nunnery that we were just passing by. "Yes, indeed", I said immediately, thinking what a rare and unique opportunity that I should not let pass by. We backed up on the narrow road and pulled into a dirt driveway leading up to the nunnery perched on the hill. There were some old buildings and a small courtyard where we sat in the shadow of some willow trees. As we took rest and absorbed the quiet ambiance of the place, I suddenly heard the sound of robes flapping like bird wings in the air. "That's one of the nuns," my guide explained as I saw a fleeting figure run from one building to another. "It's difficult to tell the difference between the monks and the nuns." Indeed, the fleeing monk was indeed a nun, head shaved with the prominent Mongolian features of slanted eyes and moon face, smiling demurely at the elderly pale-face sitting in repose under the tree. I could hear running water in the background and the guide led me over to a small waterfall that cascaded over a rock ledge in the hill. "Have a drink," he encouraged me. Indeed, I took up his offer and drank deeply the crystalline waters of this glacial stream. The Chinese would call it "qi" and the Indians "prana"; I call it a poem in motion. By all accounts what I experienced in these clear refreshing waters was a life force that was original in quality and from a unique source. I do not exaggerate when I say that I could feel the energy of the snowmelt mountain stream course through my veins, depositing its clear and pure essence like some electrical charge through the meridians of my body. This was the true nectar of Shangri-La.

* * *

The longer a traveler journeys through a place like Ladakh, the more one takes on the enchantment of nature and the spirit of the sacred traditions that are the essential reality of such a place. The mountains, the valleys, indeed, the primordial wilderness are all there as ancient artifacts that are timeless and eternal, and yet having had the privilege of passing through such a primordial wilderness, I did not feel as though I were leaving this miraculous place behind, but rather that something of the wilderness itself—whether it be the ink-blue sky, the flooded, swift-moving river, or those cloud-free, snow-capped mountains—had entered and become a part of me as an experience that would stay with me and endure as a sign of a new sensibility. As such, I returned without regret to the familiar surroundings of the capital city of Leh and the hotel I had stayed at earlier, the faithful hotel attendants there once again to greet me as we pulled up to the front door in the jeep, as though I had just journeyed across the mountains of the moon only to arrive back at this familiar and most welcome setting to be greeted as a prodigal traveler now returning from the edge of a lost horizon.

Now at the end of my stay, the driver and guide brought me to a village nearby Leh that happened to be the homestead of the driver himself. I didn't know this at first, but soon realized that something was not the same when people began to greet him, while the driver beamed his smile in return as we made our way deeper into the village. The guide and I eventually left the jeep to walk into the center of town. There was a great crowd of people gathered together in the town square. At first I didn't know what was happening, but soon enough the guide explained that a famous Lama had arranged a town meeting of the community to give them instruction on the Buddhist doctrine of compassion for all things in this life and the possibility of escape from the "wheel of existence" through good works and honest living. We soon discovered that the Lama had just left and people began to walk about and have lunch. We briefly visited a temple on one side of the square, but at this point I was much more interested in taking in the ambiance of this rare and unique gathering.

At one end of the square, a kind of throne was set in place, covered with carpets and adorned with flowers. The Lama had sat there to address the crowd. Now, of course, this area had been cleared with his departure, but the entire square was still full of people, sitting here and there in groups on carpets that had been laid for the occasion. Clusters of people were having lunch and chatting. There was the scent of incense in the air and overhead the entire square was covered in great colored awnings of cloth to block the direct rays of the sun. In addition, from one side of the square to the other, prayer flags were strewn, sending their prayerful messages into the air as the wind blew through the square. The entire scene had an enchanting quality to it, like something from another time and place, proving that there are ancient traditions that are still living and real in the hustle and bustle of today's modern, secular world.

As we roamed about, my guide and I were invited to sit down and partake of some lunch. People were snacking on buttered bread and I was offered a taste of a thick, flat and weighty brown scone, called a *taki*, followed by the traditional tea of the area. As I sat there cross-legged on carpets taking in this unique experience, a woman passed by carrying a young infant. Suddenly, the child looked down upon me, beamed an angelic smile, and reached out to be taken up in my arms.

Those sitting around the carpet were astonished by the child's behavior, and I secretly wondered if this weren't some instance of a young infant remembering some connection to me from some previous lifetime, since by now I was beginning to think that anything is possible in these places. I took the adorable bundle into my arms and basked in the warmth of his endearing infant sentiments for a few minutes, then passed him back to his mother. I later learned that I looked like the child's grandfather, whose white beard, closely cropped hair, and eye glasses resembled my own.

We eventually left the village scene behind to return to the city, but I have carried away with me the image of that child reaching across chasms of age and culture and language to convey a universal truth to my unsuspecting soul. We are all one in the universal scheme of things, interconnected on subterranean levels of experience by the forces of deep-seeded spiritual traditions and the enchantment of virgin nature and human expressions of good will. It may take a journey to distant lands and the experience of its silent places to realize that a virgin wilderness of spirit lies within us that awaits discovery and exploration, permitting the weary traveler to transcend borders and cross chasms of experience to arrive home at the end of a journey as a changed soul, ennobled by this encounter with people from other cultures and enriched by this visit to distant places in the shadow of Heaven.

3

INSIDE
PATHAN COUNTRY

FOREWORD

AMID THE STRONG FEELINGS and surprising events of this Pathan diary, there is perhaps some room for a brief forward. The episodes in the following account might have been the random notes of a stranger in a strange land; instead, they have become the genuine impressions of a rare and unique experience. The world was approaching the turn of the millennium and, in addition to the world-wide crash of computers, I had been warned about venturing into the northern frontier regions of Pakistan. The harbingers of doom had shouted dire warnings in the civilized world I inhabit. My family was worried, my friends either skeptical or alarmed. The threat of terrorism and the spirit of anxiety that accompanied the approach of the new millennium seemed to focus in particular on the Muslim world. Stark images and sinister innuendo, I thought unconcerned, are like the bullets of a gun: they can be invasive, determining, and even fatal to the integrity of one's deep-rooted attitudes and beliefs unless you are vigilant.

Muslim terrorists, Islamic militants, the Khyber Pass, the intransigent Taliban, mysterious Pashtu tribesman—all well publicized elements of an allegedly grand scheme of terror and intrigue that had become a primary focal point of the international media, highlighting a part of the world I was intending to visit as a lawless frontier and focusing on a form of militancy among remote and little known tribal peoples that is portrayed in the media as rigid and unforgiving. Americans were being warned to keep a low profile and avoid large crowds in both Europe and the Middle East. In particular, people intending to travel abroad during the holiday season were advised to avoid potential hotspots such as Pakistan. Nevertheless, I brushed aside these warnings and resolved to fulfill a promise I had made to my Pathan friend, Farman Allah, to visit him in his village in the North West Frontier Province of Pakistan.

I have journeyed to many foreign places, but on this trip, a strange thing happened that the diary itself will have to reveal. When you travel to a remote and distant land, you fully expect to enter an unfamiliar and intriguing world of people, places, and events that may interest, entertain, and challenge you beyond the comfort zone of your former experience. In retrospect, I now realize that I didn't enter Pathan Country; on the contrary the spirit of the Pathan had entered me. The truth is, one takes away from such a rare encounter more than a memory that can be expressed in words and phrases. One comes away feeling changed somehow and different, as if the experience had become a rite of passage into another, a more traditional world, whose ambiance and spirit still remain in my soul in noble contrast, and as an anachronism of time, to the cultivated fields of Western civilization and the prevailing spirit of the modern world.

Behind the fragile façade of a country in transition and behind the noble face of a people in search of a place in the modern world lies the ancient and enduring spirit of a traditional, Islamic way of life. If what we suffer in today's world is a kind of invasion of the modern "spirit" into the very heart and soul of the individual, then I can similarly affirm that this unexpected journey has resulted in the incursion of another kind into my heart, of a phantom spirit from a distant past, permitting this rare passageway into a frontier-land from another era, into a world of people and events in which the vicissitudes of the modern world could be momentarily forgotten and left behind. For a few brief days, you are privileged to enter a world that remembers and emulates the spirit of the traditional world where one's word becomes a bond, where a promise is still sacred, where the world is transparent; where generosity is the norm. In return, that world enters you.

This diary is a journey into a forgotten world where a common humanity is inscribed in the way of life and a mutual respect is reasserted before the terrible darkness of spirit that exists within the modern world. In return, this brief encounter with the traditional world of the Pathan may serve as a vehicle of understanding among men in which the spirit of the modern world actually reflects something of the traditional world of the spirit.

NOTES FROM THE PATHAN DIARY

For Pakistan, you is foreign guest; but for me and all the uncles and cousins and friends in my village, Yahya, you is friend and brother. Welcome! (Farman Allah, Pathan Tribesman)

Nothing could have adequately prepared me on all the levels of body, mind, and heart for my encounter with the great Pathan tribe and the profoundly moving experience I had at the turn of the millennium in the North West Frontier Province (NWFP) of Pakistan. A brief hint and perhaps a premonition of what was to come began to take root after my initial introduction to a Pathan named Farman ibn (son of) Saleh Mohamed while working at a university in the Emirates. Fascinated by the sight of a Western Muslim such as myself praying at a local mosque, Farman introduced himself and initiated a friendship that soon grew and deepened. The incredible solidarity and camaraderie of the Pathan people began to unfold as I was slowly taken into the inner sanctum of their unique brotherhood whose integrity they have religiously preserved even amid the hardships and severe working conditions in the Gulf countries. The developing story culminated in an invitation to visit Farman and his extended family of mother, brothers, sisters, in-laws, uncles, aunts, cousins and other close childhood friends in a small village outside of Peshawar.

You come, Yahya. The people in village is waiting for you. If you not come, whole village is very sad and I will kill you.

I thought for a minute, then looked at my Pathan friend and beyond to the inner being of the man. At a glance, he could have passed as a tender giant of childhood fairy tales. His frame was larger than life, well-proportioned, solid and suggesting a feeling of strength and nobility that went beyond the normal course of a man. There was a bigness in him that transcended his body. Dark-skinned and toughened by hours of hard work out in the grueling elements of the Emirate desert where he worked as a foreman for an irrigation company, he wore his thick dark hair closely cropped and had a well-trimmed jet-black beard covering his face, offsetting the brightness of his eyes and the light of his facial expression. I knew he was kidding about killing me, not because of the broad smile and the gleaming row of white teeth, but rather because within that incredible body was a simple, innocent, uncorrupted, noble soul incapable of committing any true outrage. Indeed, he was a formidable being by any account and a rare and unique friend that I truly valued and trusted, even with my life. When he invited me to visit his village, I accepted, knowing full well the import and implications of such a rare invitation. He was drawing a line in the sand by inviting me to cross over into a very private and conservative world that few have ever seen, much less experienced.

I arose at 4:00 a.m. on the day of departure, to have the pre-dawn Ramadhan breakfast (*suhur*) and say the prayer. The Muslims were now in the final days of Ramadhan when my trip would coincide with the Eid Festival after the holy month. I was scheduled to fly out of Muscat, in the Sultanate of Oman where I lived and worked, at 8:00 in the morning for the two and a half hour flight. When I got to the airport, however, I was informed that the flight was unexpectedly delayed. The plane eventually left at 1:00 in the afternoon, jammed packed with Pathan tribesman and the incredible amounts of luggage, blankets, cartons, and oversized bags, some of which had to be left behind. I thought with relief of my friend waiting to receive me with his friends at the still unknown and mysterious destination of Peshawar in the North-West Frontier Province.

As we approached Peshawar, I could see the dramatic range of the Safed Koh mountains that runs along the border with Afghanistan and through which the famous Khyber Pass winds. The range of cliffs was shrouded in mist. The pilot attempted a landing, but apparently thought twice about it since the fog at the airport was so dense that it made a safe landing questionable. He then turned the plane around and we soon landed at Islamabad, the capital of Pakistan and the seat of the government. Needless to say, this was a little alarming. I was supposed to be met upon my arrival and there was the question of "security". I knew that my friend would be beside himself with worry.

My friend Farman was taking the security issue very seriously, since that part of Pakistan was traditionally considered to be a wild and ungovernable area. Americans had been warned during the millennium festivities about travel, particularly to Pakistan, and there had been bombing incidents against American interests in Pakistan recently. There were the heightened security concerns surrounding the whole Osama bin Laden affair since he had issued a call to kill Americans world-wide, and the year-end hijacking of the Indian airliner to Afghanistan had recently heightened tensions in the area. The still unidentified hostage-takers had allegedly passed anonymously across the border in the area where I was headed.

Against all expectation there I was, being bundled into a small transit area of the aging, single-runway airport at Islamabad. We passed through immigration and I was shoved unceremoniously over with the other tribal horde, all bedecked in turbans and shawls and talking agitatedly in a foreign tongue to await further instructions! Oman Air didn't have any representative there as understandably they don't fly into Islamabad. I soon gleaned that the luggage was being offloaded, indicating we were here to stay.

Dark thoughts began to emerge. I managed to approach the sole person who seemed to have any wits about him and spoke some English. When I suggested that I take a taxi to Peshawar, he quickly advised me not to. "It's very dangerous," he whispered. He then added ominously as an afterthought, "you will never make it to your destination!" Word soon arrived that buses would be provided to take all 200 of us, including the mountains of luggage to Peshawar. Before I could ponder the possibilities of an endless night of hassles, and thinking of my friend who has been waiting to meet me since 11:30 that morning, I was confronted with a well-dressed and charming employee of Shaheen Airlines who informed me in a clipped British accent that my friend Farman had managed to call and wanted the message passed on to me that he would come down to Islamabad himself to pick me up, a 175 km trip that with the terrible road conditions could take up to three hours!

Now the real Pathan experience began to unfold in its truest dimension. I was escorted through the airport to the restaurant and offered a delicious complementary dinner of rice and kebab (I had been fasting through all of this!), and thereafter invited down to the airline office to await the coming of my friend. About 9:00 that night, I finally met Farman and his two other "bodyguards", all three of whom arrived sporting armed rifles and guns. Indeed, they were taking my security seriously. Farman had a revolver tucked discreetly into his "cloth", Farouk and Babu both had Kalashnikov rifles hanging discreetly along the folds of their woolen shawls.

Indeed, the winter weather was freezing beyond belief. Cold, damp, record-setting temperatures had been recorded that winter in the region. I was delighted to see my friend, guns and all, as he muscled his way with his two brawny friends through the crowds of the terminal and never was the sight of a friendly face so endearing. They all embraced me in great bear hugs, wrapped me into a spare wrap-around-foot woolen shawl typical of the area and escorted me out into the raw elements of the night, only to be confronted with a commotion of people, cars, taxies, rickshaws, horses, donkeys, and bicycles whose cacophonic sounds were all draped in a shroud of near total darkness, not exactly the mirror reflection of the gleaming metropolis I was coming from. We hadn't walked five steps when it became clear that the car, which they had quickly left by the curbside to fetch me from inside, was being taken away. It had been raised up on a forklift that looked like it was attempting to lodge it on top of a tree. This inspired much argument, protestations that I was a foreign guest and much more, then with a wink and a nod (and a few hundred rupees), the car was dumped back down onto the road, whence I was tucked into the back seat for the return trip to Peshawar.

People here drive as they like. There is no law on the road. And everyone is government of one.

Only God could have prepared me—or saved me—from the wild ride back to Peshawar along a road that was poorly lit, two way, accommodating a multitude of cars all attempting to pass each other at incredible speeds while avoiding the carts, animals, bicycles, and potholes that littered the road. Doesn't anyone sleep in this country? I wondered. I sat mesmerized by the sight of the on-coming headlights heading straight for us, only to be brought out my trance by near-death experiences in which we passed in and out of the on-coming lane at the last minute. It seems to be a question of pride to take chances and show no fear, but as we careened down the road into the dark night heading toward the North West Frontier Province and ultimately my friend's village, I was petrified. I had finally arrived inside Pathan country.

By the time we arrived at my friend's tiny village about 30 kms outside of Peshawar, it was nearly midnight and I was exhausted, but the end of the day was not yet in sight. A great crowd of people, men I should say, awaited my arrival just outside his ancestral home and were there to greet me with a garland of wild flowers that they placed with a great show of spirit around my neck. Everyone was beaming with happiness as we crowded into the "guest room" the family had prepared for me to use while I was visiting the village.

I was ashamed to learn later that these "poor" village people had actually built and refurbished this spacious room at the entrance to their living compound, complete with separate private bathroom, running hot water and shower, all American amenities they had never had in the main part of the house even. I was ensconced in front of the little electric heater, thoroughly wrapped up in the woolen shawl, and so were the others sitting in random semi-circles around me, including Farman's brother with whom I could communicate in Arabic, his father in law who was an educator and sometime doctor who spoke fair English, his uncle, his cousins, his nephews, his childhood friends and other close members of his village. As I began to drift off into the total exhaustion of sleep, I noted the clear, strong sound of their native tongue, Pashtu, which belongs to the Iranian linguistic group. It later became clear to me that these tribesmen are great story-tellers and the story of my arrival was even then being spread far and wide from the crowded room on that dark, sober night from village to village across the area.

All food is original and fresh from farm. We visit tomorrow the land around village and you see for yourself.

As a city boy from the suburbs of Boston, Mass., I had never drunk milk from a cow much less from a goat or water buffalo; I had never eaten fresh yogurt or unprocessed cheese made by some mother's hand; I had never tasted a farm fresh chicken or a freshly laid egg; nor had I ever eaten meat stewed in buffalo oil! Where had I been all my life to have missed out on this exotic, "original" fare? Indeed, I had never eaten the amounts of food I was called upon to eat in the name of hospitality, for the Pathan people pride themselves on hospitality without bounds and its success is measured in the amount of food the guest can eat. Gratefully, the first four days of my stay were the last days of the fast of Ramadhan, so I had a brief respite before the really serious eating began after breaking the fast in the evening.

We awoke early to have a hearty breakfast, although understandably the word for this meal in both Arabic and Pashtu means anything but "break-fast". Rather, it is the meal that commences the fast and seals its sacred intention. After eating not only the fresh eggs, yogurt and honey, but also the steaming rice, lentils and meat that were to preserve us during the rigors of the fast, we made our ablutions and found our way to the mosque for the early morning, pre-dawn prayer, walking in groups through the dark, eerie village. The narrow little streets were shrouded in a thick layer of mist and fog which passed like spectral ghosts through the tall, thin poplar trees that lined the near-by fields with their sentinel presence.

We went on a tour of the environs surrounding my Pathan friend's village that morning. The countryside itself was lush, well-tended and green with ripening winter vegetation in spite of the winter season; but I was even more impressed with the number and variety of trees that highlighted the bucolic setting, particularly the wide variety of fruit trees that crowded around the more stately poplars, cedars, and oaks. Springtime I was told brought a blaze of flowers, so I would have to return once again to see them. On one side of the narrow path, a field dense with the tough-looking leaves of the cauliflower; on the other side, purple-skinned potatoes, what we used to call in my Irish-American family "new" potatoes, lay steaming in the newly-overturned soil. In the distance the courtly stalks of the sugar cane were blowing lazily in the light wind.

The farmers all waved and then went about their business, cutting, pruning, digging the rich earth and tending the animals who wandered about in this natural setting as though from some primordial past. Great water buffalo stood under well-thatched, open-sided sheds exuding an air of detachment and contentedness, an archetypal example if there ever was one in nature of an animal teaching man the meaning of both contentment and calm. Little lambs frolicked in the grass while one proud villager introduced me to his pet sheep, a magnificent looking animal who sported a well groomed, chocolate colored coat with a lush verge of sheep-down that hung along the back of its legs and sashayed as it moved like the bustle of a woman's skirt. It nudged its head affectionately against my leg in response to my greetings and looked up at me with clear, intelligent eyes as if it wanted to make friends.

This is all natural and original setting, Yahya. Now I take you to see sugar cane factory where they make sugar.

Factory, I thought puzzled, entrenched as I was within a fixed mindset that thought only in modern cityscape terms. What I was about to see was a "factory" in the same sense that we say that the discovery of certain tools in pre-historic times was an advance in "technology". I nearly slipped on a patch of buffalo manure and skipped over a gurgling stream before we came upon the "factory" just over that slight incline covered in sugar cane stalks. A more natural setting could not be imagined and a far cry from the bleak and dismal factories of the Western world.

A primitive apparatus set up in the fields squeezed the juices of the sugar cane in a large tub. This raw nectar was then transferred to large copper vats that were heated to boiling point underground in a series of tunnels fueled by the crushed residue of the cane. Two old Pakistanis sporting their traditional beards knelt beside one great vat and stirred the golden creamy broth with flat ladles in what must have been backbreaking work, but their smiles belied their effort and the light on their faces was matched by the rays of the sun that stole through the cracks of the thatched roof to settle and glow on this frothy sweet nectar. On the other side of the enclosure, I saw a similar vat that contained the end result: small, rounded brown sugar balls that I couldn't taste at that moment as we were all still fasting, but every house sweetened their tea with this natural, home-made sugar. Out back, we saw where the fire was stoked, where the fresh ripe stalks were gathered, and where the used cane was prepared for re-cycling, but all was a mere after-thought after the sight of those two old men smiling in the fullness of their years. Factory, indeed!

I have new cloth for Pakistani suit and we buy you waistcoat and shoes and sandals. All must be new for Eid festival.

The next day, we were scheduled to visit the city of Peshawar, including the famous Mogul fort built by King Akbar in the 16th century and of course the grand bazaar. The fort we saw from the distance, a sprawling, magnificently constructed structure in the style of the period that could not be visited in its interior because it is still being used as a military encampment and headquarters. The bazaar we saw by plunging headlong into the labyrinthine puzzle of side-streets and by-ways all jam-packed with every manner of buggy and vehicle from horse, donkey, and bullock-drawn carts to vesper-driven rickshaws that attempted to weave their irritating way through every available space. The amount of pollution thrown off by these vehicles created thick pea-soup smog that clogged the nos-trils and seriously affected my breathing.

The Eid was several days away and the city was in the final throes of shopping in preparation for the end of Ramadhan celebration, known as *Eid al-Fitr*. I was very concerned during this shopping spree about the money situation. I had first consulted with Farman at the airport about changing money, but he refused to dignify the discussion with words. I asked him again early that morning, hop-ing for the opportunity of trying out my famous bargaining skills in the money markets of the Peshawar bazaar, but not wishing to insult him somehow by breaking the protocol of the "guest", I soon fell silent. I was to have no such experience with the money-changers. In fact, I never touched Pakistani money and never laid eyes on it while I was in Pakistan. It was this Pathan villager Farman who saw to my every need and was ready to buy anything that concerned my well-being or desire. That needless to say included outfitting me for the Eid with new "cloth", shoes, and a woolen Pashtu vest and their traditional distinctive hat which I hoped to wear by way of disguise.

A further word on the question of money could not be broached without causing serious insult.

We spent considerable time roaming like locals through the maze of streets and stalls, with every kind of clothing and cloth hanging down from overhead awnings, much of the work was tailor-made by people sitting at their sewing machines right there in the narrow alleys of the bazaar. I was in the market for a smart Pakistani waist-coat that has since become world famous, in the style of what we often saw Nawaz Shareef wearing before his downfall and incarcera-tion. It is a sleeveless coat that comes in different materials and col-ors, but we were looking for a heavy one made of wool with a matching Pashtu cap. I was already wearing a Pakistani suit of my own and soon enough, thanks to the bargaining skills of my friend, was sporting the woolen waistcoat and cap.

I was fully expecting to stand out in the bazaar "like a sore thumb" as I looked about me in the crowded confusion of the bazaar, especially in light of the hysterical warnings on CNN over the holidays to avoid crowded places and keep a low profile against the event of terrorism. Here I was in the midst of what some people consider to be terror-terror land, plunging into the frantic pre-Eid crowds with aplomb. However the truth was quite different, I real-ized a little sadly: no one took any notice of me. I was as invisible and anonymous as the next bearded and turbaned person. I men-tioned this to Farman as we pushed out way through the bazaar. He smiled happily and beamed a bright light. *You look like people who come from secret valley in North Pakistan, near Hunza, descendants of Alexander the Great. They have same color like you. White color for the beard to make you old; red color for the skin to make you healthy; sky color for the eyes to make you happy*, he said. In the life of simple truths that he lived, he considered me to be one of their own people, for I was a Muslim, a brother and a friend.

In the evenings of the final days of Ramadhan, we always returned to the guestroom where I was staying, to break the fast and sit with Farman's relatives and village friends. The guestroom itself reveals an inner dimension of the family's invitation. I had asked Farman where I would stay when I was there and what sort of arrangements could be made that would not intrude on the integrity of the household. I was concerned because I knew with what strictness the Pathan tribesmen preserve their "traditions", particularly when it comes to home life and the sanctity of the family, what the Arabs call the *harem*, (literally: that which is holy) or inner sanctum of the household where the women and children live and that constitutes the hearth (and heart) of the home.

Only after my arrival was I to discover the reality of the situation. Farman and his brother had built up a storage area of the household into a fully furnished living quarter complete with an attached bathroom that included a shower with hot water, clearly an incredible concession to my particular western needs since the rest of the house had no running water. A well serviced their needs set off in the corner of the inner courtyard near the kitchen. The freshly-laid plaster on the walls of the room was still damp and this accounted for why it wasn't painted yet. Farman and his brother apologized profusely for the fact that the walls were still in such a condition; but it couldn't be helped. The room was amply furnished with two beds, a carpet that covered the entire floor, a divan, and a number of Arab style pillows and cushions to service the people who visited since they all sat on the floor. I never slept alone—either Farman or his brother slept in the other bed with the Kalashnikov for protection against any unexpected intruders.

I was profoundly shocked to learn that for a one-week visit this poor family had gone to this kind of expense and clearly in my naiveté I didn't realize that these people didn't have "guest" rooms. The houses in the village were made of red brick, resembling solid, rectangular mini-fortresses. Rooms fanned out around an inner courtyard reflecting a tempo of additions as the need arose for more space: one room for the mother where the grandchildren often gathered, another for the oldest brother, wife and family, another for his other brother Mohammed who lived in the Emirates, housing his wife and four children. Farman and his wife occupied another room with their two young children, the oldest sibling, a sister who had never married and had taken care of her younger siblings when their father died, also had her own room. Finally, there was a communal kitchen used by all the wives and his mother and a latrine used by all. The guestroom was well separated from this hub of activity, being on the other side of the courtyard and adjacent to a small garage that led onto the street.

Tomorrow we go into the mountains of the famous Swat area. We visit my friend Akbar and his family in mountains outside Swat. You know Akbar from Emirates.

There was a rhythm to this journey and an ambiance of well being and meaning that comes from a number of factors including intelligent planning and purposeful design. To Farman, we were not visiting the area as tourists marveling at the sights; we were visiting friends who happened to live in a region of the country whose natural beauty could be enjoyed as a by-product of the journey; but what really mattered was the visit with friends. It was the first day of the Eid, a day for visiting loved ones and friends above all. We said the early morning prayer in the mosque. I was embraced by just about everyone in the mosque, the elders and the youth alike, great bear hugs punctuated with heart-felt greetings and *salaams*. The way they shook and embraced me attested to the sheer delight it was for them to encounter an American Muslim under these circumstances in their tiny mosque on this special day of rejoicing, celebrating the end of a month-long fast. The elders had given me a place of honor in the front row behind the prayer-leader (*imam*). In every instance, great care was taken to preserve the "protocol" of the moment.

Farman and I, his brother-in-law Babu, Farouk, a close friend who did all the driving in the "borrowed" car—in fact my three bodyguards were still armed to the teeth with revolvers and rifles—set off around mid-morning for the foothills of the Himalayas beyond the northern side of Peshawar, whose soot and suffocating smog I was glad to leave behind. We stopped for lunch and sat outside on wooden benches wrapped in our woolen shawls against the bitter cold to sample the local *kebab* that we scooped up with fresh, piping-hot Pakistani bread. Farman had bought some tomatoes from the vegetable stall and hand washed them himself, knowing of my passion for tomato salad. Nothing was overlooked and everything was remembered. The *kebab* actually looked like an oversized burger, but didn't taste like one, being seasoned in the local style with onions, tomatoes, peppers, herbs and spices, putting to shame the stale, overcooked burgers served in fast food places in the US. We washed this down with thick black tea before bundling ourselves back into the small car for the next leg of the journey, feeling fully satisfied and well fortified against the winter chill.

I had the overwhelming sense of "living" rather than "touring", of being a part of something real rather than acting out a role as journeyer and casual tourist. As I sat in the back seat and looked out over the increasingly more beautiful countryside, I listened to the conversational banter of Farman and his two friends. One thing worth noting is that these people are great conversationalists as well as great linguists, and I was able to witness this in person as we drove deeper into the mountains of the northern frontier. Farman himself speaks five or six languages, but he never made much of this ability, as if it were second nature to everyone. I know for a fact that he spoke his own native Pashtu, in addition to Urdu which is the national language of Pakistan officially spoken by everyone in the country, but actually used by only one-tenth of the population on a regular basis, Hindi which is similar to Urdu but written with a different script, Farsi which is the Iranian language in which his own language of Pashtu shares an ancient legacy, fluent Arabic and increasingly proficient English, not to mention several other dialects and languages of other tribes of the area that he was familiar with.

However, it was in the style of their conversation that their true characters were revealed, for these people love to converse with each other more than anything. They sit together; they talk together; and they are silent together in a manner that doesn't exist in the Western world. Above all, in spite of the language barriers between myself and the others, a sense of balance was preserved. Farman concerned himself with his friends but somehow never forgot me and made every attempt to include me in their banter. I couldn't understand their conversation as such, but what with my own linguistic ability, my background in Arabic (for Pashtu has Arabic influences) and from a context that was often briefly outlined by Farman, I was often able to glean much of what was being said, at least in its general meaning and import. The truth is, the details didn't matter to me that much. It was enough to witness the incredible camaraderie, friendship, and mirth that flowed from one to the other. It was obvious that much of what they were saying consisted of stories and tales of earlier times and places, humorous and/or serious events that had happened to them that required dialogue, drama, emotion, and talent to recreate as a living memory. But I was never left out. Farman would ask after my well-being, translate particularly interesting points, and comment on the countryside. Babu made courageous attempts to refresh his English in his unselfconscious and bold style. Farouk showed himself to be the imp that he was through a cascade of words and intonations that I couldn't understand, but that somehow had the power to mesmerize me with their intonation and charm. When he laughed, everyone laughed, for his smile was too infectious for words. Whenever I repeated a few phrases of their beloved Pashtu, they made much of it and were as overjoyed as children.

It was growing dark and I was getting concerned. After all, someone had to worry as my companions were so carefree and trusting to fate that nothing seemed to bother them and certainly not the approaching night. The mountains were getting more rugged and the landscape more primitive looking. The road narrowed and the cliffs drew down steeper into the valleys. The sparkling waters of the Swat River wound their way down through the hills and cliffs with a clarity and vitality that suggested some kind of living presence and we could hear the roar of the swift-moving current as it made its way through the valley below. Soon enough, dusk turned to darkness and in the pitch-black night of the sky, the big dipper rose once again to reaffirm a reality that is greater than our own through the presence of the stars as a celestial awning of divine light peeking through the darkness like pinholes in black velvet.

The final few miles turned into a search for the small village in the mountainous Swat area where Farman's friend Akbar lived with his large family. Have you been here before, I asked Farman. *Yes*, he said firmly as he peered out the clouded window, *once, about fifteen years ago, when I was sixteen.* But these people have good memories attested to by the multiple languages they remember. We were soon making our way in total darkness through the street of a tiny village built along the contour of the mountain. Densely packed houses crowded along the side of the village street that was very narrow with very little room for a modern vehicle such as we had. Our expert driver Farouk negotiated the cramped passageway with precision, careful not to let the car slip into the open drains separating the street from the houses.

We were soon well ensconced in a typical Islamic-style sitting room, what the Arabs call a *majlis* that is always the first and outermost room of the house, invitingly furnished with carpets and cushions. It was bitter cold, but this was offset by the incredible warmth of feeling and hospitality afforded by the host, Akbar who I knew from the Emirates, together with his father and brothers and a number of other men from the village who had came to welcome us. We sat around on the floor of course, a habit that I have grown accustomed to over the years, and within the hour, the floor was spread with a cloth and Akbar's brothers brought in a piping hot array of foods, a specially flavored rice famous in that area, meat and vegetable dishes, and the much favored *raita*, a yogurt dish flavored with chips of cucumber, onion and green pepper, all washed down with the strong black tea that they seemed to favor there. I noted that the bread, as in all Pakistani homes, was lovingly wrapped in a cloth bundle and set in a basket, to keep it warm.

When it was time to retire for the night, the four of us were led back out into the elements further up the hill and deeper into the village where we passed through a gate into an inner garden with various rooms for sleeping. When I entered the room, I saw five beds lining the walls. All the beds were hand-made from rope woven across a wooden frame, and each came well equipped with a simple cotton mat covered with hand-embroidered sheets and hand made quilts that were very heavy. Under that mountain of hand-packed cotton, no one was cold. The host slept with us in the room as a courtesy to the guests. My companions quickly nestled into the folds of their weighted blankets and after various shifts and turns fell into a seemingly heavy sleep. I lay on my back listening to the regulated breathing of these rough mountain men who seem to live life to the fullest; but when they lay themselves down are quick to abandon their daily cares for the peace and potential dreams that deep slumber affords the pure of heart.

During the night, I had to go to the bathroom, so I got up quietly, not wanting to disturb the others, and especially not my three commandos who like babies slept the sleep of the innocent. Once I had left the safe haven of the blanket, it was bitter cold outside, but I had no choice and donning my sandals at the door, I made my way across to the little outhouse that stood at the other end of the garden within the walled enclosure. Simple bodily functions were never so difficult, but finally relief was at hand and I stepped back out into the cold dark night of the garden to find my friend Farman standing guard several feet away with the Kalashnikov sitting on his hip and a sleepy grin on his face.

In the morning, we made our ablutions and said the early morning dawn prayer, which is recited at the first light of day well before the actual light of dawn creeps over the horizon of the world. Hot water was prepared and the host himself actually poured the water over my hands and feet to facilitate the ritual since running water from a tap was not available. Thereafter, and ready as we all were for more food, we sat down to a sumptuous breakfast of fruit, yogurt, a flaking and nourishing oil-based bread well known in the sub-continent as *paratha*, which we used to scoop up the thick, fresh cream and the raw, unprocessed and pure honey.

I asked my host about the honey because not only was the taste exquisite and as my friend Farman liked to say "original", but it also seemed to have bits and pieces of the hive itself mixed in with the gooey sweet mass. Akbar told me the honey came from within their very house. It seems his eighty year old grandmother can communicate somehow with the bees and had been able to coax them into the house to set up their hive. The bees come and go as they please given the nature of their "duties" to the household, I was told, and no one seems to notice, least of all the bees themselves. You can even play with the bees and they don't bother you, Akbar told me wide-eyed. Now that's original honey, I thought.

When I stepped through the door of the garden upon our departure, the land spread away in front of me into the distance to form a magnificent panorama of snow-peaked mountains and clouds. As the pale disk of the winter sun rose in the distance, I saw our next destination, the rugged, white, mountain peaks of the Karakoram, the land of the snow cloud and the traditional, northern spice-route to China. We said our good-byes and prepared to take our leave. There had been a light rain during the night, the first in many months and the village street had turned into a sea of mud that we had to trek through in order to reach the car. The old man, Akbar's father, gave me a warm embrace and was the last to pass his hand through the car window to offer me one final hand-shake. Through hand gestures, he gave me the traditional signs to indicate that he wanted me to pray for him. I quickly nodded the customary sentiments, but felt humbled by his request. He was the model of benevolence, the host in the tradition of the Prophet and the generous one reflective of one of the names of God in Islam (*al-Kareem*). His prayers I thought would fall more readily at the foot of the throne of God than mine, but the Muslims have a favorite saying: *Allah knows best*.

In some strange and unexpected way, the highlight of the journey and its true *raison d'être* were the people we encountered along the way, while the magnificent setting we passed through only served as an afterthought, in keeping with my friend's notion that travel was for visiting people, not places. Akbar packed his tremendous hulk into the back seat with Farman and myself to accompany us during our tour of the area and a good thing too since we kept each other warm in the bitter cold. As we made our way up the valley deeper into the mountains, the weather became colder than before and eventually we passed the snow and tree line and found ourselves deep into the snow clad territory of the Karakoram. We were now journeying through a wild, mountainous country setting. The snow was coming down hard and as we advanced, it was getting much deeper and the road more treacherous. Yet, in spite of the remoteness of the area, I realized that our whereabouts were being constantly monitored. At one point, we stopped at a kind of check point, and my bodyguards jumped out and consulted with the local authorities as if they were expecting us. When I questioned Farman about it, he just said that my security was "under control" and refused further comment. I was amazed, to say the least, at the thoroughness and seriousness with which my safety was being taken. All throughout the course of my stay in Pakistan, our whereabouts had been monitored by the special security forces of the government in cooperation with my Pathan companions.

We finally reached the end of the road at a town called Kalam, a scenic mountain village with a mountain river rushing headlong through it as it made its way down the mountainside. In the summer, I was told, this place was packed with tourists and holiday-makers. Today, the town was nearly empty and fairly desolate; it was snowing hard and threatening to seal us in with an impassible road. When in doubt about a course of action, food was always suggested, so my friends set about finding the best place to eat by fanning out in different directions to make inquiries, each of them comically wrapped up in their woolen shawls, but not before packing snow down each other's backs.

Soon enough, I was being led into what appeared at first sight to be a dingy little place, but unexpectedly it opened out in the back to become a spacious dining room that seemed to be hanging on the edge of a precipice on one side of the town. A fine array of windows provided ample views of the houses of the town that were nestled within the contours of those craggy mountains. Great chutes of water made their way down the side of the mountain near the windows of the restaurant and created a tremendous roar within as the water cascaded outside the window into the gorge below. After marveling at the unbelievable views, we were served up some fresh trout that had been grilled barbecue-style over hot coals out in the snowy street in front of the restaurant. This was served together with a curried chicken cooked in a wok and the inevitable freshly-made and piping hot Pakistani bread served as a satisfying lunch before making our way out of the town and out of the mountains altogether, to escape being sealed indefinitely within the winter landscape. We eventually left Akbar in a town near his village from which he intended to make his way back on his own so as not to delay our return journey. After leaving him by the side of the road, we began the long trek back to the village nearby Peshawar in the late afternoon. True to the Islamic tradition, the needs and comfort of the traveler are sacrosanct and Akbar had fulfilled his duties well.

The next day was to be my last complete day in the North West Frontier Province, in what had become for me the beloved Pathan country. These tribal people are fully conscious of the demands of intimate relationships and respond with deep feeling to the subtleties of the moment. After a full week of what amounted to well orchestrated touring and visiting, we would spend a quiet final day in and around Farman's village. The following morning, I was scheduled to fly back to Muscat.

The day began as always with a tremendous breakfast of fresh, original farm foods including bread, cream, laban, cheese, fruit, farm-fresh eggs, and tea. Thus fortified, we piled into the car and began to tour the countryside for one last nostalgic glance at how people live within this remote, country setting. The memorable images still pass through my mind's eye. The horse-drawn carriages jingled with bells as they carried their passengers to local destinations along that dusty road, the trotting horse in silhouette against the rising sun like an ancient pictogram. The great cumbrous water buffaloes, the heavy folds of flesh hanging down from their necks like a woman's shall, pulled their heavy loads without any sound of complaint. We passed through a village even smaller than Farman's where the houses were all made of clay and straw and whose inner enclosures traditionally housed the farm animals. Along the outer walls of the houses in this and other villages, I saw sizable mud patties flattened like burgers on the side of the wall to dry in the sun. And what were they, I wondered aloud? None other than the "spoils" of the water buffalo, I was told, carefully preserved and left to dry, to be used later as fuel for cooking and hot water. *Nothing is wasted in village life*, Farman told me solemnly and I believe him. A hard-working donkey pulling a heavily-loaded cart passes by looking young and boyish and enduring. I think I have learned something about virtue from the sight of this animal. In the village itself, we squeeze the car through the narrow streets. A little dead-end child with a dirty face walks past the car window with a chicken squished in her arms. Their two pinched little faces look up at me. We stop and wait for a cart to pass, packed with sugar cane stalks drawn by a great water buffalo. The little boy on the back of the great beast grins at me and waves hello, or is it good-bye. I do not know. These are the pictures that were not taken by my camera, the pictures not of my imagination, but of my discerning mind, pictures I could not have created on my own.

Even on this my last day, there was no such thing as idle touring. We were on our way to a destination, another visit, another friend, another group of people who wanted to see the "foreign guest" and talk with the "American Muslim". On my own in this little village, the clay walls of the houses looking old and run down, I would have been as out of place as an alien being on an outer planet. Under the protection of a local Pathan family and as their honored guest, I was everything that mattered to the village.

We descended from the car and tip-toed through the mud of the street to enter the grounds of the house beyond the wall. I was advised to be careful to avoid a great smudge of buffalo waste that was still steaming near the gate of the house. Beyond the grim reality of the outside setting lay all the charm of a truly bucolic existence. An inner courtyard revealed a variety of farm animals. Two elegant, gray colored cranes posed for my stunned vision and fanned their wings in protest at the interruption. A number of chickens provided a frantic counterpart to the detached serenity of the cranes as they scurried about the courtyard in their perennial search for food. Yet nothing could compare to the noble-looking black water buffalo that peacefully munched its hay on the other side of the courtyard as it gazed into the distance beyond the limited horizon of its mind. This was a picture I simply had to have, and the host obliged by stepping into this rustic farm setting to lend the image of his own self-possessed nobility and calm appearance to this charming scene.

He then gracefully ushered me and my friends into the interior beyond an open door. I was amazed to find myself in a small rectangular room that was fully lined on every wall with glass-enclosed wooden bookcases that housed a complete collection of hard-backed, leather-bound books whose titles and authors were inscribed with the exotic gold lettering of Arabic and Pashtu and Farsi. Perhaps it was the unexpected quality of the experience that left me bereft of words. The man's son spoke good Arabic, so after we had sat ourselves down on the plush, hand-woven tribal carpets and cushions that were strewn randomly around the room, he busied himself with me, displaying with loving care a number of books in Arabic including a few hand-written and embellished Qurans. Of course, every visit must include a meal, so we ate our second break-fast at 11:00 in the morning, a feast that included steaming rice and chicken roasted and stewed in buffalo oil. After a brief prayer of thanks initiated by the host that this happy encounter had been made possible, we took our leave. The remembrance of God is never far away from the rituals of their daily life.

By the time we left the village, the sun had passed the meridian, we had said the noon prayer, and the day was beginning to die. There was a feeling in the air of closure and departure. No one wanted the moment to pass—not of course the individual moment, but the totality of the moment that summarized our experience as a moment of encounter and exchange. For me as a Westerner and American, it had been a kind of surreal dream of a vanished time and a passageway emerging out of the remote past. For my Pathan friends, the monotony of their lives had been interrupted with this unique encounter, and they had been able to express and show the best of themselves. No one wants such moments to pass, but pass they must, at least in their linear and literal reality, if not in their enduring remembrance.

It was past two o'clock and we were going to buy some fish and have lunch at Farouk's house. Not another meal, I thought as I remembered the liberating quality of the Ramadhan fast. Give me the true satisfaction of hunger any day, I prayed, rather than the false satisfaction of being sated and full. However, this was my last day and Farouk and his family considered themselves honored by my presence. We sat outside on cushions and a carpet in the court-yard of his house. Farman showed me the water pump in the corner and filled a pitcher with water. *Every house has a well*, he told me. So this is the source of the water supply, I thought, remembering the armies of tourists I had seen in my travels carrying their own water bottles.

Farouk's father came to join us together with his little daughter. Farouk brought in the food, including the steaming fish just cooked by his wife. I tried to make a brave show of interest in eating, but my heart was in it and I couldn't face another meal. In fact, my friend Farman and the other guests made matters worse by pilling more food on my plate and encouraging me to eat more. In true Pathan style, Farouk also offered me the choicest morsels of fish and encouraged me to eat more. Perhaps I was distracted by all this attention, but suddenly and unaccountably, I swallowed a sizable fish bone. I felt it scratch the back of my throat, and immediately tried to spit it out, but it was too late, and I realized that it was lodged precariously beyond the back ledge of my tongue. I was beginning to choke.

My friend Farman, Babu, Farouk, his father, the child, all were struck dumb and jumped up from the floor. To their collective horror, the guest was in distress; this was their responsibility. I excused myself and went to the latrine on the other side of the courtyard to see what I could do and try to pull myself together; but there was nothing to be done. I couldn't swallow and I couldn't expel the sharp bone. I stepped grimly back out into the courtyard and they immediately took in the reality of the situation. They resolved to take me at once to the local doctor. We left the rest of the meal spread out uneaten on the carpet. As we left the inner courtyard, I noticed the worried face of Farouk's father as he held the little girl in his arms and a Kalashnikov left abandoned in a corner of the inner courtyard. They were no defense against this.

A doctor at a small dispensary in a nearby town shook his head. He couldn't handle it and we would have to go to the hospital in Peshawar. I groaned audibly. The thought of going all the way to Peshawar, at least 45 minutes away, through that nightmare of pollution, traffic and congestion, was enough to make me sicker than I was. It was as if a curtain had been drawn and a new act was now unfolding, an unexpected denouement to an otherwise perfect play. But Farouk was up to the demands of the moment. He stepped on the gas and leaned on the horn as he made his way at breakneck speed along the road to Peshawar, defying every possible danger and every unexpected circumstance. The world seemed to fall away from our path as our car advanced with the horn blasting a perpetual warning for the cars, carriages, carts and countless pedestrians to get out of the way as we made our way through the smog into the congested city.

My three caretakers rush me through the crowds and the injured milling about an emergency room that seemed dark, run-down and uninviting. An x-ray was quickly taken. It was determined that a bone was caught in my throat and we were sent upstairs to the eye, ear and throat department. Throughout the course of this unwanted adventure, my friends were silent and clearly worried, like children struck mute in a situation they couldn't fully comprehend and over which they had no control. Gone was the happy banter of the previous days and a grim forbearance seemed to settle over them until we got through this harrowing experience. I marveled at the ability of my friends to respond to the needs of the moment. These were no country bumpkins, but people with sharp instincts and sound intuitive reactions ready to respond to any contingency.

The calm atmosphere of the eye, ear and throat department upstairs was in sharp contrast to the frantic air of chaos that had prevailed in the emergency room. Farman quickly assessed the doctor of the situation, then took my hand and sat down next to me. The doctor briefed me about the probabilities of resolving such an encounter and with a true feeling for the psychology of the moment, tried to calm me down before proceeding to attempt the extraction of this discomforting fishbone. "There is nothing to worry about," he assured me with professional calm. "These things happen and we should have it out in no time. Even if we can't manage to extract it, the bone could stay there for several weeks without doing much harm before eventually slipping down into the stomach. So don't worry," he assured me in good English.

He heated a dentist-style mirror and positioned it awkwardly at the back of my throat. "You will have to help me," he said, "because I only have two hands, one for the mirror and the other for the tweezers. Secure your tongue and hold it out as far as you can." I did as I was told, breathing deeply to calm myself. "I see it," he exclaimed as if he had discovered a gold nugget. Several attempts to seize the bone brought me up gagging, and we were all beginning to wonder whether this was going to result in the happy ending we all prayed for. On the fourth attempt, however, and with a deft maneuver, he slowly withdrew the offending bone. "Here it is, you can save it if you want," he joked good-humoredly. It didn't look like much, sharp and oval, like a pared fingernail, but inside my throat, it had felt like an old shoe. I breathed a sigh of relief and uttered the traditional

Islamic epithet, in chorus coincidentally, with the others, *al-hamdu-lil-Llah* (all praise to Allah), and never was a phrase uttered with more heart-felt sentiment and collective relief. We thanked the doctor and praised him for his skill. He embraced me warmly, and we took our leave from the grim environs.

The ride back was a leisurely affair, with much relieved laughter and banter. They kept asking me if I felt better, as if they couldn't believe that the ordeal was finally over, that I was whole again and myself as before as though nothing had happened. I never knew what it cost, if it cost anything at all. I never saw any of my three companions pay anyone any money and no one was forced to fill out any paperwork or show any documents. In the end, there are some advantages to a system in chaos. Just before entering the house upon our return, Farman told me not to say anything about the incident to any of the guests at home because everyone would be very upset. We soon discovered that everyone, not only in the house but in the entire village, knew the story of my ordeal which in true village fashion had spread like a brush fire.

It is a humbling experience to be fully accepted and taken into the inner circle of a family and the warm embrace of village life, indeed into an ancient and traditional tribe who practice very conservative customs and follow strong religious beliefs. The Pathan people seemed to me larger than life, physically, mentally, and spiritually. Physically, the appearance of many of them was that of the lovable giants of legends and folk tales. You come to know them, however, through their actions and not their words, for the extent of their generosity knows no bounds and the needs and comfort of the guest takes precedence in all matters. The face you see is their true face. The words you hear are their true words. If they take you in, you are one with them. They showed an attitude toward me that made it clear they considered me their brother and friend. It was unexpressed in words, but spontaneous and freely offered through their actions and behavior. No matter who I was or where I had come from, to them I was Pathan and one with them. This was no journey of a stranger in a strange land. On the contrary, this was a journey in which my soul felt at home. If I were asked where I was and how I got there and why, I could have given a clear answer because I had found one in the encounter with these simple tribesmen.

On a number of occasions, I was asked, perhaps a little self-consciously, what I thought of the Pathan people. It was a question I was instinctively reluctant to answer, partly because I felt that no simple answer existed or came to mind that could do justice to the experience I was having, and partly because it would take serious consideration and the right words to portray the greatness and nobility of these people in their true light and could not be summarized in a few superficial words. In writing this tribute, I have finally answered this question as I promised I would, a promise that needed to be kept in view of the profound outpouring of sentiment this great tribe had extended toward me.

The next day, I said my good-byes to all the friends and relatives and villagers who had troubled themselves over me during my brief stay with them. Feelings were muted and subdued and there was a genuine sense of melancholy in the air. They put a brave face on what was a sad parting. As I approached the car that was to take me to the airport, I passed through a line of Pathans who each in his turn embraced me, shook my hand and bid me the traditional Islamic *ma salaam* or "go in peace". With a final smile and wave, I was gone and so was the moment.

At the airport, Farman and his friends carried my luggage up to the check-in counter. I had been loaded down with gifts, but the grandest was the hand-made blanket Farman's mother had made for me, a dark and rich maroon-colored quilt that seemed to weigh a ton, heavy enough to service those bitter Peshawar winters. In addition to this, Farman had procured for me 10 kilos of the fresh mountain honey that is favored in the area. When I protested the inordinate amount, he grinned broadly. *This is Pathan style.*

I managed to get through all the many formalities, the baggage checks, the embarkation forms, the x-ray machines, and finally the immigration line. It was time to say good-bye. *Thank you so much, Farman. It has truly been an experience of a lifetime. You have been too kind.* But Farman has no use for these awkward English pleasantries and finds refuge in one final act of generosity. *I leave when plane leave, Yahya, and not before.*

At parting, words finally fail. What remains is an embrace that wouldn't let go, a final raising of the hands, and then the traditional gesture of leave-taking, namely the right hand over the heart. This final symbolic gesture must now seal the narrative closed, just as it allowed us to leave behind with each other the best of ourselves, without the need for another word.

4

TRADITIONS OF A
TRADITIONAL BARBERSHOP

PATHAN TRIBESMEN maintain the tradition of not cutting the child's hair until he reaches his first birthday when the head is summarily shaved of its curly locks. "This is Pathan style," my mountain man Pathan friend told me solemnly. This is the story of little Wajahat's first haircut, who in keeping faith with an age-old tradition of his Pathan tribe also came to witness the social traditions of the tribal barbershop.

Out of their relentless probing down into the inner heart of physical matter and amid the welter of infinitesimal particles they have managed to unearth, physicists have come to learn about the uncertainty of measurements contained in Heisenberg's principle of uncertainty and later amplified to the limits of probability brought by quantum mechanics. In so doing, they have uncovered an astounding truth, that there are unclear boundaries to the space-time reality suggesting a higher reality of eternity and infinitude, and that human perception not only misunderstands the meaning of shapes, but alters the way we understand that reality. Although we like to believe in this modern age that reality is rooted in the physical and the material world, even modern scientists are coming to realize that there are dimensions to our universe that we cannot sense, regardless of how clever and precise our instrumentation may eventually become. Infinity may not be within our reach, but a sense of unity is there for all to behold if we only had the eyes to see it written within the fabric of this world with a golden thread, binding together the universe that we experience as an expression of the oneness of God.

You may wonder what the principles of uncertainty and indeterminism have to do with a child getting a haircut. Let me try to explain.

This little excursion to the barbershop is going to spell trouble, I thought to myself, as we piled into the olive green Nissan Maxima for the drive to the barbershop. Today was Wajahat's first birthday and according to age old traditions of the Pathan people, a day to be reckoned with. "Get ready for a nightmare," I said jokingly to my Pathan friend Farmana as he settled his great hulk into the seat next to me. "This is Pathan child," he said gravely, as though affixing to the child and the moment a noble insignia foreshadowing bravery and courage. "I doesn't cry my first haircut and Wajahat doesn't cry his first haircut. You see." Indeed, I thought, what charming bravado set against the complex backcloth of culture and tradition. I was not one to argue, content to let events tell their own tale.

I had met Farmana, a Pathan tribesman from a village outside of Peshawar in the North West Frontier Province of Pakistan, many years ago while coming out of a local mosque in the UAE where we were both working. I worked as an English lecturer at a local university and he worked as the foreman and kingpin of a small Irrigation company in Al Ain, the university town outside of Abu Dhabi, the capital city of the United Arab Emirates affectionately named by the local people the "Father of the Antelope", a small island off the coast in the Arabian Gulf that has become a futuristic metropolis thanks to the oil economy of the world. Apparently, my Pathan friend was intrigued in his noble heart by the sight of a white bearded American Muslim searching hopefully through a welter of footwear outside the mosque for his sandals. That I was a foreigner and some kind of alien being there was no doubt; but true to the traditions of his tribe, Farmana was a fearless soul and full of curiosity.

Now, after many years of close friendship, I had been taken into the remote and intimate world of the Pathan people whose origins date back millennia in the mountainous regions of northern Afghanistan and Pakistan. To be taken into this close tribal society and anointed as the symbolic grandfather was a rare honor indeed attributed to the fact that I was a long-standing Muslim. Our friendship has endured throughout the years and survived the onslaught brought about by the politics of terrorism that now dominates the ambiance of our world, becoming a cultural artifact and prevailing tradition of our modern world in its own sinister way.

Wajahat's two older sisters sat submissively in the back seat without uttering a sound. They both had dark black eyes and a mop of black hair. Najma, the little star according to her Arabic name, was intelligent and helpful, lifting the chubby Wajahat up and away from the street and depositing him awkwardly like a cumbersome bundle on her lap. Zahra, the little monkey according to her *abu* (father), was a little *shaytan* (devilish jinn) who experimented in trouble like other children invest in natural innocence. She looked out onto the world as if she wanted to interrogate it for its faults or blame it for its troubles, her black eyes giving off the sharp light of a wild thing in the forest. For now, she sat quietly attentive suddenly to my admonition not to touch and disturb anything in my precious car or else. They had grown up with me as a familiar member of the family. They referred to their father as *abu,* while they referred to me as Papa, in deference to my white beard and grandfatherly status.

Like many aspects of social life and behavior in the Arab and Islamic world, the ambiance and coloration of the barbershop was far different from what you would expect to find in a Western barbershop. Granted the large red-and-white swivel chairs and cacophony of mirrors were the same reflecting a thousand different images from every conceivable angle for the onlooker to behold; there are the usual condiments of cheap cologne, scented powder, a small bottle of face cream called "Tibetan Snow", and the bushy face and hair brushes that you might find in an American shop, together with the sterilization tray with straight-edged razors and a cavalcade of gleaming scissors, but that is the extent of the similarity. Otherwise, the traditional, tribal experience of the barbershop has all the components of a village social gathering, complete with one's most favored barber, a complement of friends, and an ever moving stream of passers-by and well wishers who come and go from the shop greeting the barbers and their customers with equal sincerity and aplomb.

As we entered the barbershop aglitter with reflected neon light and smelling of cheap eau de cologne and stale cigarette smoke, our

little entourage included my friend Farmana and his little son Wajahat, who was tucked in the niche of the arm of this Pathan mountain
man like a gnome in a tree trunk, where he sat sleepily surveying the
alien environment from the protection of his father's familiar cloth,
the two sisters as protectresses and myself as the grand patriarch taking up the protective flank. We were ceremoniously greeted by both
the barbers and customers inside the shop like long lost relatives
who had suddenly appeared from nowhere. Everyone "salaamed"
each other in their traditional Islamic greeting of "salam aleykum"
(peace be on you) and the traditional reply "wa aleykum as-salam
(and on you also peace), sent back and forth in a manner that lent a
formal, almost Quranic quality to the proceedings, in keeping with
the tradition of the Quran as a living presence in the daily lives of the
people. We were warmly embraced and kissed on each cheek, the
children were patted and teased until they managed to escape
behind the refuge of my billowing pantaloons, a light weight cotton
Pakistani suit that I wore for comfort's sake as well as to blend in
with the communal environment.

Wajahat was merrily ensconced with much fanfare onto the special children's board astride the swiveling barber chair to mark the
completion of the first year of his life and the maturing of a full
hair's dark growth curling down his shoulders with a ceremonial
hair cut, shaving the head completely with a straight-edged razor.
The barbers and customers were abuzz with interest at the ceremony that was about to take place. I took up my position as protec-
tor and village elder next to the somber child sitting astride a special
board running across the arms of the chair. I now awaited the kind
of spontaneous outrage and indignation that infant children are
unashamedly capable of in fulfillment of my prophecy at the outset
of our little excursion; but I was soon to be disappointed. My own
little revelation awaited my worldly wise mind.

Wajahat sat there in the chair in solemn introspection, as if he
understood the moment and was fully prepared to meet it. He
seemed to belong there and didn't want to be anywhere else. As he
settled himself into the oversized chair far beyond his means, he
looked out unconcernedly at the world around him as if he had
already taken possession of it. He then looked at himself in the

mirror with a self awareness that lacked all curiosity, as if the human image he saw there held no mystery he did not already know. There he sat, noble and content with his lot, as if he had brought from his mother's womb a knowledge of his own unity, as if the sea itself flowed in his veins and he wore a crown of stars on his head, as if the mystery of God's creative hand was still near at hand and he was still one with the Spirit of God.

In the detached gaze of an infant child, the wisdom of the world that I thought I possessed was wiped clean. It made me think just how fragile the experience of a lifetime can be, and just how powerful knowledge and truth can be when it is perceived by a pure mind untouched by the world. Watching the child at rest and free of care as he sat there taking in the world around him, I began to realize it is not what a person sees, but the way he sees it that marks the difference between a pure, virgin mentality and the corrupted, overworldly veneer that envelopes the adult mind weighted down as it is by the experience of the world. In fact, what does the child see but the same world as we do; but in a manner infinitely different in which everything is at first new and strange, inexpressibly rare and delightful, and above all beautiful.

The infant child is a little stranger unto himself, but his entrance into the world is compensated by the world itself saluting him and surrounding him with innumerable joys. He knows nothing of sin and protest, illness or government laws. He does not dream of poverty, contention or vice. Everything seems at rest, free of sorrow and having an immortal quality. He knows nothing of sickness or death, rents or other tributes to the hardships of this world. All things abided eternally as they were in their proper place. Everything was manifest in the light of day and behind ever created thing something infinite lay in waiting. Time is still a part of eternity, the universe itself is an Eden, and the world that he is beginning to experience makes him heir to the mysteries which the books of the learned never unfold. The proud father stood behind the child and look at him with tender affection, his thick, strong paws resting protectively on the infant's shoulders, just below the forest of curls that were soon to become part of the historic lore of Pathan tribal history.

I have never had children of my own, but that does not preclude my special interest and fascination with them and their manner of being and acting. Contrary to virtual observation, I still held the secret desire to hear the screams and cries of the child reacting in defiance to this strange, invasive encounter, but it was not meant to happen. The children led me back to the scruffy, worn out armchairs in the rear of the shop where customers and their friends could while away the empty hours waiting for service or just socializing with friends. Indeed the area was full, but several men quickly deferred to my age and foreign aura in spite of my traditional clothing and offered me one of the engulfing chairs which I promptly got lost in. There was a coffee table strewn with Bollywood movie star magazines and the alien Arabic/Urdu script of the Pakistani newspapers looking like a conflagration of letters without sound or meaning. Tea and dates were immediately served and I settled back for an evening of social accommodation to these customs and traditions so alien to my own experience in the Western world.

The traditional, tribal barbershop serves a kind of sanctum sanctorum for men of all ages, a respite from all the cares in the world, a refuge from domestic problems, nagging wives and familial misunderstandings. Entering this inner sanctum of fraternal friendship and bonding amounts to entering a world of camaraderie and companionship that one does not always find at home or in the street. One respected and love one's barber and the barber in return petted and massaged and pampered the beloved crown of the head, the supporting shelf of the shoulders, and the sturdy and faithful pillar of the neck that fulfills its own sacred function by keeping the weighty head afloat the body. There was tea and cigarettes and friendship there, someone to hold a light for you against the invasive wind, trim your beard, shave your street-worm, emotion-clad face and wipe it clean of all care and worry.

When I go to a Middle Eastern barbershop, I know that there is nothing finer than the hot towels laid over the face, the broad strokes of the razor, and the deft shears of the experience barber, his fingers expertly working pomade through to the scalp, the final whisk of the powered brush against the back of the neck. I am greeted like an old friend and they do not forget my name when I return. Three brothers run this particular shop and day after day, hour after hour, beard after beard and head after head, they never seem to tire and always accord everyone their due treatment. I consider myself an educated man and have lived and worked in many different countries. I have written books on education, religion, and philosophy and have lectured in countries across three continents. Yet, these simple people have something to teach me. As I watch them work, I have learned from them what it means to be patient, how to be friendly in the face a routine monotony, and how to remain devoted and concentrated to the work at hand. Would that I could come to my every routine tasks with as much fortitude, sensibility, and attention to detail as they seem to do day after day. They shake my hand, kiss and hug me as if I were a long lost brother and lead me to enjoy their ministrations to the extent that I gladly and trustingly put myself under the sharp edge of the razor. The barbershop becomes a weekly appointment I am reluctant to miss. If I don't show up because of a holiday or an unexpected lapse in my routine, I am missed in return and greeted with extra effulgence when I finally come back.

However, as soon as the Pathan child Wajahat was astride the board on the oversized chair and bundled up with protective paper napkins secured with a silken polyester bib smugly tied around his neck against any wayward and offending hairs, his older sisters rushed to his aid to attend to his every need, squeezing his pudgy legs and affectionately pinching his nose, all of which he endured with detached serenity. In addition to making sure that he was comfortable and well positioned in this alien perch, they were to provide the in-house entertainment and any diversionary tactics required to assure a smooth and uncompromising investiture into the world of the monthly haircut. Najma, the little star, began to chirp an aria of bird songs, while Zahra, the little monkey, began to climb the barber chair and leer into the little boy's face with grimaces of doom. His head, bedecked with a year's growth of curly black hairs, was about to lose its pride. The king was ensconced on his throne, attendants ready for his every need, as he began to nod off into the netherworld of dreams, oblivious to the ceremonious tradition of his first haircut about to happen.

Amid the whir of overhead fans and the constant chatter of the multiple languages and dialects of the subcontinent including Pashtu, Urdu, Hindi, Farsi, and Arabic, a number of people were already being attended by the busy barbers in various stages of cosmetic enhancement of the unruly growths of hair on head and visage. One fellow was having his head completely shaved, not an uncommon custom in this traditional environment where temperatures can become very hot indeed and where a shaved head is considered a blessing as well as a means of self-effacement. I detected a look of introspection and satisfaction on the face of the sleeping customers, arousing in my mind the inquiring insight as to why people always gave up their spirit and tended to float away into oblivion in the barber's chair, as if cast away from all turmoil as by some magic spell. Another fellow was having his faced scraped in an elaborate ritual of skin purification in which the barber manipulates a fine thread through this teeth and fingers that virtually relieves the facial skin of unwanted hairs, excess and dead skin and any blackheads that may lie in route of the swath of the swift moving thread. There seemed to be no end to the arcane rituals being enacted upon the customers as though from a secret cult. One of the barbers had just prepared a cotton ball at the end of a long pair of tweezers that was steeped in alcohol that he alighted in flame. He waved this flaming torch in close proximity to each ear as a way of effectively scorching away any offending hairs on the ears without much ado.

Two other men sat in nearby chairs and had come for regular maintenance of their beards. Now it needs to be understood that beards in the Islamic world take on a symbolic and sacred quality. To don a beard is not only a sign of manliness and dignity, it is considered the practice or *Sunnah* of the Prophet, upon him blessings and peace, meaning that the wearing of the beard is in imitation of the habit of the Prophet and any imitation of the beloved Prophet brings with it is own corresponding blessing. Trim the mustache and leave the beard uncut was the advice of the Prophet. Out of deference to his words, many Muslims grow elaborate beards that over the years take on a kind of "personality" of their own. I am there to witness the high maintenance through clip and trim of beards that will never be fully cut.

The first fellow, asleep in complete repose of course and therefore oblivious of the skilled craftsmanship being affected on his facial hairs, has grown what I call a manicured beard. This beard over the years has taken on the quality of a finely nurtured and well mani-cured garden, thick, rich, and lush with foliage in a dense and well-developed pack of facial curls. One recalls in mock terror perhaps the close proximity of the straight-edge to the throat and the unyielding theoretical power of life and death the barber wields as he works his way across the path of the jugular, recalling the verse of the Quran that proclaims Allah to be nearer to you than your jugular vein (*al-hab lil-wareed*). The second fellow, fully awake and critically surveying every individual snip of the scissors, monitors the actions of the barber with careful scrutiny through the reflective mirrors as the tentative barber moves across the field of the beard without missing a clip. This beard has a classic, sculptured look, boxy and full, with a kind of descending shelf that is densely packed with tufts of hair and uncompromising in the statement of its mission. Over the years, this beard has taken on the bearing of a work of art, to the extent that the beard seems to take precedence over the man and actually wears him, rather than the man wearing the beard. The bar-ber hovers anxiously over this man and snips away hair by hair any offending growths that over time have actually begun to destroy the symmetry and perfection of this facial work of art.

These observations lead me to recall the somnolent effect the pampering attentions of the barber can have on the shop clients and to speculate upon my own experience in the barber's chair. Cer-tainly the fact that one is remembered, greeted like a long lost friend no matter how often you have attended the shop, in my case weekly to trim the edges of my mustache and beard, and pampered and pummeled with all the artistry of an experienced and dedicated sculptor, creates an ambiance of satisfaction and trust that is condu-cive to the total relaxation that leads to sleep. It is the only explana-tion I can come up with why I always dose off in the barber's chair, no matter what time of day I go there, whence the trussing up begins. My neck is wrapped in protective tissue, then the entire upper torso is covered from neck to knees in an elaborate bib and tied securely across this tissue at the neck. To complete the bun-dling, a towel is placed across the shoulders to dry the fingers of the barber and to periodically whip clear the head, neck and ears from excess water and hair.

Once the hair is dampened down and the head is thoroughly massaged, I feel my head loll back on my shoulders as the initial sign to my dozing off. With this kind of treatment, does anyone need the contingencies of this world? One enters a kind of nether-world of daydreams, half in and half out of the experience being undergone. My beard could be characterized as manicured, mean-ing that areas including the checks and at the base of the neckline, and a more profound styling of cut under the lips and over the hori-zon of the mustache needs more serious attention. The barber applies a shaving jell to their areas which he proceeds to massage into the skin to facilitate the movement of the straight-edge. By now, I am well on the edge of eternity, fully receptive to other-worldly insights as well as the attentions of the barber.

The close proximity of the straight edge to my neck and throat draws me briefly back into the real world of cutting and snipping. First the throat, the checks and under the nose get this raw razor treatment, in some instances hair by hair. Once finished, the barber moves on to cutting the hairs inside the nose, in itself an alarming if not hair-raising experience. Then, the mustache at the lips are trimmed, hoping that the lips remain assaulted but without bleeding after being pricked several times by the sharp point of the wayward scissors. Finally, the bushy eyebrows are given their due, ever fearful that the scissors and/or the attention of the barber may slip for a second while in such close proximity to the eye. But all's well that ends well. Just as I am about to slumber off again into the netherworld of sweet dreams, the barber sprays my entire face with ice cold water from a spray can to the point that I think I will lose my breath whence he pats down and dries with meticulous care every parameter of my countenance, including the pouches under the eyes and the remote crevices of the nose. This has got to serve as the climax of the entire experience I thought. As denouement, well aware of what's coming and amid a lingering reluctance to leave the cocoon of the barber chair, the face was now ripe for the final barber-ic indulgence. First the barber doused his hands with medicinal smelling cologne and rubbed the alcohol based spirit deep into the sensitized pores with stinking results. This was followed by the soothing nourishment of a sweet smelling facial cream which the barber proceeded to work into the raw skin of the face and neck with the massage strokes of a professional masseur. The final touch of the barber comes with the evocative smell of a fine, silky powder to soothe and comfort the age old visage. On that note and having paid my fee of 5 dirhams ($1.25), the friendly brothers send me on my way with a handshake and a smile, while the echo of the traditional, blessed salutation *salam aleykum* follows me out the door of the shop.

I leave this mesmerizing reverie of past grooming to return to the scene of the traditional first hair cutting of the infant Wajahat, half expecting a howl of outrage by the infant at the sight of his shorn tresses. Surely, the infant was not up to internalizing the splendor of this meditative experience. On the contrary, he sat perched complacently on his wooden throne astride the red and white barber's chair and gazed serenely at the world around him as the barber swiveled the great chair around several times for effect nearing the end of the shaving ceremony. In my mind's eye, he momentarily resembled a Red Indian, shorn on both sides clean to the skin with a swath of thick black hair running from the base of the neck to his forehead. I caught his attention for a second with a smile and a wink, but he had no inclination to disturb the serenity of this first haircutting because of the antics of a dotting grandfather. He seemed to be lost in meditation during the intrusive scraping of the unsuspecting hair by the razor-sharp straight edge blade, lulling him into a deeper world of somnolent experience far beyond the vanity of this world. He was even dozing off beyond the world of care, and thus giving the lie to my prediction of trouble earlier in the day. Alas, with a few more deft strokes of the straight-edge, the job was done. The beloved urchin bedecked with a head full of black curls was now stripped clear of his year-long growth of baby fur at the summit of his being. He resembled nothing less than a Buddhist monk in miniature or a Red Indian in cameo, ascetic in outward form to complement the nobility of his true Pathan nature and the sweetness of his infant heart.

I went over to retrieve the courageous little infant from the barber's chair. Having suffered the close attention and scrutiny of all the rough comrades of the Pashtu tribe who pinched and prodded, squeezed and kissed him as they came and went from the shop, he gladly retired from the field of observation and fell into the anonymity of my arms where he could now rest in peace. His mountain man father, my friend Farmana, grunted in satisfaction. "Just like his father with no word of complaint. This is Pathan style," he affirmed with pride, as I witnessed yet another example of the incredible tenacity Farmana and the close companions of his village in holding to their traditions and the sincerity with which they preserve and fulfill their obligations to themselves and their society.

As the little entourage of my Pathan family left the camaraderie of the traditional barbershop, I began to sing lightly the traditional German lullaby *Guten Abend, Guten Nacht* that I learned nearly 40 years ago while working as a teacher in Germany. The busy Afghans and Pashtus making their rounds of the Pathan suk (traditional marketplace) stopped in their tracks and stared at the unexpected scene before them, enchanted at the sight of a Western-looking person dressed in Pathan cloth singing a lullaby in the busy suk to the bald-headed infant Pathan sleeping on his shoulder as though he were at home snuggled safely in the robes of his own blanket. And I thought: invested in the sweet repose of the child lies the secret mystery of an unfathomable trust between infancy and age that is as true and as real as any truth or reality could be. Hidden within the slumber of the child and the melodious 19th century German lullaby lies a communion of souls that transcends distance and time and cuts across the horizon of the world to reveal a oneness and a unity at the heart of all true experience. In that sleeping human frame lay a bridge that crosses the grave distance of age and nationality to create a meeting of two minds and hearts, at one with each other in the heart of a tribal marketplace.

5

THE GIFT OF NO RETURN

SEVEN YEARS have now passed into the mists of time since I first set foot in what I affectionately termed Pathan Country in an article I wrote at the turn of the millennium, a tribal area evocative of the wild, lawless region in the far North of Pakistan, traditionally called the North West Frontier Province. My first trip began four days into the new millennium at a time when there was a recent plane high-jacking in nearby Afghanistan that made headline news across the globe, a time also when the world had just passed through the well anticipated IT crisis by avoiding the much heralded computer melt-down that seems fabricated and silly now in retrospect, as if the world had nothing else to worry about than the world's computers going haywire. When people asked where I was going during a busy time approaching the end of a long Spring semester at the university where I work in the United Arab Emirates, I jokingly told them Osama bin Laden country since there is rampant speculation the most famous arch terrorist of the century lies tucked away in the vast spread of rugged, inaccessible mountains that form the border between Afghanistan and Pakistan.

As I climbed out of the hot sun into a taxi on my way to the air-port in Abu Dhabi for the three hour flight into Peshawar, I felt a lit-tle on edge. There has been a rash of recent bombings in both Karachi and Peshawar due to sectarian violence and the politics of the country had been recently volatile at best and downright chaotic at worst, a kind of cauldron of sectarian violence and political tur-moil that the average Westerner has very little experience with, and I was certainly no exception. From my perch as a university profes-sor in a Western-style university in the Gulf region, I had enjoyed an era of unlimited prosperity and safety in the country, as thought resting in the eye of some infernal storm with an unsettling war being waged in Iraq and nuclear storm clouds hovering over Iran not far away and yet far enough for the horizon of my daily routine to resemble the strife of another planet, something to turn on during the evening news as a token gesture to the realities of the world.

Not surprisingly, the taxi driver was himself a Pathan as are all the taxi drivers in Abu Dhabi. True to my expectation, he immediately asked me in rudimentary Arabic if I was going to "my country" and from his broad smile and eager face, he had no reason to believe that I wasn't heading home to America. This seemed to bring joy to his heart, judging from his animation and readiness to talk to this foreign devil. I knew otherwise, however, thinking that I didn't want to shock or disappoint him; but that I was heading to his home inside the heart of Pathan country. He would undoubtedly find it hard to believe that I was going to Peshawar, sitting there next to him in my crisp white shirt and summer woolen slacks looking every bit the American, clutching a soft leather briefcase between my knees with my ticket, passport and money, the three essentials of any trip. "No I am not going to my country," I replied in Arabic in a deadpan tone, and then, as if it were the most natural thing in the world, I told him I was flying to Peshawar. He looked at me aghast. "Where are you from," I asked innocently, knowing full well that he came from Peshawar or some nearby village like all the rest of the Pathan taxi drivers in Abu Dhabi. He appeared to have been struck by a stun-gun and he drove the rest of the way in silence until we approached the apron of the airport when I advised him to head toward Terminal Two, "the flights to Yemen and Pakistan fly out of the cargo terminal," I ventured; but he already knew, having used the terminal himself many times on the way to his country and was well familiar with the short cut to this less used terminal.

It reminded me of my experience at the Pakistani Embassy when I went to get the visa. I was fully expecting to get a multiple entry visa for a reason that will soon become clear. When I told this to the clerk who was filling out my application form on the computer in a small crowded office peopled with every manner and shape of turbaned tribesmen, he immediately stopped my plans of multiple entry short by telling me that I could only have a single entry visa. "But I will be flying over to Peshawar about once a month," I implored, but his flat, disinterested face immediately told me that I was speaking to the wrong person. "I need to see the First Secretary," I said with a polite air of determination. "Of course, Mr. Faisal, outside and in the main embassy building, second floor." After passing through a battery of security and donning my security pass on my shirt pocket complementing my tie-clip with its officiality, I made my way upstairs wondering whether it was the American second floor or the European second floor. As it happened, it was the Pakistani second floor beyond a mezzanine and first floor. I knocked on the closed door and made my entrance to encounter the first secretary standing at his desk talking with an aide. He immediately deferred to my presence as though I were some kind of dignitary and after shaking my hand invited me to sit down. I hesitated for a second, my thoughts roaming through a complicated maze of explanations and reluctantly coming to the fore to make sense of what I needed to tell him. For one panicky moment, it all seemed too implausible to articulate in real words the unique experience of my becoming the grandfather of a family of eight, including six children, mother and father, a story with no past and no future, only an inner truth that could bear no verbal explanation without destroying its reality, like trying to explain the quantum enigma or the presence of eternity within the reality of time. Its plausibility simply couldn't be reconciled with convincing ease; only its implausibility stood forth as a striking sign of some false pretense.

Nevertheless, I took leave of this shore of incertitude and made my way through the delicacies of my unexpected tale; it seemed incredible even to me as I heard myself begin to recount the story of an unlikely and unexpected encounter that turned into a true friendship, while the first secretary listened to my narrative with attention and interest. I had met this Pathan tribesman over fifteen years ago one Friday in the mosque after what the Muslims call the Juma Prayer, the prayer of congregation that takes place every Friday noontime with a brief sermon by the imam followed by the simple Islamic prayer ritual. This particular prayer is a crowded affair with practitioners spilling out onto mats in the courtyard under the stark mid-day desert sun, a testament perhaps to the intensity that ordinary Muslims still feel for their religion in this post-modern age of secularism and material progress. When the prayer is finished, people linger around for a while socializing, performing the extra Sunnah prayers and alternatively sitting cross-legged against a pillar to read the Quran.

On one such Friday afternoon as I sat reading the Quran after prayer, a dark shadow crossed the page of my *moshaf* forcing me to look up at the unexpected intrusion. A virtual mountain man towered over me, broad-shouldered and barrel-chested; he leaned down with a benevolent smile spread across his face, offering me a great gorilla paw of a hand to shake. I had grown accustomed to people greeting me in and around the mosque; the Muslims feel great happiness when they learn that someone has converted to Islam, especially a Westerner such as myself. Not only does it open their hearts to a natural feeling of communion and camaraderie; but it also strengthens their own faith in a kind of reverse way, since Arabs generally respect the intelligence, discipline and technical know-how of Europeans and Americans. A Westerner's free willing entry into the true spirit of Islam gives them pause and always recalls to their mind the traditional saying (*hadith*) of the Prophet Mohammed that a Muslim convert has the sins of their past wiped away and will be entitled to enter the paradise without question.

I sensed immediately that this was no casual encounter and no common man; but rather an occasion that happens rarely in a lifetime and has the capacity to reverse tides and change destiny. There was a light on his face that was impossible to ignore, as if someone has turned on a lamp inside his head. The darkly bearded man looked down upon me with a full-rounded face that was as sweet and honest as the day is long; his smile shone out of him like sunlight falling on the full moon. Squatting down with ease next to me with his feet flat on the ground, he asked where I came from, always the first question amid such encounters. When I told him America, he clapped his hands irreverently and topped onto his backside and back like a playful gorilla. "I very happy with this news," he beamed with an earnest pleasure that was intoxicating, if not infectious, once he had set himself aright. He raised his hands in front of himself as a gesture of formal leave-taking, then put his right hand over his heart, saying: "I not want to be bother you reading Quran," and with the hint of a wink and a "*ma salama*", he disappeared silently among the pillars of the mosque.

We met up again on numerous Fridays and soon enough he invited me back to a small villa he shared with his two brothers and a number of other close relatives from his native village in Pakistan, Tarkha by name, the very place that I was now on my way to visit once again, deep in the hilly countryside of the North West Frontier Province. The First Secretary of the Pakistani Embassy seemed to listen to me with skeptical interest as I related the development of a very long relationship that started many years ago in that mosque and that has now grown to include his fully extended family of six children, all of whom considered me as their grandfather and affectionately called me Baba, the Pashtu term of affection for grandfather. Mr. Faisal eventually began to warm to this unique situation, an American sitting in his office, a Muslim convert for some 35 years now, a story as fantastic as it was improbable of the initial friendship and now familiar love of the Pathan family who had taken in this stray expatriate as one of their own. Could the incredible be more believable when it seems too farfetched to be false, containing truths that one finds in fiction that can hardly bear the light of reality in fact?

At first, I was slow to recognize the rarity of his unique Pathan mentality and the manifestation of his simple and uncorrupted heart. I too like many others allowed myself to be misled by his awesome size, shape and bearing, for all appearances, he seemed to be a rough cut and a person of formidable bearing. One of the inevitable effects of living in the modern world is that we have hardened ourselves against the intrusion from the outside world of anything that could invade the serenity of our routines and upset the narrow setting of our conscious minds. In our initial encounter, the hurly-burly Farmana approached me with the openness and spontaneity of a child, not as if we were perfect strangers—for a child everything is strange but harbors a latent familiarity waiting to be discovered—but rather as if we were long lost friends who had suddenly been reunited after a span of decades. Who was this strange fellow befriending me with an unrelenting fusillade of expectation and candor, as if I had everything he could ever want and as his friend I would gladly give it to him because that is how he understood the world and that is how he approached the people he encountered. I mistook his child-like spontaneity and seeming innocence for the clever ploy of a con man moving in on silent wings over his prey, ready to gather in his claws the unsuspecting waif. I had not been too long in the world, but too long in the modern world if you will, where a person quickly learns to hold him or herself in reserve, to guard against the unwanted encounter and the unpredictable stranger as an instinctive means of protection against the unexpected nature and contingencies in life.

Over time, I was to learn that his inner nature was so rare and unique and his personality was so natural and true to itself that I could not fail to be drawn to him, especially in an age such as we live in today when the majority of individuals are self-serving, superficial, and inaccessible on some deeper and truer level beyond the superficial mask that most people present to the world. He said what he meant and meant what he said. He fulfilled his promises and kept his appointments. He gave the broad field of the traditional virtues their name back, including generosity, truthfulness, faithfulness and a natural inborn dignity, being incapable of lying, cheating, or talking about others behind their back. He taught me the meaning of the Quranic verse: "Allah is with you wherever you are." He was devoted to his family, his village friends and his tribe in that order. He accepted what life offered to him and he never complained. All of this set him apart from the standard of modern individuals and made him an individual worthy of note. Even his physical statue seemed to take note of his singularity and uniqueness, for we should not fail to mention that he was in his physical presence a giant of a man.

In my initial association with him, I came to learn what it meant to be a giant among men. We don't mean to imply necessarily some exaggerated physical amplitude that we read about in childhood fairytales in the form of the elusive giant who walks through the forest pulling up trees by their roots, but a kind of traditional man cast from the mold of the universal man who appears larger than life, partly because he was larger than the average man, his noble bearing and vertical stance heightened by such traditional clothing as a turban and flowing caftan, and partly because he is larger than life and in so being has taken on the physical presence of a giant as the outward projection of an inner magnitude. That he was also an unsuspecting giant who did not know his own size only accentuated the endearing contrast between his physical prowess and the boundless inner child-like presence that heightened the pure and uncorrupted quality of his personal nature.

I had moved around a lot in my life and could measure the progression of my years by the places I have lived in. I used to smartly boast that I have lived and worked in three continents, 9 countries and 19 different institutions of higher learning, but I don't do so anymore, not since the day I met my Pathan friend Farmana, through whose association over time I came to know the ultimate wisdom, namely that in truth one doesn't know very much at all and if somehow you have acquired some wisdom, you let it shine through your actions and your behavior and not through the proud boasting that is the sugar coating of empty words. Over the years, I had encountered every size, shape, color, personality and temperament of individuals from innumerable backgrounds and cultures, enough to fill the universal book of man with all the mug shots of a disturbed and vainglorious humanity. In addition, I had been a teacher all my life. I have considered myself what is called a natural-born pedagogue, and countless students have sat, figuratively speaking, at my feet over the fleeting years to learn the message of the day, its significance, and its application. I prided myself on the fact that I have taught much more than the subject at hand, namely English in all its facets of proficiency and skills. I have attempted to guide my students, set the example, and through whatever means available to my limited mentality and experience, to instill in them the very best of myself, for whatever that might be worth.

Then I met this unsuspecting giant and learned how very little I actually knew about the key elements that form an accurate self-image of man and actually constitute the knowledge of how to live a good life. For once, I had the instinctive intelligence to become the ear rather than the voice, the lantern and not the light, as he taught me without knowing that he did, without effort, unconsciously and indirectly, through his simple words, his integral actions and his very physical bearing, the meaning of a life and the meaning of his life. Was he a philosopher, a theologian, a purveyor of words and ideas beyond the normal course of a man? Far from it. Was he a lama, a sheikh, a guru or a saint cast into the magnificent corporeal form of a man under the halo of sanctity and the product of a rarefied upbringing that had singled him out as a man among men? The answer is an unqualified no. He was a son among four sons, orphaned by his father when he was six and left to help his brothers support their mother and family as he walked barefoot the byways of his village with his donkey and its load of grasses.

The years passed by and during this time I got to know him better than perhaps anyone else in my life. I came to learn that in his presence I experienced a rare and unique soul without pretension or guile and that indeed he was a unique individual among the people of our time. In fact, he was the living representative of the saying of Christ that unless you become like little children you cannot enter the kingdom of Heaven. He was, in every vital respect, like a child, with his simple innocence, his unpretentious quality, the spontaneous joy that accompanied the simplest of his pleasures. In children, these reactions are everyday occurrences of an uncorrupt and in some way inexperienced soul in which the primordial aura of beginnings has not yet dimmed and the sweet remembrance of first origins keeps alive the true identity of our inner self. In this unsuspecting giant, they were a sign of another world, a higher dimension and an alternative reality that for him served as his beacon of light whose luminescence remembered the one God of Islam as the only true reality worth living for.

He married several years after I met him and return thereafter once a year to his ancestral village to spend time with his young wife Shaista, a childhood sweetheart who was an infant when he himself came of age, putting nearly 14 years between them. His first two children were girls whom he named Najma and Zohra. By the time I made my first visit to his village at the turn of the millennium, Najma was several years old and Zohra was an infant in arms. As she began to grow older, Najma hardly knew her father when he returned home for his once yearly visit; she preferred the arms of his brother or father-in-law and this slight touched deeply upon his soul. Zohra befriended her father upon his return and in the true spirit of all infants, she was ready to extend her love at the slightest provocation. Finally, about six years into the marriage, there was another child on the way; this time, Farman had returned to his village because he was between assignments in his work.

One night, as they lay sleeping, Shaista shook her bear-like husband awake and whispered in his ear that she was ready, and so was the baby. Farman jumped up and ran to awaken his brothers who all rushed into the village to get a Nissan pickup they had arranged in anticipation of the impending birth. The three brothers climbed into the front cab; the three women, including Farman's mother who was an experienced wet-nurse in her own right, his sister and the belabored Shaista, breathing heavily, climbed into the open-ended rear of the pickup truck. It was a seasonally clear night in early October. The moon and stars shown down their benevolent pale light on this expectant party; there was a chill dampness in the air and a creeping fog along the edges of the dirt road lending an uneasy atmosphere to the proceedings. The women were well fortified with woolen shawls and the heavy chador draped over their heads like a shroud. The brothers set off through the village and beyond its fringe on the way to the hospital in Peshawar about 45 minutes away. They were but a few miles outside the village under the blackness of the brisk night sky when there was a tap on the rear window of the cab. "Turn around," Farman's old mother cried out from outside the cab. He maneuvered his way around the narrow pathway and immediately headed back without a word. Only a few minutes went by when he heard another tap on the window. "Pull over ... now," his mother shouted with authority, and Farman immediately brought the pickup to a halt by the side of the road. He later told me that he could hear the croaking of frogs in the distance breaking the eerie silence of the night, interrupted only by the heavy breathing and muffled cries of his wife beyond the enclosed cab. The brothers sat in silence and resignation, when suddenly there was another tap on the rearview window. "My son," his mother intoned majestically. "You have a son. Allah be praised. You have a boy." Whereupon, they returned to the village and went back to their ancestral home with the new addition to their family.

When Farman returned to the Emirates and told me the story, I felt in awe at the unassuming manner in which he related the story to me, as if it were an everyday occurrence. I then realized that it was time for him to bring his family to live with him in the Emirates, so long as he had work there and could sustain them in a suitable manner. When his son Wajahat turned six months old, they bundled him up with the other two girls and Shaista took herself and the three children to this strange, new country, leaving her village for the first time, and traveling beyond the borders of her country across vast mountains and oceans to reach her new abode with her husband in the United Arab Emirates. By the time Wajahat could crawl over to my legs and stand up with the support of my knees, he has fallen in love with me. When I arrived for the weekend, he ran in ecstasy to my feet to pull off my shoes and socks and when I left, he waved good-bye and cried as he sat in the crook of his father's arms. Mariam was soon to follow, dark-haired and dark-eyed. Shaista wrapped her up for the first six months and tied her like a birthday package, as she had done with the other children so that she would not flail about unnecessarily in her infancy. When she was about 8 months old, she turned to look at me while in her mother's arms and reached out to me to be held. From then on, she was my girl and was completely taken with me. When I arrived, she clung to me; she sat in my lap all through the weekend, and when I left at the end of the weekend, I did so when she was taking her afternoon nap to spare her the heart-rending sobs at my departure.

By the time of Shaista's next pregnancy not a year and a half later, no one said anything out loud because one accepts the will of Allah; but there were secret, unspoken aspirations for another boy, since the family already had three girls and poor Wajahat was sorely outnumbered. Sure enough, my Pathan friend called me at 3:00 in the morning one Friday to announce the arrival of Raouf, making the 25th of August forevermore a day of remembrance for the family. This new "bundle of trouble" also fell in love with Baba, the Pashtu word for grandfather. It was the first word to emerge from his lips with distinction and he took to marching around the room and pulling down my photograph from the bookcase, calling out Baba, Baba all day long. When I arrived for the weekend, he joined the rest of the army under the shade of the mango tree waiting for Baba and when my car emerged from around the corner, his little feet danced in the dust, his excitement rushing headlong through all his extremities in a fit of joy. And when I left for home at the end of the weekend, he climbed into the arms of his mountain man of a father to see me off, crying inconsolably as if it were the end of the world and not just the end of his world.

Unbeknownst to myself and my own invention, I now knew that I had my own adopted family, including mother, father and six children, if you include little Laylah who arrived a few months ago and is still wrapped up in swaddling clothes and hasn't recognized her Baba yet. A confirmed bachelor all my life, I had not sought out the joys of domesticity for a number of reasons, not the least of which being an inborn disposition for privacy and solitude that precluded my getting married and making a solemn commitment that true marriage requires. However, knowing now what I know and having responded to the reality that presented itself, I am grateful that this beloved family had quietly and without fanfare crept into my life and become a part of my world before I had a chance to protest. A gift is given to you and you cannot decline its offering without betraying something fundamental in yourself, not to mention the one who is giving. It is a gift of love and devotion and faithfulness that clears the air and clarifies the day, that brings the light of dawn and the darkness of twilight together into a single unity by the reality of this frank outpouring of emotion that is raw, pure, and unqualified. I can hear the voices of the children now even when they are not there and they come and go within my mind without asking for permission, freely and happily, bringing with them their own happiness and well being into my waking consciousness with their natural grace. They are there and they are gone, but I am among them even when I am alone. "I could stay among them," I think to myself. "Yes, I could stay with them forever and watch them grow. Even as I grow old or perhaps because I grow old." Who could turn away from such a gift and not feel regret at its passing away? It is the thought of going on without them that would turn my life into an unexpected trial that might be too much to bear.

* * *

Of course, I didn't extemporize to this extent the qualities of my friend and what his family meant to me to the First Secretary of the Pakistani Embassy, although admittedly I tried to convey the essence of this unique, eternal friendship as the foundation for my desire to visit them in Pakistan. Some ideas cannot bear the harsh reality of being spoken out loud, particularly to strangers. They express knowledge so fragile and emotion so raw that sending their vibration into the air could shatter the serenity and purity of their meaning and significance. Yet, there are ideas and experiences that lie in waiting to shed of their essence when it is needed, to be seen and listened to in the form of people, places and the natural beauties in the things that surround us and are absorbed into our beings as the essential quality of their transcending truth. The significance of people, places, and things suddenly make themselves known on a day as unexpected as a summer storm. You see a shadow along the path, hear the sound of the sea in a seashell, feel the breath of wings on your neck, or through a lingering smell a fragment of memory enkindles a spark within your heart and you remember . . . what is it precisely, but the spirit of the giant who did not know his size that lies sequestered as a promise within each of us, a presence that you know is there, but cannot see and do not always remember, even if you wish to take hold of it and never let go. Yet it quickly escapes into the netherworld of potential promise and vanishes once again below the first tier of ordinary consciousness, to remain a harbinger of blessing for the aspiring soul. Indeed therein lies a presence that you are afraid to acknowledge and may not even want to see with the eyes, lest the shadow image in the dark recesses of your consciousness dissipates into thin air and the vague premonition of something great within you disappears forever.

I never told this embassy official the story of my great love for this Pathan tribesman and his beloved family and my place within their hearts as their grand patriarchal Baba, the story of the unexpected gift of this family coming to a man who had lived alone most of his life. It is a story whose final page, when closed, will preserve its sweet memory even thought it has long since ended in time. It is the story of a great gift that stands in silhouette as it were against a greater light, since we are but shadows standing against an eternal flame, giving evidence once again of the vagaries, the uncertainties, and the beauties of the human condition.

With the colorful, full-page visa stamped in my new 10-year passport, and armed with my roundtrip ticket on Shaheen Airways, I made my way to the airport to discover upon arrival that the flight would be delayed, a delay that sank into my heart like a stone falling into a well. A very obliging Shaheen Air agent singled me out from the crowd to give me his mobile phone number. "Call me tomorrow morning around 8:00. I will have a better idea of when the flight will be taking off; it hasn't even left Peshawar yet," he whispered conspiratorially while eyeing the other nearby passengers. I abruptly turned myself around and caught a return taxi home to sleep off the disappointment. I have traveled the globe for decades on long haul flights across vast oceans and mountain ranges only to arrive on time in almost every instance; but I was having trouble making my way toward the Khyber Pass, famed in the 19th century for being an impossible barrier to cross in those remote mountains. Many years living in the Middle East has taught me to be flexible and I have steeled myself to be resigned to the forces that are beyond my control. In that spirit, I fell that night into a deep slumber as though it were part of my written destiny and not to be trifled with without disturbing the harmony of the universe.

I did eventually take off the next afternoon at 3:00 PM. Shaheen Airways treated me like a first class passenger although the plane, a Boeing 737, had only economy class configuration. The obliging agent wrapped a VIP tag around the handle of my suitcase and put me without asking into seat 1A and kept the other two seats beside me unoccupied. On the other side of the aisle sat two middle-aged pilots who had undoubtedly flown the plane into Abu Dhabi and were now ready to sleep through the ride home. Everyone displayed extra respect to my presence on the plane, from the pilots, stewards and stewardesses, to the horde of male Pathan passengers all decked out in their regalia of headgear, turbans, shawls and cloth Pathan suits, looking wild and unruly in their extravagant attitudes of the mountain man, coming as they did from such areas as Hunza, Swat and the Karakoram. All looked benevolently upon me with genuine smiles as a most welcome intruder, a foreign guest, an unexpected traveler in their midst. The pilot himself came back into the cabin during the flight and sat chatting with me. As the aging, rundown plane lumbered toward the take off point, there was a loud rumble of noise coming from the chaotic cacophony of gruff voices speaking an alien tongue in back of me, a language that was surprisingly becoming more familiar to me to the extent that I could now isolate individual words and actually understand them: "Move over", "Turn off the light", "Wait a minute", the Pashtu phrases came to my mind now like old friends. However, as the plane suddenly sprang to life with a loud roar and lurched forward down the runway gaining speed, the garbled chatter came to an abrupt halt and silence suddenly reigned throughout the cabin amid the spell-bound passengers as they sat and listened respectfully to the road of the engines. We lifted off and headed northeast toward the Khyber Pass of the North West Frontier Province of Pakistan.

Three hours later, flying low over the city on the approach to the airport, the extended city looked dark and forlorn, low-lying buildings and sheds, deep shadows and flat contours that created an undistinguished, poverty-stricken landscape of mud huts and corrugated iron roofs, a far cry from the dazzling display of light that greets the nighttime traveler into any one of the Gulf countries, where every street is flood-lit and every house awash in the glitter of a thousand illuminations. My Pathan friend Farmana had warned me that if I didn't see him in the outside line awaiting me that I was not to leave the security of the inner arrivals hall. However, there was no cause for concern for my safety or convenience. He had arranged for me to be met by a representative of Shaheen Airways who stood waiting for me at the foot of the plane. He introduced himself to me like a long lost friend, before we walked way from the plane on foot into the dark, aging terminal. Without a question or a word, I was passed through Passport Control and taken to the luggage collection area where my VIP bag was quickly retrieved with the snapping of fingers and a careless wave of the hand to the skinny porter. Before I knew where I truly was, I was whisked through the arrivals door to see my three body guards anxiously awaiting my appearance, my friend Farmana, his brother Wali and his brother-in-law Babu who each in their turn embraced me in their great, lingering bear hugs that wouldn't let go. With a wink and a knowing glance, Farmana showed me the revolved tucked within the folds of his Pathan cloth suit. "No need for worry," he assured me and I thought "no indeed", the gun will solve any problem, if not create a few of its own. Still, it was comforting to know the extent they were prepared to go to take care of and protect me, and hijacking for random, if nothing else, was a genuine concern.

We piled into the small Nissan for the 45-minute trip into the outskirts of Peshawar, down the four lane highway on the way to Islamabad full of the commotion resulting from every manner of transportation, including three-wheelers, cars, trucks, motorcycles, bicycles, horse-drawn carts, oxen, chickens, turkeys, truant pedestrians and vendors selling fruits and vegetables along the side of the road, all of this activity filling the highway like some mad road thoroughfare to Gomorrah. Soon enough, we pulled off what passed as a highway, pitch dark except for the beams of the cars penetrating the night like swords of light and plunged into the night bazaar of a small local town. "This is the last town before village," Farman confided with me. "We will pick up more protection now." I was alarmed, wondering what he was talking about. The car pulled over to the side and I found that we were bounded on each side by jeeps full of young men dressed in cloth suits and turbans and heavily bearded of course, totting Kalashnikovs in various stages of readiness. "The last stretch into village very dark and dangerous. Bandits sometimes waiting," Farman confided nonchalantly. And on that comment, the car sprang to life again and we lurched forward in a protected caravan toward the ancestral home of my friend in the remote village of Tarkha.

The village itself was in various stages of shutting down for the night. It was dark enough as we made our way through the one dirt road full of cracks and holes and framed on each side with the crumbling mud walls of the houses and shops of the village. The lights had apparently gone out and inside the shops I could see the flickering of candles. People were making their way through the darkness on foot or on motorcycles slicing through the darkness with their headlights and noisy clatter, but everyone deferred to the movement and progress of the car. Suddenly, we had arrived and I was unceremoniously shoved down the dusty path between two drains and around the corner between tall trees. I heard the chatter and singing of children and then saw them standing in a cluster in silhouette against a hanging lamp in front of the door of the house in which they now lived. When they saw me, they came running forward in a cascade of glee, sounding like birds in a tree at sunset. Shouting Baba, Baba in their unrestrained excitement, they threw flower petals over my head and shoulders as tears came to my eyes. Then each of them salaamed me respectfully and extended their little fingers for the traditional handshake. I noticed through the hubbub that they were scrubbed clear and neatly dressed, the girls' heads wrapped discreetly in the colorful Pathan shawls. My arrival was an event that they had anticipated and prepared for the entire day, indeed the entire week.

Raouf, the baby now near two years old, sat contentedly in the arms of Farman's oldest brother, Niaz Mohamed, who himself stood next to the children looking like the Grand Mufti of Al-Azhar, the famed Islamic university in Cairo, with his majestic face and sculptured white beard. Raouf sat there as if he owned this niche and had every right to be there, his little legs dangling barefooted from the shelf of Niaz's strong arm in careless abandon. Niaz Mohamed walked over through the darkness of the night and immediately handed the baby over to me. It was three months since Raouf sat contentedly in the arms of his beloved Baba. Once there, he could have stayed there for all eternity to the extent that whenever I wanted to put him down, he protested mightily, kicking his legs in protest. But children can be unpredictable and know what they want and what they don't want and it is not always the right of adults to fathom the what and wherefore of their desires. Would the beloved baby Raouf remember after a three month hiatus this aging bag of bones that he had once clung to and cherished as his beloved Baba?

I had been told by Farmana that in order to perpetuate my memory, they would show Raouf my photograph and he would proceed to march around the house showing everyone and pointing to his

Baba, the first and only word that he could yet articulate, uttering the sound like some secret, lost revelation newly discovered. In my mind as I had prepared for the trip and now as I stood there at the true moment of my arrival, I wondered if he would remember me. I had lived a long and interesting life and done many things that I could be proud of and a few things as well that I shouldn't be proud of; but the recognition of the baby and his sweet remembrance had suddenly become for me the only moment worth waiting for. Worlds could turn and eternities pass us by, but if this beloved infant didn't remember me, it would lay waste my new world and shatter the fragile expectation we having of loving and being loved in return. There is something primordial and unique in the outpouring love of an infant baby. There are no conditions or attachments associated with this fragile emotion and like sweet fragrance it emerges from the noble presence of the child with its own raw and unconditioned truth. It seems to ask nothing in return, and in so doing opens a world of love and emotion that pour out willingly from soul to soul like flood waters spilling over a dam. Infants recognize true love in others and give it back freely in return.

Judging from the size of his eyes and the hint of his smile, Raouf was clearly caught up in the excitement of the moment as he was passed from the arms of one grandfather to the other before he had time to think about it or protest. As he settled his chubby frame into the crook of my arm where he had spent so many weekends during what seemed now like the ancient history of our time, he wasn't sure he was having any of this. I could see it in his eyes and attitude that he wasn't sure who I was at first and was going to take his time about making up his mind. He sat there in my arms eye to eye and face to face and began to scrutinize what he was seeing. I have always marveled at the child's ability to be fully in the moment without the excessive baggage that adults usually carry around with them, and this moment was no exception. Raouf took me in with all the native instinctive powers available to him as an infant presence, like some regal prince surveying one of his subjects. At first, he seemed to roam the topography of my face for some familiar landmarks, and for a second he raised his pudgy little hand and touched my beard, as though feeling its texture for hints of the identity from this strange person causing so much excitement; then not getting a satisfying reply from this brief survey, I felt the child look straight into my eyes and I stared back, as if his head were surrounded by a halo in a mist of light shining forth from a lamp over the door of the house.

This was no casual glance; I could feel him probing deeply into the well of my being for a signal that would awaken what he was looking for, as though he were searching through the forest for a glimpse at a passing deer or scanning the horizon of a great ocean for signs of land. For a moment, his gaze was so penetrating and direct, I felt as if I were suspended in mid-air without any ground under my feet, held aloft by the scrutiny of his pure, uncluttered gaze; my heart had become merely a string that was being pulled taut so that I could actually feel pain. Then, without further ado, this boy wonder made up his mind. His face became aglow with infantine delight and gave me the most beatific smile imaginable and uttered distinctly the word Baba, as though he were reading notes from a piece of musical script and Baba again and again, setting up echoes in my heart of a distant bell whose reverberation ran through my being like the sounding notes of some grand musical prelude. It felt like we had just journeyed together to the world's edge to see what lay beyond, and had come back with smiles on our faces. It filled my heart with joy to know that the traditional loyalty and faithfulness was already there in the little heart of this Pathan infant. We all made our way into the house together; but my eyes were glistening and wet as I carried this little mountain man in my arms through the door.

The intimate moment passed into eternity and true pandemonium broke loose as the other five children all clambered for my attention, everyone pulling at my pockets and grabbing for my hands, each of the ragamuffins wishing to be the chosen one to escort me through the house. Farman pointed proudly over the top of the maroon and gold painted entry to the message written in elegant Arabic set within the inlay of a triangle framed above the door: "This is a blessing, the house of the son of Saleh Mohammed." On each side there was another message in Quranic Arabic embellished with arabesques and florals: by the will of Allah. Indeed, I thought, there is a will higher than anything imaginable that guides us and leads the way with infinite knowledge and mercy. I bowed my head as I was hustled through the metal transom of the doorframe and humbly entered this new world that is the immediate consequence of my own making. As though suddenly awaken from some deep slumber and not knowing precisely were I was, I gazed about me at the interior courtyard of these surroundings endeavoring to take in the reality of what I was witnessing, but all I could think of was the evening more than a year before, when my friend Farmana and I had resolved to build this great ancestral house made with a love that could withstand time and last for generations.

His mother, widowed now some thirty years, Farman's father having died when he was about seven years old, had given her son Farman the deed to some prime land in the village, just far enough off the main street so as not to be troubled by the noise of the buggies and motor cycles that occasionally picked up the dust of the road. There was a small knoll in the middle of the land that would form the foundation site of the building and the entire area was surrounded by cultivated fields and fruit trees, especially plums and peaches. At the time the children numbered six and there were bound to be more. Farman's wife Shaista was a robust 16 years old when she married her childhood friend and now eight years later and six children richer, she were a mere 24 and not the worse for wear. She was a tall, strong-looking woman with a matronly face full of strength and character.

Farman's work situation in the Emirates was demanding at best and miserable at worst. He had on-going battles with his Syrian boss who was part owner of a small irrigation and lighting company. As foreman for the company, he saw through the irrigation projects from initiating the bid and securing the tender to laying out the farms in the desert with his team of Pathan workers all hand-picked from his village. When there were no irrigation projects, he sought out lighting contracts for the company such as setting up the garden lighting for the local sheikh's palace or handling the lighting for some real estate entrepreneur who was building ten or fifteen buildings. He had earned millions for the company and never got a penny extra by way of bonus for his efforts. His boss called him his right hand man when Farman was pulling in the money or finishing off projects ahead of time; but if the slightest problem arose, he was a running dog, lazy and good for nothing. For the proud Pathan such as my noble friend, such talk is the kiss of death. We both knew that there would come a time when this love-hate relationship would finally be broken. When that happened, they would have to return to Pakistan and take up life once again in his ancestral village. To prepare for this eventuality and with a view to my fast approaching retirement, my friend and I resolved to build a house for the family, for the future, for the children and their children's children, a house made of stone and brick but sealed with the mortar of brotherhood and love that would last as long as the mercy of Allah prevailed.

The planning of the house had a surreal quality to my inexperienced mind. Who was going to design this imaginary edifice? I naively asked my friend Farman. Who will be the architect, I wondered to myself, setting the design and laying down the plans in detail? But my Pathan friend had a level of practical experience tucked away in his back pocket and a native intelligence that permitted no barrier to fulfilling what he had set his mind to accomplishing. For a simple, village boy from just east of the Khyber Pass and armed with a high school diploma, this Pathan mountain man had a native sense of what he wanted in a house in terms of light and space and airiness and no attention to detail was left unspecified. Planning and designing a house came as second nature to him and he set about it with vigor and speed. I sat with him as he drew up a floor plan and we discussed the number and kinds of rooms that he envisioned, the traditional style of the house with its open inner courtyard, its size, the number of floors, the village workers who would take part in its construction, and the building materials that would make its frame and substance. Once the design was set down on paper, we passed it back and forth making adjustments and alterations as the ideas came upon us. When I saw the finished drawing, I marveled at its conception, traditional functional style and spacious and open design.

The house itself, in the style of the Pathan tribe in those areas, would be completely closed off to the street without a single window looking outward. From outside, the structure would give the appearance of being a kind of fortress and with good reason, as the area is not referred to as "lawless" without reason. Indeed, I had noticed during my first visit to the area that the houses themselves that lined the street were closed off and inaccessible. As such, the village itself became a maze of solid structures that were closed to public view. The only sign of life were the shops built into the walls or the contours of the land and the goods that spilled out into the street in trellises and fruit stalls. Once inside the walls of these miniature citadels, the visitor enters another world of domestic life that resembled a kind of symphony of sound and light and movement. That is why when I raised myself up full height and still carrying the heavy baby Raouf in my arms who was scrutinizing my every movement as I pass through the door of this new house, and while the other children pulled at my pockets and ran around my knees, I gazed in wonder at the interior setting that we had poured over in pencil tracings on white paper fulfilling our dreams of the future for the family. I stopped dead in my tracks and gazed about in wonder. The children broke away from me and ran up ahead and Shaista, Farman's wife, approached to offer me her Salaams and welcome. "You complete this house with your presence," she said, "and bring it blessing."

The last time I had seen Shaista was in the cramped quarters where they lived in a small town in the Emirates, with a sitting room that mercifully led out to an outer courtyard which was surrounded by a wall separating the small villa from the street where the children often played. There was also a small kitchen and two bedrooms, one for the two of them with the children and another bedroom for Baba that I occupied on the weekends when I visited the family from the capital. No one dared enter my room when I wasn't there. When the decision was taken to return to Pakistan, it was Shaista who gave voice to the melancholy that we all felt on their impending departure. It was true that they would be returning to their beloved country and they were excited about that. Three of the children had been born in the UAE and had never seen their own country, and Wajahat, the five year old, had come to the Emirates when he was six months old and remembered nothing of the country of Pakistan whose name was often invoked within the household, much less the wild midnight ride under a moonlit sky that had witnessed his birth in the back of a pick up truck. The world of his ancestral roots really meant nothing to him beyond the invocation of the name. Even the two older girls had only faint recollections of their time in the village, the mud-packed ground inside the house, the great water well in the outer courtyard, taking long afternoon naps under the plum tree that shaded the courtyard, and the soft lowing of the cow in the room next to the kitchen; the kitchen itself with its great fireplace where all the cooking was done and the great scorched black mark staining the wall that ran from the fireplace to the ceiling, the result of cooking kufta and seasoned briyani in great pots sitting on the burning embers of chopped wood in the fireplace.

One morning, we all visited Farman's ancestral home where he grew up and laid ourselves out under the all-embracing shade of the densely leafed tree. The women set up a fan and served chilled drinks and grapes freshly picked from the rooftop arbor. Peach Tang in chilled metal cups never tasted so good as we lay supine on brightly colored cotton cloths and pillows, protected from the intense sun and overwhelming heat by the mercy and generosity of that noble tree. There was something proverbial in the shade of this tree covering a good portion of the inner courtyard, mocking the sun in its own heavens with its amber coolness. When the modern accoutrements such as electricity gave out, somebody's brother or son or nephew was there to fan us unto a cooling redemption. The children played with the baby calf and approached its mother with caution as I gazed up into the density of the tree, marveling at the gnarled knots in the branches of the trees, reflecting years of experience and the onslaught of weather, heat and cold to mark the tree with the wisdom of the ages in that it faithfully gave forth of its fruit for these poor people to eat freely from.

One of the teenage boys had an affinity for nature and had brought home a parrot that he had stolen from its nest when it was just a baby. It was a scrawny looking bird; but was a parrot sure enough with its green coat and red beak. The boy loved the bird that he called Tutee and talked with it lovingly, imitating to perfection its attempts as vocal sound to the extent that it was difficult to decide who was imitating whom. The bird was loose and rummaging freely among the leaves in the corner of the courtyard when suddenly Raouf emerged from the crowd of children and ran over to the squawking bird. He was excited beyond belief and jumping up and down when suddenly he jumped upon the unsuspecting parrot and crushed the life out of it in a second without so much as a squawk in protest from the feeble bird. Not knowing fully what he had done, he turned around and stared at the rest of us with a look of triumph, the same look that he assumed when he killed an ant and shrieked in delight. The family later told the boy that the baby calf had unwittingly stepped on the wandering Tutee by accident. When the boy heard the news, he ran over to the calf and beat it to its knees to give vent to his anger. Raouf kept silent.

When Farman had his classic blowout with his boss and made a sacred vow to sever once and for all the relationship that had been an exercise in restrained compromise for years, Spring was upon us and the buds of the mango tree outside in the courtyard were offering their spuds to the wide world of sun and air. I was scheduled to fly to the US to attend a teaching conference that would bring my return very close to the time of their sad leave-taking. As it happened, when I visited them one last time on the weekend before my own departure from the country, it was my 62nd birthday. On that final weekend, Shaista became the mistress of last times and final things that would never happen again in this time and place, turning all of the little routines of my weekend visit with the family into a last time event that would never happen again. "This is the last weekend you come to us in this little house, Baba" Shaista bleated with a look of sadness spread across her broad face like a map she didn't understand. It would be the last time that Farman and the children would gather under the mango tree in front of the wall of the villa to greet me on my arrival, the little feet of Raouf dancing in the dust in a physical rush of excitement and those pudgy little fists working the invisible air as if he were conducting a symphony of joy and infant delight, when the children saw my car turn the corner of their back alley; the last time we would gather inside the house on the late afternoon of my arrival and feast on the sliced home-made cake that I always brought with me, topped with frosting that glittered in the yellow light of the late afternoon desert sun streaming through the courtyard door into the living room as the children spread out across the floor like a living, agitated fan surrounding the magnificent cake with cries of joy and screams of protest at who got the biggest piece, followed by murmurs of deep satisfaction as the cake quickly disappeared, washed down with great gulps of tea. Years could go by and worlds would turn; yet the memories of these last moments would live on in the heart of my beloved family. Shaista perpetuated the melancholy feelings of the weekend with her pronouncements of "last things": this is our final evening meal together, the last kufta ball stuffed with egg and dripping with tomato salsa, the final plateful of chapatti and yellow dahl seasoned to perfection with burnished onions. It would be the final time that Mariam and Raouf would clamber for a place on my lap during dinner, both of them receiving the morsels of meat that I placed on their little tongues, with Mariam giggling with delight and clapping her hands when I shouted "wacha, wacha" (the Pashtu word for meat), and Raouf grunting in satisfaction as he munched on his grilled lamb shank, bones and all, then pulling my scented handkerchief from the beast pocket of my cloth to fastidiously wipe his nose and mouth clean.

For the last time, I crawled out of bed on Friday morning, the Muslim holy day when the faithful gather together in the mosque for the noontime sermon and communal prayer. Tradition had me slipping away in my car to buy the newspaper and pick up fresh hot zatar croissants from a famed local bakery, the attendants always smilingly amusedly at me when I showed up in my traditional Pathan cloth to order the same thing every Friday, like clockwork. On this last Friday, I returned to the house with my parcels to find the house in silence and the door to the sitting room closed. Something was afoot on this final Friday and when I entered the sitting room to peruse the newspapers before the rest of the household would awaken, I was confronted with a hushed silence and the burning candles of a cake. The six children and their two Pathan parents were standing around a little make-shift table singing "Happy Birthday" in a variety of rhythms and tones to the astonished Baba, a last time for such happiness before we all embarked on a new adventure into the unknown destiny that we must face in our lives with determination and courage. I drove away that afternoon, knowing full well that upon my return from the conference in the States, my beloved family would be gone, the dusty little villa with its brave mango tree would be abandoned, and the history of our lives together there would be engraved in the silence and dust and silhouette of the place against the light of the unrelenting desert sun, a place that would hold no return.

The world that had quickly receded into the past as fond memories was now superseded by this new world of spaciousness and light. The first real thing that I noticed after greeting Shaista and feeling the warmth of her welcome was the pale light of the moon and the twinkling stars that shown down their mystery on the inner courtyard of the house. Just beyond the entrance to the house and under the sparkle of an overhead chandelier there extended the short length of an L-shaped avenue that framed two sides of the inner courtyard. I was greeted by a multitude of guests – all uncles and grandfathers and in-laws, nephews and nieces and children of other close friends, all gathered together for the arrival of the "foreign guest" and the beloved patriarch of this place, the one who had made possible the construction of this magnificent edifice that sits amid the serenity of this bucolic setting like a sleeping animal, full of life and color and incredible purpose. We walked past the pillars on one side, past the screened in grille of the windows of the kitchen with its great oven and floor freezer and wooden cabinets lined across every wall filled with the condiments and spices of the exotic East. Amid the commotion of my arrival, dinner continued to simmer on the stove, sending up great wafts of steam amid the scents of cumin and cloves. I put my head inside to make my inspection and make a little joke amid a flurry of giggles and the tightening of veils and head shawls. Simmering eyes gazed back at me in amazement and terror from sisters and aunts as I moved on deeper into the inner sanctum of the mansion.

As we came to the end of the lip of the L that met at right angles the broad avenue of the main concourse of the house, against which lay all five of the rooms, the two older girls, Najma and Zahra showed me the room that was prepared for me and that would forevermore be identified as the sacrosanct quarters of Baba, never to be traversed unless he is in residence in the house. The next room housed all the children and Farman's mother, the beds were lined up against the walls of the room like sentinels of the night, each with their pillow and blanket. Moving down the marble avenue of the broad concourse of the courtyard, the next room was Farman and Shaista's bedroom and beyond that a room they had set up as a Western dining room with an oaken table and eight chairs, out of deference to Baba's strange habit of sitting at table rather than the Pathan tradition of sitting on the carpet on the floor and eating with their hands from the communal plates. Within the courtyard itself, Farman had planted a garden with roses and jasmine with an extensive lawn surrounded by a wrought iron fence. He had also planted lemon and plum trees, now in their infancy, but soon to grow strong and tall with the aging of the house. "You can bury me here in the garden," I joked with Farmana, but he only shook head and refused to think such thoughts, saying: "You will live forever in the hearts of the family and the people of the village," he murmured. "We never forget and will never forget," he emphasized, shaking his head.

The house itself was tiered with three levels. From the distance, because Farman had laid a strong dirt foundation and raised the house considerably off the ground so that it dominated the entire neighborhood and could be seen from various vantage points within the village, it looked like a Tibetan pagoda, according to the comments of one person I met. To my reckoning, it looked like a modern-day citadel with its tiled roof bedecked with fresh maroon paint set in contrast to the cream-colored walls facing the pathway leading to the street. Stairways on each side of the broad concourse of the inner courtyard, lead up to the second floor where there are two more sizable rooms still empty, with kitchenette and bathroom, and a broad terrace overlooking the surrounding countryside of the village. Another stairwell led up to the third floor where there was one room with another kitchenette, outside sink and bathroom and yet another terraced sitting area that caught the cool breezes of the spring night. One final flight of stairs led to the roof where I found a little house painted in distinctive squares of green and red that housed the water tank. From the tiled roof of this little structure flew the flag of Pakistan in its vivid green broadcloth decorated with the white crescent of the moon and a single star, flapping majestically in the wind and announcing its faithful allegiance for all to see.

From the roof of the house, I can see the countryside of farmland and fruit trees clear to the horizon. In the distance, there were rows of serene poplars, standing tall and stately, like sentinels of the village, ancient souls that have undergone a metamorphosis into these noble trees, surrounding and protecting this little pocket of domesticity, of life and lives being lived, with all the grandeur of its natural setting. The air is clear and very still; the trees stand in eerie silence and not a leaf seems to move. Down below, the layered tiers of the house spilled down to the ground like multiple balconies in an opera house. Far down below, I can see again the little garden that Farman had so quickly and lovingly constructed with its manicured lawn, rose bushes sprouting buds, and infant jasmine trees. Already the buds of the white jasmine were making their way into the world to grace the house with their fragrant spirit.

One evening before my departure, my Pathan friend Farmana and I have tea upstairs on the roof terrace to watch the evening sunset and survey the grounds from this vantage point. The stars shine down upon us with their detached grace and the silence of the surrounding trees murmur their mysterious presence through image and not word; but I give my mind back to the moment when the idea for this house originally came into my mind. "This is what you have done," I said to my friend; but he is a noble soul and will not let this pass. "This is what we have done, Yahya, not me alone." A gift that will last for the generations, I thought, in return for the gift this particular family has given me in return. In the true spirit of an eye for an eye and an ear for an ear that the Quran speaks of, this is a gift of one heart to other hearts, without attachments or conditions, except for the incredible bond that has grown over time between people from alien worlds, like those jasmine flowers in the garden, an unspoken mystery that buds and blooms into an emotion and an experience that has become a gift given in mutual respect whose spirit will endure.

I wish I could encapture the defining quality of the experience in words as I gaze upon the product of the collective effort of me and my faithful friend. Instead I silence my mind and listen to the sounds of the night that float through the countryside, listen to the hooves of the donkey pulling a cart full of grasses down the village thoroughfare beyond the fringe of the premises, listen to the song-like voices of the children below as they fill the house with their blessed laughter. I listen as I let my mind run like a stream through the sounds of the house and the surroundings, everything speaking for themselves until we begin to listen and hear, in order to enter into communion with that deep and peaceful sensation that ultimately gives voice to a higher reality that speaks only of what is valuable and true, remembering and fearing and wishing for nothing for myself alone. Only giving, and being given in return.

Alas my stay is but a long weekend and I must return to the Emirates and my duties at work. As we drove through the village on a sultry afternoon on our way to the airport, flashes of the house come into view in the distance. Through the trees and beyond the ridge, I witness one last time the newly built ancestral home constructed on the knoll of some remote village, a home I have been searching for all my life and never knew I would have in such an unexpected, indeed unlikely place. It is a small wonder of destiny amid the great wonder of a higher presence, reminding me of the wise insight of a Sufi saint that entreats the faithful to read the unity of the universe in every created thing. When blessing comes to us, we are lucky if we recognize it for what it truly is, namely an internalized happiness that nothing and no one can take away. Life can be sweet when we least expect it. You work hard all your life without true recompense, you have expectations that are never fulfilled, you seek and never find; you wished things would happen and when they do, you wonder why you wished them. You never thought of things that did happen and in happening, changed you in ways you should have hoped for to begin with, but didn't have the mind to imagine.

The car sputters forward as the house flickers in and out of view beyond the trees. It seems disembodied in my mind, curiously detached once more in the distance and something not my own, but only part of this strange village, only to realize that this is what I have created for this family, my family, who will live on here for generations to come, into a time when my precarious journey on the edge of time will have pushed me over the edge into the eternity I have always dreamed about as the only reality worth pursuing.

I am once again taking my leave of all that I hold dear as I have done many times in the past; but I take with me in compensation my hope to return, just as the fleeting images of the disappearing house on the hill remain alive in the mind as a sweet remembrance and a living reality, something that will now be a part of me until my final days drift away, just as it will be apart of the children and their children when I am gone. Such a little piece of the world as I see vanishing before me now would be worth a man's long life, as I watch and listen and remember the echoes of all those voices that still animate the house, until I sense that I will never be satisfied with seeing, nor my ears filled with hearing, until I can return once more to this inner sanctum of love and life and friendship. "I could stay here a long time," I say to myself as we turn a final corner and my vision of the ancestral home vanishes behind a cluster of fruit trees, leaving only a fragment of wishful thinking to roam amid the unwritten pages of a destiny yet to unfold. "I could stay here a long time indeed."

6

RAINDROPS
ON KAMPUNG ROOFS

IN THE FAR EAST, there still survive elements of alternative medicine in the form of traditional massage that can be found in India, Thailand and Malaysia among other places with which I have had first hand experience. I can therefore safely and honestly attest to the veracity of the claims that traditional massage such as you find in these and other places seeks to cure the patient by focusing on the source of the problem which according to ancient approaches to medicine find their root cause in intoxification of the blood, poor circulation of the blood which is directly related to the congestion of the blood and atrophy of the internal muscles, poor aeration of the blood as a result of shallow breathing, inadequate sleep together with sleeping at the wrong times of day and night, unsuitable nutrition of the body, and finally unsuitable life-style in general, not to mention the noise and pollution that we must live with every day of our lives in today's world as a matter of course.

The human hand and the subtle intricacies of the sense of touch play a major role in the healing process, although you would never know it judging from anyone's experience in a doctor's office in the Western world. Doctors make investigations with rarefied machines like MRI and Cat Scan; they probe invasively into the inner sanctum of the body through every available orifice; ply you with pills and tablets to deaden the pain and hide the symptoms; but they never actually lay their hands on you, and if they have to for some reason, they now wear latex gloves. However, in ancient Tibetan medical traditions, for example, a doctor could effectively diagnose the ailment of a patient by merely feeling his pulse.

The healing skill of ancient medicines can be found in a variety of traditional massage techniques that go back thousands of years and find their roots in the sacred revelations of the various Far Eastern religions that still exist today in places like Thailand and Malaysia as a genuine form of alternative medicine. For example, there is an abundance of wisdom in the knowledge contained within the sacred scriptures of the Vedanta. The medical science of Ayurveda that can be found faithfully practiced to this day in the South India state of Kerala has preserved a philosophy of medicine that focuses its applications on prevention and longevity in addition to the standard practices of healing and cure. It is in fact the oldest and most holistic medical system still available to modern humanity. What truly makes Ayurveda unique is its professed association with the spiritual tradition of a religion such as Hinduism. The knowledge itself has been transmitted to humanity through the divine revelation based on the four main books of the Vedas, including *Rik*, *Sama*, *Yajur* and *Atharva*. At later dates, the knowledge of Ayurveda was organized into its own compact system of health as an auxiliary branch of the Vedas called Upaveda or "limb of the Veda", because it deals with the practical healing aspects within the realm of spirituality.

Using massage, internal herbal medicines, hot oils, cooling treatments, diet, life style, and a harmonious natural setting, Ayurveda leaves no stone unturned in coming to terms with the health and well being of a person. With its holistic philosophy of medicine based on traditional sources, Ayurveda uses everything within its means to affect a cure or better to achieve prevention of a disease affecting the body, mind, psyche, heart, or soul of the individual. All of these components interact in subtle ways of correspondence so that the disease or health of one aspect of the person necessarily affects some other aspect, and draws upon the principle of Supreme Unity that lies at the heart of the traditional doctrine of Hinduism as well as all of the other orthodox religions of the world. As such, Ayurveda draws upon everything that influences these various components that make up the human person, including massage, medicated oil, internal herbal medicines, heat treatments for certain diseases such as muscle and nerve problems, cooling treatments for arthritic problems and the like. As such, the importance of touch in the pursuit of these treatments plays a paramount role in affecting the cure.

Homeopathy is another traditional approach to cure that, while discovered by a German, has been taken up by people in the sub-continent of India, among other places, as an alternative approach to healing and cure. I had a brief encounter with the benefits of homeopathy nearly twenty years ago that is worth relating in this context as a parenthetical aside before embarking on our main theme. I am not one to suffer from chronic colds and flu and I have been spared other typical ailments that others have to suffer from such as asthma, diabetes and blood pressure, not to mention the dreaded cancer that many people fall victim to. Over the years, however, I have noticed a tendency to suffer from muscle and nerve problems and that my body is prone to these ailments, for what reason precisely I have no idea. It has been enough to have to seek appropriate alternative cures for such ailments because Western solutions tend to fall short of the mark in these areas of application.

It must be over 20 years ago now that I was living in the Middle East when I succumbed once again to a chronic ailment that came suddenly on feathery wings and landed on some area of my body with a vengeance that was difficult to ignore. On this particular occasion, it was stabbing back pain that made itself manifest in the upper back, midway between the spinal column and the so-called wing of my shoulder, that protruding shoulder bone that distinguishes both sides of the upper back. I would have liked to extend one or another of my arms either over my shoulder or coming up from behind to reach the offending area; but it was impossible by my efforts alone to draw out the knife of back-stabbing pain that aggravated my days and spoiled the slumber of my nights with unrelieved agony. I had just taken a 20 hour flight from New York to Jeddah in Saudi Arabia on my way back to work after the summer with this outrageous feeling of pain nestled between my shoulder blades, as though induced by an impaled scimitar.

Once back at work at a university in Jeddah, I mentioned my suffering to a couple of Indian friends as we sipped "black tea" and munched on shortbread cookies early one evening after work.

"We know someone who can cure that," they replied jauntily, shaking their heads from side to side Indian-style to affirm in no uncertain terms the truth of their assertion.

"That would be worth experiencing," I deadpanned a little sarcastically, thinking from experience that this was pain that would never go away until it eventually disappeared.

"No seriously," they insisted. "A friend of ours has these little sugar nodules that have been steeped in the liquid extract of roots and herbs of some sort that, taken in the right proportion, and quality will actually cure certain ailments."

"It's worth a try," I answered with resignation, willing to try anything as simple as sugar nodules to affect a cure to this outrageous pain I was experiencing morning, noon, and night. "Take me to him."

Interestingly enough, the Indian doctor himself, although a genuine Indian from the Kashmir, was not a doctor at all, but a professor of Chemistry at the university. He was also an attested homeopath and took a special interest in this alternative approach to cure. I was introduced to him one evening soon after and he spent quite a bit of time asking me questions about my health, my life style, my routine, the quality, nature and extent of the pain, how often it occurred, whether it was perennial and so on. He seemed to be gathering enough information for him to be able to make an informed decision. Finally, he announced that he had decided upon a course of action. I remember him pulling a wooden box out from under his bed and opening its golden latch to reveal and large number of vials, perhaps thirty or forty of them, glistening in the night light, that contained the mysterious sugar nodules as the sweet instruments of cure I had been promised earlier. The homeopath counted out a number of the flecks of sugar, nodule by nodule into a variety of pieces of paper representing different kinds of medicine. He then folded them into small hand-held packets with strict instructions on when and how many of these nodules to take during the day and advised me to come see him again in two days.

In two days I went back to see him. "What have you experienced?" he asked with great interest. I told him that I had taken the nodules as prescribed, painlessly and effortlessly slipping them under my tongue as he said. The first night I awoke in the middle of the night with a feeling of intense pain in my upper back, much more so than usual, a pain that I explained to the doctor was very curious indeed. I told him that it seemed as though the medicine itself was attacking the atrophied area, blasting the area with its crystalline vitality. While the pain was there as always, this was a pain of a special cloth that harbored within its folds a mysterious promise of cure, as though it were necessary to close some invisible threshold of pain itself on the promise that there would soon be relief.

Thereafter, I continued to visit my Kashmiri friend and related to him the story of how, little by little, nodule by nodule as it were, the outrageous pain that I had suffered for months got weaker and weaker, fainter and fainter, until it gradually disappeared like summer mist in the light of day. I remember that he had the foresight to write down precisely the specific prescription that he had used to effect the cure, in case that should the ailment ever return, I would have the exact prescription that had effected the original cure that any homeopath could follow and prescribe with ease. This did, in fact, happen. Years later, when I was living in Malaysia, the old problem came back again, in a milder form no less, and when I presented the prescription to a local Malay homeopath on the weathered scraps of paper that I have religiously kept with me over the years, he was able to follow the guidance of the original treatment and thus was able to bring about a second and so far permanent cure.

* * *

Malaysia is another country that has faithfully preserved its tradition of massage as a legitimate means for affecting cure for many ailments such as muscle and nerve pain by addressing the medical problem at its source in order to bring about an effective cure. Anyone who has suffered the agonies of lower back pain will appreciate the unexpected encounter I had a number of years ago while I was working at a university in Kuala Lumpur. I had suffered for years from chronic lower back pain and it periodically came back to haunt me like an uninvited guest. It always arrived unannounced and stayed for months with an insistence that was hard to comprehend or ignore. The unbearable pain would be etched upon my face as stark evidence of my suffering. I would undergo every treatment under the sun from electric shock and to heat treatments to ultrasound. After several months, the pain would eventually subside, but I was never truly convinced that it was the rarefied technological treatment, but rather sheer time that effected some kind relief and temporary cure until the pain would come back once again a year later.

One evening while drying my feet in the bathroom after a shower, I felt with impending dismay the old familiar stab of sciatica pain run down my back like a rip at the seam of my body. By the next morning, I could not turn around or lift myself from the bed. In desperation, I crawled to the telephone and called a Malay friend for help and advice. "Do you want to have a traditional massage?" he asked me. "Why not," I replied, immediately receptive to such an intriguing offer? Of course, I had no real idea what he meant, but I was soon to find out.

As a group of villagers gathered to witness the unusual spectacle, my Malay friend, Zainul-Din, and several of his companions somberly carried me into the Malay kampong house, raised on stilts against invading insects, snakes and the inevitable tropical dampness. They wrapped me in a *batik* sarong and laid me on a floor mat on my back. The village elders sat down cross-legged around me and gazed meditatively and with concern at my supine body wracked in pain.

A traditional Malay masseur (called *dukun* in Malay) entered the room, and with quiet majesty knelt on his thighs by my side. He was a powerful-looking man for his modest size and advanced age, with clear skin and a round moon face that expressed the wisdom of his years. With short-cropped white hair, he was stripped to the waist revealing a well-proportioned brown body for his age, and he wore a colorful batik Malay sarong folded tightly around his stomach. For all appearances, he could have been an aging pugilist with his small fighters frame exuding vitality and strength. He put his thick, paw-like hands on my arm as if he were handling a dish rag. There was authority in his grip and a sense of presence to his touch that was distinctive and unmistakable. He solemnly asked my name in simple English, repeated it aloud, and made several invocations in Arabic which I later learned were epithets and verses from the Quran, in order to actively invoke the presence of God into the proceedings. In truth, nothing happens in such traditional environments without first invoking the name of God in any event, a ritual that is still very prevalent within the Islamic community across the globe. Then he touched the palm of my hands with home-made herbal oil and proceeded to pressure point his way along my forearm from shoulder to wrist and back again.

There was no denying the pain generated by his powerful hands as he followed the line of muscle and nerve down my arm; it was excruciating, as if he were touching the raw nerve of my being. I cried out briefly while the group of villagers chatted and giggled nervously as they sat around and witnessed the proceedings. He worked on both arms and then moved down to the sides of the legs from hipbone to knee. The old Malay *dukun* radiated vitality and I could feel the power of his concentration and the force of his energy pass from his fingers into the tired and painful sinews of my body. He worked the muscles as though he were kneading dough, and he could have been plucking the strings of a violin the way he pulled the meridians of muscles and nerve that run up and down the body back into their natural line of energy flow.

A vital aspect of the cure and one of its essential components is the encounter and relationship of the masseur affecting the cure and the person receiving the cure. It must be a relationship of complete acceptance and surrender, acceptance that the masseur has the ability and the power to bring about the cure through the power of the traditional laying on of hands as a medium of benediction and blessing, combined with the absolute surrender of the will of the person being treated with the body in a state of complete relaxation to the ministrations of the masseur. Without this interaction of complete connection and acceptance, no cure can be affected according to the traditional approach to healing.

Angin, the Malays call the problem, wind. On the physical plane, they believe that wind caused by many toxic elements, including the icy cold drinks everyone loves accumulates in the body to ill effect. Indeed, as he proceeded with the massage, it did feel like wind as the pain shifted, diminished and ultimately disappeared under the pressure-pointing and stroking of his capable hands. Even the pain of the cure had a curative component that made the experience bearable to some degree. On another level, traditional Malays believe that devils—what are called *jinn* in the Islamic tradition—enter the body and set up residence to create havoc on physical, as well as psychic and spiritual levels. The notion is comparable to our beliefs concerning "possession" in which a person can be "possessed" by an evil spirit on mental or psychic levels.

Curiously, the masseur never actually touched my lower back; the pain was the final destination rather than the origin of the problem. Instead, he moved down and began to work his magic on the soles of my feet as if he were handling a rag doll. He began to knead and press against the muscles in the arch of one foot then the other with a focused stroke, causing an outrageous pain to run through me like a knife or some kind of electric shock to the system. He seemed to stop instinctively at some pain threshold of unbearability that held the promise of relief and healing. Still, I felt the need to give voice to my distress and I yelled like a banshee in fright and howled like a wolf in distress, much to the amusement of the villagers, curious about the identity of this *mate sale* (white devil in Malay). Throughout the ordeal, the *dukun* proceeded serenely with his work as if he were in some kind of otherworldly trance and periodically he would recite verses from the Quran or laugh to himself as I howled in outrage.

Malays are great talkers. My Malay friends and the other villagers carried on a running dialogue about the treatment, much of it in response to my questions. Such traditional masseurs believe in a holistic approach in which the interaction of both the physical and spiritual serve to effect the best possible cure. To that end, the masseur whispered a litany of Quranic incantations designed to raise the level of the experience and call upon the higher powers as protection against all evil. Finally, after an hour's worth of intense therapy, the old Malay sat back, indicating with a grunt that he was finished. A sublime feeling of relief surged through my body that was overwhelming and pure. I could hear in the distance the entreaties of the masseur to rest for a while before attempting to move. I lay quietly on my back, seemingly in some kind of yoga trance, and surrendered to a rare feeling of absolute peace that coursed through my body, as though a reservoir of well-being had been released in compensation for the outrage of the ordeal I had just endured.

Then, as suddenly and unexpectedly as a summer storm from some deep well within me, there emerged the inexplicable urge to cry. The source of this impulse was completely unknown to me although its impending presence was real enough. To my shock and amazement, I then began to weep aloud, first quietly, then in great choking sobs that shook my whole body in embarrassing spasms, although the origin of this emotion remained a mystery to me, leading me to wonder who within me was crying in this way and why, as though some other voice had taken possession of me and wanted to give expression of some sort. I had the feeling not I, but something inside me was giving voice to a terrible sadness. Perplexed, I let myself go and surrendered to the experience with curiosity and detachment, as I watched myself cry my heart out, with real tears.

The great heartbreaking sobs eventually subsided as I shook myself free from the grip of some uncontrollable experience and I was once again calm enough to inquire what had happened, for I could not understand or explain the reason for my outburst. "It was the *jinn*," my friend Zainul-din told me. "Whatever do you mean?" I asked incredulous. "The bad *jinn* are reluctant to leave the body and cry out loud when forced to do so," he replied casually. Improbable as it sounded, I was not in a position to counter his theory with an explanation of my own. In any event, I was suddenly summoned by the old *dukun* to rise from the bamboo mat. He indicated with gestures to bend forward and backward, then to stand up altogether and walk around the room. I looked at him in surprise as he smiled knowingly. The outrageous pain that I had suffered for weeks, indeed for years, had completely disappeared.

For three weeks thereafter, I continued to have a "session" with the Malay *dukun* at his kampung home when he would go through the routine once again of massaging my arms, legs and soles of the feet. But I never again experienced the kind of pain that I went through on this original afternoon, when the old Malay was able to drive out the evil spirit from my body. The follow up treatments were merely a concession to routine inflammation that would take a little time to subside, although I no longer had "active" pain in my body. What I do clearly remember was the sound of the rainfall on the tin roof of the kampong house. Tropical rain is never quiet. First the light of day suddenly darkens with angry-looking overhead clouds. Then the heavens open and the rain descends in sheets in such abundance that you think the earth itself will drown under the deluge. As I lay quietly on a mat on the floor, I could hear the roar of the tropical rain as it flooded down upon the tin roof of the old village house and imagined the blessings rained down upon us as one of the major sympathies of the natural world. When I think of Malaysia, I think of the roar of the rain on kampong roofs.

Was it the rare communion of body, mind, and spirit culminating in an experience of healing that seems alien to the realities of the modern world? Was it a foreign presence as suggested, not of alien beings from outer space but rather evil spirits from an inner space with the capacity to transform well-being into chronic and debilitating pain? Malays, indeed many Muslims, are fond of saying when they are confronted with some inexplicable mystery: "Only God knows!" As for myself, while I had been carried into the village house like a sick lamb, there was no denying the special light of this unexpected encounter and miraculous cure that shone down upon me that day. I expressed profound gratitude and with feelings of humility took my leave of the old Malay masseur, walking out of the house and into the wilds of the jungle village on the strength of my own two feet, feeling that I had been touched by more than two aged hands. Indeed I was touched by a benediction and a mercy that was invisible to behold.

7

THE MIRACLE OF AYURVEDA

ANCIENT TREATMENTS
FOR MODERN AFFLICTIONS

"For every disease on earth there is a corresponding
cure in nature." (Traditional Islamic Saying)

WE MAY NOT live in an age of miracles, but that does not preclude
their still occurring. Perhaps what we have lost is not the prevalence
of miracles in our lives with the power to increase our faith and
heighten our perception of reality; what we have lost is our ability
to recognize and appreciate the significance of a miracle whenever
we encounter the truly miraculous in today's world. In appreciating
the blessing of a miracle, we can dissipate the sense of shadow and
mirage that is perpetuated in today's modern and sophisticated
world by those who would disbelieve the sacred wonders that are
still within our reach.

   A true miracle does not necessarily signal the abrupt overturning
of the natural order and the arrival of the supernatural within the
natural to reveal an ultimate truth that no one could otherwise deny.
God knows we witness miracles everyday in the coming of the dawn,
the descent of night and the stream of life that flows within our
veins; and yet we never stop our frantic pace to answer their sacred
summons with a moment of introspective silence to the mystery of
the natural order and the holy enchantment that surrounds us.
Only when it is forced upon us through sickness and affliction do we
stop to consider a deeper reality beyond the world of sensation and

superficiality that we live by during these times. Only when the reality of sickness and the possibility of death make their presence known do we pause to realize that neither we, nor the world we live in, are what they appear to be.

The miracle of Ayurveda[1] in our title represents a miraculous functioning of the natural order, rather than some kind of overturning of nature and refers to a science-of-life philosophy of health and well-being in India that dates back over 5,000 years. This account hopes to recreate the remarkable experience I once had during a three week stay at an Ayurvedic Medical Center about 100 kilometers outside of Cochin in the State of Kerala, an area in southern India just south of Goa on the Western coast of the Subcontinent. I had come down with an upper arm and shoulder injury while playing competitive tennis and squash. When I first felt the injury, I paid no attention to it. A devoted player doesn't stop playing every time he feels some discomfort in the body; but I soon realized that this pain was not going away. I stopped playing all racket sports for a few months only to realize that this ailment needed some serious medical attention.

At first, I went to the doctor who ran me through all the usual tests, including x-ray for bone problems and MRI scanning for such things as arthritis or a torn ligament. When nothing showed up on the screens of our latest technological marvels, I underwent several months of daily physical therapy, including ultrasound, heat and electrical treatments that were intended to relax and soothe what appeared to be inflammation of the muscles and a classic case of tendonitis. Rest and time will cure all ills, I was soberly told. After nearly two years of aggravation that I endured with stoic patience, I was beginning to wonder whether the pain and the limited extension of the arm would ever surrender to rest and the inevitability of time as a healer.

In consultation with a doctor at a local Ayurvedic Center in Muscat where I was living at the time, I decided to contact and book a

---

1. *Veda* means "science" in the traditional sense of the word in the original Sanskrit, namely true, higher, spiritual knowledge that originate in the Vedas or sacred scriptures of India.

room at the Vaidyaratnam Nursing Home located an hour's taxi ride outside of Cochin deep in the heart of the Kerala countryside. The philosophy of Ayurvedic medicine was not unfamiliar to me. Dr. Deepak Chopra, a best-selling author and popular lecturer, draws much of his inspiration from its principles and to a degree has popularized its application in the US in recent years. I knew, for example, as many people probably know, that it is an alternative medicine that has ancient and traditional roots that originate in the state of Kerala in Southern India. I also knew that as in other alternative health practices that are available in China, Thailand and other Far Eastern countries, traditional massage forms the backbone of a number of therapies that are based on the theory that many human ailments arise from basically two things, poor circulation and toxicity of the blood stream. The variety of therapies aims to heal the root cause of illness rather than to only deaden the pain. In addition, I was familiar with the fact that Ayurvedic medicine has its own forms of prescriptive medicines that are based on the natural roots and herbs found in the nearby surroundings and have no side effects whatsoever, unlike most if not all Western medicines. Finally, the treatments could be described by using the two words everyone wants to hear: they are (relatively) inexpensive and effective. My three-week stay at the Ayurvedic Center, including the room, the therapy, the medicines, all food, and finally all the medicines and oils that I took away with me and lasted up to a month after my stay came to less than 20,000 rupees.[1]

What I have come to learn about the Ayurvedic treatment through first-hand experience has turned into an unexpected personal awakening about the possibilities of such ancient alternative medicine. Ayurveda treats a broad range of ailments and afflictions affecting the blood circulation, muscle and nerve systems of the body. It employs traditional treatments including mud-pack bandaging, poultice and massage that affects not only muscles and nerves, but the entire nervous system and ultimately the brain itself,

1. An incredible account by any reckoning. At the time of this visit, the Indian rupee traded at roughly 47 to the US dollar.

as I shall soon relate. It approaches the concept of sickness and cure with the age-old adage that both time and patience are fundamental to the healing process and that the quick fix of a drug or a pill is a modern Western myth that deadens the pain while it obscures the symptoms and the cure. It builds on the intelligence of the body to respond to the natural cures that exist in the world of nature and the ingenuity of a positive mind to support the body in this process of cure. Most importantly, it counsels the patient to adopt the right attitude toward the treatment including a belief in its effectiveness, a willingness to endure the lengthy treatments, a trust in the doctors to monitor and advise, and the establishment of a sacred interaction between the patient and the masseurs to effect the full course of the treatment and cure.

Ultimately, the Ayurvedic philosophy of approach to medicine and good health turns the entire process of ensuring health and well-being into an allegory of the outer quest of healing for the inner harmony of health. It is based on the ability of the body, mind, and soul to interact in such a way as to affect the totality of the human spirit through a holistic approach to the establishment of well-being within the person that is total and complete. If the body is sick, then the mind, soul, and spirit need to take part in the process of healing and rejuvenation by way of compensation and balance. This holistic approach is essential in the Ayurvedic system of medicine. The body cannot be true to itself without the interaction of the mind, soul, and inner spirit. Similarly, a healthy mind interacts and ultimately depends on a sound and healthy body to support it. The soul as summary and the spirit as substance reflect on physical and mental levels the essence of what lies within as the very best of the human being.

* * *

Although I have traveled extensively in many parts of the globe, I had never been to India, so my imagination was running wild and my expectations were unsure and apprehensive. I landed in the seaside city of Cochin in the late afternoon and took a taxi about 100 kilometers into the interior of Kerala to the Vaidyaratnam Nursing

Home,[1] passing through dense tropical foliage, extensive forests of swaying coconut palms interspersed with lush rice fields, a natural setting that gave the appearance of being wild and untamable. The anachronous Ambassador Deluxe taxi, squat and classic in the style of a sedan car of the late '40s, summoned thoughts of a by-gone era, but the sight of the rich tropical landscape was already a balm to my soul. I was arriving from Muscat in the Sultanate of Oman where I live and work, a country in which the hot, humid climate and relentless desert sun provides no mercy and little relief to the arid and mountainous lunar landscape that distinguishes Oman.

In marked contrast to Muscat and as an auspicious beginning in a region of the world where rain is considered a blessing, a torrential downpour complete with thunder and lightning provided a spectacular backdrop to this lush setting as we drove through the entrance arch and down the long driveway fringed with flowers and spreading lawns to the main building. In fact, the day of my arrival marked the first day of operation for this entirely new medical center whose traditions and roots pass back through father and son into the middle of the nineteenth century when, as the story goes, the great grandfather of the existing owner cured the ailment of a high ranking British official. When asked what he wanted in return, he asked for the honorary title Vaidyaratnam which remains to this day as the name of the center. Dr. Mooss, the present owner, director, and chief resident, who was known affectionately as "the old man" by the mostly local patients, had overseen the establishment of this new center to replace the much older and more traditional wooden building that had served the family for most of the 20th century. The modern three-story building with wings to left and right was tucked away in this quiet, rural setting surrounded by lawns, fruit trees and of course the tall and stately coconut palms that provide the oil base for the treatments.

Beyond the elaborate entrance and through the great wooden

---

1. I later advised the senior physician how misleading the term "nursing house" would be in the West where people would immediately think of an old age institution, but he assured me that in India the term meant what it said, a place where continuous nursing and medical attention was available and nothing more.

doors lay a spacious reception area whose centerpiece contained two large photos of the father and grandfather of Dr. Mooss. Photos bedecked with flower garlands flanked a golden statue of the god of health and healing before which stood a golden urn inset with a burning candle that flickered in the breeze like some beckoning promise. It was in fact a sober setting that cast a hallowed and almost sacred ambiance to the business at hand, namely the healing of long-standing afflictions that seemingly have no other cure. When I entered the building and was quickly assigned a simple, well-appointed room with an overhead fan on the second floor, I too joined this community of people in search of a cure that was intended for the patient and the serious-minded. Little did I know when I entered the premises that I was not to leave the building for the full extent of my three-week stay.

I had arrived on a Thursday evening and was no sooner settled into my room and unpacked, when one of the young doctors visited me to advise me about the protocol of the moment. Dr. Mooss was scheduled to visit the patients that evening and would conduct a consultation with me. He told me that I had arrived on an opportune day as treatments traditionally start on Tuesday and Friday, these days being considered propitious for the commencement of a cure. I was later to come to understand just how sacred an undertaking the doctors, nurses, and masseurs who administer the various treatments consider their vocation of healing to be. Of a sacred and symbolic significance were the rectangular medallions painted across the forehead and throat of the Brahmin doctors affected with a mixture of colored powder and water. The vibrant colors red and yellow gave the appearance of a hieroglyphic cartouche and served to refresh the eyes (for powers of observation) and the voice (for the purposes of advice and prescription) of the doctor. Later, a patient told me that the doctors regularly visit the Hindu temple that lay just on the other side of the road beyond the gates of the center, the business of healing being for them a sacred trust.

After a simple meal of several chipattis with curry sauce and salad served to me in the room, Dr. Mooss and his entourage of doctors and nurses arrived to consult with me about my ailment. Somewhere in his 70s but giving the appearance of being in his sixties, he received me graciously with a smile and a nod. He was dressed in a shirt, a white doctor's coat and wrapped in a floor length white dhoti which is the traditional dress of the area. The young doctors and attendants deferred to his every utterance and the patients sat patiently in their rooms during the course of his twice-weekly visitations respectfully awaiting his arrival. Nothing was done without his permission.

With a thoroughness that one would expect from this setting, Dr. Mooss wanted to know the full history of my ailment in all its detail, including the kind of climate I lived in and how well I slept. I explained to him that I had a weakness in the upper arm and what appeared to Western doctors as tendonitis of the shoulder that was chronic, with limited extension and profound weakness of the right arm. He listened carefully, asking questions about the kind of pain, the extent, the length, and duration of the ailment, my dietary habits and movements. All were crucial components that contributed to his prognosis. He then consulted with his assistants in rapid-fire Malayalam, which is the local language of that area of India. He spoke fluent English of course, but I had great trouble understanding him, as I had with many others while I was there in Kerala. They spoke English with the same speed that they spoke their own language and with an intonation that was so strange and unique that it actually sounded like a foreign language to me. In many instances, to cover my confusion and inability to understand my own native tongue and to avoid embarrassing them as well since they understandably prided themselves on their linguistic ability, I resorted to the trick that they themselves use so often, the shaking of the head from side to side that seems to outsiders so comical with Indians from the Sub-continent. I discovered was an effective body language that covered all questions of doubt and effectively conveyed a feeling of assurance, even when you didn't have a clue about what was being said. When Dr. Mooss shook his head back and forth smiling his assurances of a cure as he left my room, I knew that I had arrived and was now on the road to recovery.

A "minimum" stay at the nursing home usually consisted of a full four weeks and often longer for more serious conditions such as arthritis and paralysis. Because I had only three weeks leave from work, and because my ailment wasn't considered as serious as some of the other patients, an exception was made in my case and an accelerated three-week program was set up by Dr. Mooss under the constant supervision of the other doctors and implemented by the attending masseurs and nurses. The heart of many of the treatments calls for internal medicines consisting of the herbs, oils, and roots grown locally in the surrounding countryside, various kinds of massages using hot oils and a strict vegetarian diet. I could have no fried foods, no fruits except boiled bananas, and certainly no chemicals or preservatives.[1] The food was brought around to the rooms on a cart that was delivered from a canteen on the ground floor that exclusively serviced the building with special preparations. Gratefully, morning coffee was permitted in this otherwise austere dietary regime, and I enjoyed the luxury of tea and dry crackers in the later afternoon.

The next morning, on Friday, my first week of treatment began with the small bottle of liquid medicine that I was obliged to drink twice a day after breakfast and supper. The sight of this dark brown mixture was intimidating indeed and promised to be a culinary adventure. Every morning and evening I steeled myself for the warm bitter taste of these herbal concoctions and their harsh afterglow. Down the hatch, I said to myself, as I drank the bitter brew. The evening medicine was a milky mixture of God-knows-what with a suspicious aftertaste that quickly turned my eyes heavy and made me feel tired. Although much mystery surrounded these medicines, the procedures, the regulations and the treatments, through persistent questioning I was able to resolve some of the mystery and glean the rationale behind the medicinal brews and daily treatments. Variations depended on the individual of course and the progress of their particular treatment, but in general, the liquid medicines were intended to purge the bodily system of all toxicity, promote regularity, reduce the fat content of the body and lower cholesterol, neutralize pain, and provide either a hot or cold balance to the system in

---

1. I neither smoke nor drink, therefore both were habits I did not have to give up. For those who do, however, these habits are strictly forbidden during the treatment and during the advisory rest period after the treatment.

addition to addressing the particular body type and problem of the individual. I suspect the nighttime medicine contained a sleeping draught and a purgative, since the doctors were always concerned on their twice daily visitations to ask about sleep and regularity which they considered vital to the curative process.

My first massage treatment was scheduled for that Friday afternoon and would take place every day thereafter for the course of the first week. Another consultation would be held with Dr. Mooss when he could establish the extent of the benefit and the future course of treatment for each succeeding week. As I passed through the door of the treatment room, I entered a strange and mysterious world of sights and sounds that immediately assailed all my senses with the full force of their alien yet irresistible charm. The ancient smells of pine and tree sap, the dark herbal aroma of the warm oils, the melodious chanting of sacred Sanskrit sutras in the background, the burning candle casting flickering shadows in front of the little altar to the god of healing, the prolonged rays of the setting sun illuminating the treatment board that glistened with oil in the glow of the sun, all these elements cast an exotic spell over my mind and senses, creating an atmosphere of tranquility and otherworldliness that under the circumstances of the treatment was unique to experience. The room itself had open doors that led onto a balcony beyond which was a sight to behold, and I thought: There can be no peace like the peace engendered by the vision of this natural bucolic setting, a peace drawn from the lush, verdant fields that were encroached upon from left and right by a verge of palm groves consisting of exceptionally tall and stately palms that swayed majestically in the wind. It was the peace of the old well I saw in the distance, of grazing cattle, of cranes in flight, of thatched huts, pet goats and distant farmers tending the land or escorting their cattle back home in the evening that filled my mind with ease.

But for a bit of string and a flimsy muslin cloth to cover the private parts, I lay down on a wooden platform hewn from a single tree trunk, especially carved at front and back with drainage area to service the treatment oils. Beyond the foot of this massive plank and set to the side was a burning gas flame and a kind of wok where the oils were heated and kept hot by an attendant. I was initially doused completely in hot oil and underwent a full body massage performed simultaneously by two people for five or ten minutes while my head was completely covered in hot oil by another attendant. I was also being treated for some slight congestion in the ears and thus warm oil was also dropped from a distance into each of the ears. Thus bodily assaulted, I was then subjected to what was referred to affectionately as the "bundle massage".

The bundle massage consisted of a poultice made of cloth stuffed with herbs and a special kind of rice with medicinal properties. A goodly number of these unique "bundles" were prepared and dropped into the hot oil of the wok and then lightly pounded and spread up and down the arm and across the shoulder area in question, alternating between bundles as the hot oil at the base of the poultice cooled below a certain temperature. This procedure continued for another fifty minutes or so to complete the hour. Thereafter, I was helped into an adjacent bathroom. I need to be helped I should note, as the effect of the oil on the head and the pounding and stroking of the body and arm left me feeling relaxed and groggy to the point of exhaustion. This style of massage was said to soften the muscles. Once inside the bathroom, I was advised to pour warm water over myself in what amounted to an Indian-style bath. An attendant mixed an herbal powder with hot water to create a mud paste that was to be rubbed across the entire body to cut the herbal oil of the massage. Throughout the course of the three-week treatment, no chemicals were to be used at all, including all soaps, creams, deodorants and body sprays. Having completed the bath, I was then escorted back to my room and seen safely inside by the attendant who departed only after requesting permission in simple English to take his leave.

In following this treatment, my first week passed without incident. In fact, I had to settle into a very limited routine within the confines of the nursing home and found myself deprived of the usual outlets that I am accustomed to in the normal course of a very active life. I was encouraged to "rest" as an important component of the treatment, although I wasn't sure how that was to be accomplished. In any event I was told that I could not leave the building at all. Upon questioning, I learned from the doctors who humored my questions that, among other reasons, because of the hot oil treatment to the head, they didn't want me to have direct sunlight shining down upon the crown of my cranium and mist and rain were to be avoided as well. In general, the patients were instructed not to expose themselves to the elements outside so as not to catch any unwanted illnesses during the treatment by becoming overheated, causing excessive sweating and possibly catching cold by exposure to the rains.

In addition, I had to quickly grow accustomed to completely different foods and spices since all patients followed a strictly vegetarian diet cooked in the South Indian style, which can be strangely seasoned and spicy. Similarly, restrictions prevented me from having any fried foods, eggs, fruits, sweets and the like, although coffee and tea were permitted. A food cart came around to service the rooms. Breakfast consisted of *dosha*, a flat rice-based pancake look-a-like cooked on a dry skillet or *edili*, a kind of rice bun both of which were dipped into curry and some other kind of spicy sauce of various colors. Lunch came in a tiflin of multiple containers, one for soup, one for rice, and the other two containing vegetable curry or *dahl* (boiled lentils). The evening cart came around at 7:30 for the final meal of the day, consisting of several chipattis with which to scoop up a thimble-full of salad and a soupy vegetable *kurma* (a form of curry). These three meals, plus early morning coffee and afternoon tea, soon came to punctuate my day, the smells of the cart and its squeaky wheels signaling its arrival. I lost two kilos the first week and nearly 5 kilos during the entire stay.

While I never got used to the sparse and repetitive vegetarian cuisine, I soon grew accustomed to the multiple sights and sounds of the exotic India that formed my immediate and only surroundings. There was forever the sound of tabla, finger cymbals, and percussion forming the rhythmic pulse of the day coming from I knew not where exactly, from other rooms, from random farm houses in the area perhaps, from the Hindu temple nearby. An eerie quality often characterized the music in which the haunting melody of a solitary flute or the contemplative rhythm of the sitar floated into consciousness seemingly from some distant star. I sometimes heard a recording of chanted sutras coming from the nearby temple in the early morning before dawn, its compelling, otherworldly quality lulling the mind into a meditative trance and setting the mood for the coming day. Beyond my window, there was an active world of nature. The voice of the crow, the chipmunk, the woodpecker, the crickets and the relentless insects all spoke their own tongues and went about their business in their own inimitable fashion. In this exotic setting, I began to enjoy and appreciate the simple pleasures that awaited my attention from Jiminy-Cricket to the Daddy-long-legs spider that occasionally ventured into some nook or cranny of the room.

There was an unspoken aura of exotic mystery that formed the backcloth on one's wakeful moods. The resinous odor of burning incense, flowers in bloom, ripening fruits and hot oils permeated the air with their heavy aromatic quality so characteristic and distinctive of India. The night trains to Madras and Mumbai signaled their passage in the near distance at some late-night hour as I dozed off to sleep thinking of its passage into far-off, alien worlds. The whistle sent forth a call with the heart and purpose of a far-distant horn, the distinctive rattling of its iron feet on endless rails reminded me that people were rushing headlong to exotic destinations into the dark and otherwise silent night.

During the daytime, it was the sight of the women dressed in their saris that never failed to fascinate me, with their variety of color and formal elegance, highlighting the use of a traditional dress that has not yet lost its functionality and charm. I was told by a Goan woman, amused by my interest, that the sari consists of a one-piece five meter length of cloth that is pleated and draped accordingly for comfort and movement, carefully wrapped around the body and then hung over the left shoulder to hang down as a train flowing in the wind. All the women in India still wear the sari at every age and from every walk of life. The female doctors and nurses wore white saris under their white medical coats. They must have been hot working thus attired in that hot tropical climate, but never appeared so being accustomed no doubt to the weather. The female masseurs wore sky blue saris. I noticed a woman tending the lawns and garden in her svelte black sari and two female sweepers clearing the front driveway of fallen leaves. The visitors of the patients wore elaborate and multi-colored saris each with their own distinctive flair. The two women who cleaned my room every day wore deep maroon saris and gem-stones in their nose as they swept the room clean of insects and debris with a make-shift broom made of sticks and twigs.

From my second floor window, I was able to look down into the backyard of a nearby farmhouse. The area was bestrewn with fruit trees, the inevitable banana trees, and various kinds of shrubbery. One hot, sunny afternoon, I noticed a young woman dressed in a dark green sari with a bold orange bodice who had just come into the back yard. She was dark, capable, and sturdy-looking. She had obviously been working in another part of the garden and looked hot and sweaty; yet the rough cotton sari hung across her body in all its distinctive elegance, even though it constituted her working clothes. As I looked out into her strange world, our eyes met. Briefly in passing, she had noticed this alien being who was myself looking down at her from the open window. With folded hands, she bowed her head and sent forth this simple gesture of greeting. She then proceeded to gather together and expertly tie up the various branches and shrubs that had recently been trimmed from the fruit trees. Once readied, she threw a bundled cloth over her head, set the massive bundle of branches on top of it, and departed without further ado. The flowing train of the sari hung down from her left shoulder and accentuated her stately attitude and noble bearing as she left the yard. It is at such moments that one observes the value of a tradition upheld.

* * *

The second week marked a turning point in the treatment. On the next Thursday evening after the completion of the first week of treatment, I once again consulted with Dr. Mooss and his entourage concerning the progress of my condition. He wanted to know in detail how I felt and whether I had experienced any improvement. I expressed surprise and told him that my condition had considerably improved in such a short time, suggesting that I felt roughly 30 to 40 percent better. "Then you can take some credit for that," he told me good-humoredly, "since half the battle lies with the patient himself." In fact, the Ayurvedic philosophy sets much store in the attitude of the patient and the close positive interaction of the mind and body. He consulted with his entourage of doctors both male and female and scrutinized their hand-written notes keep meticulously during the week in my personal file. They had visited me during the course of the previous week and were well familiar with my condition and progress. He then prescribed the new course of treatment. I was to continue with the bundle massage of the previous week, but this week I would be toweled free of the oils after the massage and would no longer take a head or body bath. In addition, two new therapeutic variations would commence, namely a nightly bandage and a procedure called in Sanskrit *nasyam*.

That sounded ominous as well as ancient. I inquired what the word meant and was told that *nasiyam* was "the hot oil nose treatment". Dr. Mooss and his entourage were sensitive to the alien nature of the treatment and assured me that the procedure would be fully explained to me when appropriate and that I was not to worry. The treatment lasted for a minimum of three to five days I was told, and in some cases a maximum of a full seven day course. I ultimately received the full seven-day treatment.

The next afternoon, I had the bundle massage and head oil treatment a little earlier to allow time for the *nasiyam* treatment followed at 6:00 PM by the bandage application. This was turning into a full time job, although gratefully it kept me busy. Immediately after the massage, I was escorted back down to my room with the attending masseur and doctor who would perform the "oil in the nose" procedure. I was laid down on the bed with a pillow under my neck, thus arching my head backward to facilitate the entry of the warm oil into the nasal canal. I was advised to breathe inward while the oil was carefully poured into first the right then the left side of the nostrils. I set a standard of bravery by way of expectation that surprised even myself, but was almost disappointed to discover that while there was some discomfort, there was nowhere near the pain and outrage that I expected my nose or inner nasal passages to experience. At best, the warm oil quickly dripped down the canals and lodged into the back of the mouth and throat whence I was told to quickly expel it into a cup. Once accomplished, the doctor began to thoroughly massage my forehead and face, while the masseur rubbed hands and feet to create warmth and circulation at the extremities, all the while I was instructed to breathe in deeply and then expel as much phlegm and mucus as possible. The action of the hot oil passing through the inner sanctum of the nose created an internal flow within the sinuses and air pockets of the face and skull that facilitated the expulsion of unwanted mucus and fluid from the entire area of the skull.

This amounted to a nervous system and brain treatment that complemented the hot oil treatment to the head. Upon inquiry, I was told by an obliging doctor that there were inner corridors of nerves that passed from the brain through the nasal and sinus area down into the right and left side of the body. In my case, this treatment was called for because they had estimated that the limited extension of the arm and the atrophy of the shoulder were caused in part by a blockage of the flow of energy through the nervous system. I was told that a side benefit of this treatment would be none other than a sensation approximating "clarity of mind".

Indeed, as the days of "oil in the nose" treatment proceeded through their full seven-day course, I felt an increasing clarity of mind and a heightened consciousness on some sort of physiological rather than psychological level of experience. I can only compare it to what a person experiences when he has wax in the ear that is subsequently blown clean. There is clarity of sound within the ear that approximates, perhaps, what would be like hearing the primordial quality of every sound, as if for the first time. Toward week's end, I felt that my mind has gradually acquired a sparklingly clear "presence" that was astounding to experience, as if I had finally emerged after all these years from a dark cloud to witness the first dawn of man, and I felt ready as never before to experience the crisp primal quality inherent in the life of the mind.

After the pounding of the bundle massage and the invasion of the oil treatment in my nose, the over-night bandage was the final insult of the day. At 6:00 PM, I returned to the treatment room to have the cloth bandage wrapped around my arm and shoulder. It consisted of an elaborate cotton cloth wrapping that was coated from top to bottom in a heated mud-pack of herbal medicines. After heating this dark mixture in the wok, an attendant spread it across the cloth bandage as if he were frosting a cake. He then laid its hot and moist contents over my right arm and shoulder and secured its entire length with a cotton wrapping. Then, the fresh leaves of the castor oil plant were laid upon the arm while another cloth wrapping was tightly secured up and down the arm. The entire appendage was tied in place by a series of strings that wound around my other shoulder and arm. Thus trussed up like a chicken ready for roasting and moving about like Frankenstein before his bandages were removed, I was sent back to my room for a meager evening meal followed by a milky bottle of medicine that soon induced a sleepiness to coincide with a 10:00 PM bedtime.

The mud-pack bandage, designed to strengthen the muscles of the arm and draw out any toxic poisons, was to remain in place for a full 12 hours until an attendant came around to my room to take it off at 6:00 in the morning. At first, an alarming series of rashes and boils appeared on the upper arm and shoulder, but applications of medicated ghee soon made these unsightly eruptions disappear. This awkward and uncomfortable treatment continued every night until I left the nursing home.

In this way I passed my second week. In addition to experiencing these ancient treatments and feeling their benefit, I also learned the meaning of the relativity of time. During the nose treatment, I was told by the doctors that I would not be able to read or watch television. To use the eyes in any serious way would seriously compromise the sensitive nature of this particular treatment and, therefore, I was instructed to halt all visual activity and rest. I looked at the doctor and thought: Do I know the meaning of the word? What is rest and how is it accomplished? By denying me the pleasure of reading, a quiet companion on even the worst of days, I felt that the last vestige of my conscious awareness to "occupy myself" was taken away from me. Without any external or mental stimulus, I was finally left on my own with the silence of the inward self.

The sense of time changes. Time rushing forward as in our daily lives becomes suddenly time in amplitude, moving forward second by second and minute by minute as in the uninterrupted flow of a slow-moving river or the glacial pace of shadows moving upon the grass, forever changing, never static, always endless. Time is spread out before me like a tableland; the day becomes a field or meadow through which I wander about and roam unattended, without the props that give shape and definition to the normal course of a life such as the stimulus of books and films, the support of friends, and the satisfaction of work. As I reminded myself of the two key points of departure of this traditional form of therapy, namely faith in recovery and an open-minded receptivity to its slow and natural process, I resolved to rest as the doctor had advised and drifted off increasingly into the life of the mind and spirit. I was no longer thinking and planning and executing my desires, for I had nothing to ponder, plan or do. Instead, my imagination sets forth like a cinema reel or a player piano. The pictures of the mind, its thoughts, memories and impressions, along with a wide range of heightened and conflicting emotions, played themselves out on their own, as though they had a will of their own that were disconnected from my true self.

I was determined to see the course of this treatment through to the end, and this determination helped me to overcome the feelings of frustration and impatience I felt during the course of the second week. When in doubt or on the brink of I knew not what, I set my gaze to the world of nature beyond my window whose message reflected the broad expense of an eternal time, a world of nature I know that reflects and remembers a world of nature I do not know. Reduced to the bare bones of my inner self and the sinewy branches of the magnificent tamarind tree I see through my window, it was as though another person was standing on the threshold of another world, where one could refresh the anxieties of the soul as well as the afflictions of the body with the sense of the sacred and the eternal that is embedded as a first principle within every tree and cloud and person.

* * *

"Do you know what time it is?' I suddenly heard the clear crisp intonation of a British accent on my right. "Yes,' I said, and looked down to see a young Indian boy sitting next to me. "Would you be kind enough to tell me what time it is," he politely asked. He was deadly serious about his inquiry and didn't crack even the hint of a boyish grin. "It's cartoon time," I replied and changed the TV channel to the cartoon network. He laughed happily. It was only then that I noticed that he was a boy with a crooked smile.

I was the only Westerner, indeed the only foreigner, receiving treatment at the Ayurvedic center. The rest of the patients were local Keralites with a few others from other city centers such as Madras or Bangalore. Therefore, I was something of a novelty among the local patients. Interest in me ranged from curiosity, to shyness, to panic, to outright fear and most people kept a discreet distance as though I were an alien from another planet. One little fellow who was running around the halls in the buff with a little gold belt hanging down from his waist came up to me, grimaced and then burst into tears before finding refuge in his mothers skirts, and she also seemed dubious and uncertain; but little Manu was different. Only eight years old, he had come down from Mumbai with his young father to be treated for facial paralysis that left the right side of his face, not to mention his smile, in ruins.

Each floor had a central lounge equipped with satellite TV where people could congregate together to socialize and watch television. I sometimes spent time there as an alternative to the seclusion of my room and eventually I did get to know a few of the other patients and learned of their ailments and treatments. Due to the length of time involved in these treatments, the center had a well-conceived arrangement in which spouses, children, or a relative could actually stay with the patient in the room. In this way, husbands stayed with ailing wives, fathers or mothers stayed with their young children and visitors abounded at all hours of the day or night. I, of course, was on my own and welcomed the companionship of this little fellow.

Over time, I noticed that Manu was becoming increasingly attached to me and under the circumstances I to him. Whenever I appeared in the communal area, he always sat quietly next to me. If I was talking with another patient, he would come up and sit between us listening attentively, as if something vital were being conveyed that he could not bear to miss. Manu had had a number of Western-style operations before his father turned to Ayurvedic treatment as a final alternative. "One day when they were drawing fluid from Manu's spine," the father related to me, "I told them to stop. I couldn't bear the pain any more." "And Manu?" I asked. "He never uttered a sound," he told me.

One day, Manu, which means "man" in ancient Sanskrit, came running up and took me by the hand. "Come with me," he said affirmatively in his clipped accent, "I will be your guide." He escorted me up to the top floor where he proudly showed me the elevator engine and the array of solar panels that lined the outside roof like sunbathers on a beach. On the back side of the roof there was a small balcony overlooking the grand expanse of rice fields and coconut palm groves. We often stayed up there together in mid-afternoon before our treatments to pass the time. He named all the animals that he saw in the fields, including the white crane who was the companion, Manu told me, to the cow. "Why is that, Manu?" I asked him. "The crane always stands next to the cow all day and feeds on the insects and flies that hover near him." "That's thoughtful," I said as Manu shook his head back and forth Indian-style in agreement.

He talked to me about his interests, his friends, and his little world. He was something of a linguist at that young age. He spoke impeccable English with a British accent because he went to an English-medium school, but he was at home with Hindi because of his upbringing in Mumbai, and he spoke Malayalam, the language of Kerala which was his mother tongue. He told me about the *nasyam* nose treatment he had also undergone and advised me not to swallow the oil. "It will make you sick," he warned. He taught me a number of words in Malayalam such as "please" and "thank you" that were later to thrill the nurses and masseurs who tended me. In this way, Manu became my teacher as well as my companion and guide.

The other acquaintance who "made the difference" during my stay was a young woman from Goa in her early 30's who had come down to Kerala to study veterinary medicine and had worked as a village doctor in the area for a number of years. Apparently, she had overcome any inhibitions she may have had to speak to the man "from another planet" and I soon looked forward to meeting with her in the late morning to compare notes about our treatments and ask her the many questions I had about India, its culture and its people. She also became a vital source of much valued information about the practice of Ayurveda, the local culture, the various religions and languages of the region and much else of interest about this vast, mysterious, and ancient country.

Fabiana Lobo had suddenly and inextricably been struck down with rheumatoid arthritis over a year earlier affecting the joints of her left hand and legs and after various treatments, she decided to turn to the Ayurveda cure. "In Western medicine, they advise you to learn how to live with the pain and give you some pills. With Ayurveda," she told me, "you need faith, patience, and endurance, but at the expense of these virtues, you are promised a complete and lasting cure." She walked slowly with a limp and her left hand was a clenched fist. Her treatments, of course, were much different from mine. She underwent, for example, the buttermilk treatment in which cool buttermilk was systematically poured over her head in the treatment room for a full hour to cool her body and douse the flames of her swollen joints. She also underwent a whole series of purgatives and had to take many more medicines throughout the course of her day than I did. As with Manu, I was struck by her courage in facing the reality of her ailment, by her trust in the treatment, and by her determination to see it through and overcome its overwhelming odds.

As I entered my third week of treatment, I was beginning to realize that, in spite of the hardship, tedium and restrictions required in following through with the treatments, there was an ancient integrity to the process of healing and an inviolable completeness to the approach and possibility of cure. In talking with others, I realized that we all passed through a variety of emotions, including loneliness, bewilderment, and frustration. At odd hours of the day and night, I heard the inconsolable crying of an old, paralyzed man who stayed overhead on the top floor. These mixed emotions became as palpable as a mist that melted together into a profound feeling of hope in the promise of a cure. By the beginning of the third week, I had considerably improved and that only compounded the transforming quality of my patience and determination. I advised Dr. Mooss and the other doctors that I had made a 75% recovery.

The treatment shifted in emphasis once again during the third and final week. Gratefully, the full 7-day course of the *nasyam* nose procedure was now complete and I was reaping the benefits of this rarefied treatment to the head and nervous system. I continued with the inconvenience of the mud-pack bandage feeling profound relief in the early morning when the pack was set aside and my arm set free, to be briefly massaged with a warm oil to revitalize the circulation. My ears had cleared and dryness to the forehead that I had complained about earlier had completely cleared up.

The bundle massage of the first two weeks was now terminated and replaced with a full body hot oil massage with continued special attention to my right shoulder and arm. For this, I was seated in a chair in the treatment room for a full hour with a turban wrapped around my head as herbally medicated hot oil seeped into the head and brain cavity. This treatment gave me the opportunity to gaze beyond the open door to the balcony of the treatment room at the meadows and palm groves that surrounded the building, a scene that never failed to fill me with the higher sentiments of contentment and peace. The setting sun drenched everything in the magic of its fading light as if the slanting rays fell in prostration across the land in tribute to the dying day. As I gazed contemplatively at this sublime wonderland, I entered its otherworldly ethos and the power of its enduring message entered me.

When the treatment neared its end after my long, three-week confinement, I needed to seek permission from the authorities to leave and make formal arrangements for my discharge from the nursing home. Dr. Mooss, highly respected by everyone for creating this environment and for the quality of treatment he provided his patients, came several days before my scheduled departure for one final consultation. I told him that I had achieved a 90% improvement in my condition, and he assured me that within a short time of perhaps several weeks, any restriction in the arm and shoulder would completely disappear. I felt then and now know that he was right. I was provided with a month's worth of both external herbal oils and internal herbal medicine to continue the treatment on my own as the final follow-up phase to the entire process of this Ayurvedic treatment and cure.

As it always has, from the ancient past to the modern present, the unfolding drama of alternating sickness and health continues to be experienced as a metaphor of the human condition. We learn of balance and harmony through the experience of disparity and discord, the fragility of the human body highlights in contrast to the strength of the human spirit, the manifest evil of human sickness foretells the blessed well-being of health. It is a human drama that most of us would like to escape, but cannot any more than we can escape the yes and no of life, its polarities, its contradictions, and its final resolution in the way of some ultimate and enduring truth.

Undoubtedly, despite all the advances in science and modern medicine, there is much about ourselves and the modern world that we still do not understand. The cause of sickness with its silent and unexpected arrival, and the possibility of its ultimate cure with its dark and mysterious promise, continue to elude us in spite of ourselves and our good intentions. Perhaps that is why knowledge of an ancient and effective treatment endures as a force to be reckoned with, and still inspires people to appreciate the knowledge of traditional medicine and to turn to its holistic approach and restorative properties. My encounter with the Ayurvedic philosophy of health and well-being began with a faith in the traditional knowledge of these ancient treatments and ended with the certainty that comes with the restored feeling of health and well-being.

The morning of my departure, a happy day by any account after having successfully undergone three rigorous weeks of physical, mental and spiritual therapies, was tinged with a feeling of sadness at leaving my three new-found friends behind. Fabiana, the veterinary doctor with the clinched arthritic hand, Manu, the little boy with the crooked grin, and his father had all insisted on being awakened at 4:00 in the morning to see me off in a taxi to return directly to the airport for an early morning flight back to Muscat. Our brief encounter over the last three weeks had been close and intense in the manner of people who are confined for a period of time and pass through a hardship together. Like trains passing in the night, I was on my way back into a world far-distant from theirs in more ways than one, but this brief encounter had enjoined us together in a shared experience that would forever be remembered.

We all passed through the shadowy reception area downstairs

and out into the dark night, outside once again in the natural elements of fresh air and clear open space for the first time since my arrival three weeks earlier. We exchanged pleasantries and promises to write to fill the awkward moments as we waited for the taxi to arrive, but Manu, never at a loss for words in a variety of languages, held out his hand to offer me a gift. It was a simple key chain from which hung a glass ball.

"It has a compass inside the ball," he advised me soberly.

"Indeed it does," I said, taking note that it accurately indicated North where I knew it to be.

"If you get lost, it will show you the way," he said, and for one final moment I took in the brave little face and crooked grin.

"Thank you, Manu, I may need it someday," I replied with my own broken smile and climbed into the back seat of the antiquated car.

With the scent of jasmine filling the air and the light of a waning moon drenching the tropical landscape with its pale magic, I took my leave of the nursing home. Passing once again under the grand archway, the car drove through the great sculpted gates and made its way beyond the darkness of night toward the glow of distant light that marked the coming of dawn.

8

THE FAR ROAD TO KERALA

LIVING THE
LEGENDARY CURE OF AYURVEDA

The mission of Vaidyaratnam Oushadhasala is to pave the way for happiness by providing a healthy mind and body for all those who seek it. The family of Thaikkattu Mooss, with full confidence in the promise of Ayurveda, is on a true missionary role to propagate its excellence. Vaidyaratnam Oushadhasala has dedicated itself to give the right ambiance by uncompromisingly adhering to the core traditions to support its philosophy in the service of mankind, namely "Let everyone in the world attain happiness". (Mission Statement)

THE MODERN MENTALITY is full of romance and discovery. We explore the possibilities of genetic engineering and develop means of communication that travel at the speed of light. We believe in the predictions of astrological signs and search for messages from life forms in outer space. We destroy worlds as we build new ones. We are insatiably curious and want to explore where no one has gone before and we are willing to take any road to achieve our deepest desires. Yet the "one thing needful" escapes us, namely a true knowledge of our identity and our place in the grand scheme of the universe. We are adrift on a sea of illusion and self doubt because the facts that we uncover about ourselves and our world are as fragile as ashes and bereft of significant meaning. I recently took the far road to Kerala in South India where a healing experience at an Ayurveda Clinic brought me in contact with the ancient philosophy of medicine that combines traditional knowledge based on sacred scriptures of the Vedanta with the practical applications of herbal medicines and oils found in nature, an experience in which I was able to realize the integral part that health and well being can play in both the practical and spiritual life of our time.

The old, white Ambassador, a vintage automobile from a distant era whose classic lines recalled the getaway cars of those Hollywood gangster films of the 1940s, made its way down the winding road in the depths of Kerala in South India. Suddenly it turned off into a narrow pathway and moved through the imposing archway of the Vaidyaratnam Nursing Home, tucked far away from the main metropolises of sub-continental India at the edge of a vast palm grove plantation. The silent and stately fluttering of wings mirrored the sound of silence that pervaded the area as several exquisite butterflies made their way through the garden in search of the nectar that would sustain their own health and well being. The only noise that could possibly interrupt the serenity of the day was the rasping sound of noon time crickets at play in the grass. In the distance, the haunting cords of a harmonica floated through someone's window out into the open air to reach my alert and expectant ears.

After a four year hiatus, I was returning once again to this clinic for further treatments based on the ancient philosophy of Ayurveda, a holistic approach to health and well being that dates back thousands of years to find its source in the ancient scriptures of the Vedas. The name itself, strange as it may sound to Western ears, summarizes its meaning: *Veda* referring to the term science in its ancient and traditional concept of "true knowledge"; *ayu* meaning "life", thus appropriately identifying itself as the true science of life. In the spring of 2001, I had spent nearly four weeks here for atrophy of the arm and chronic tendonitis of the shoulder or frozen shoulder as it is sometimes referred to, and had undergone a rigorous treatment demanding patience and determination in order to reap the benefits of this ancient and traditional cure. Thereafter, I wrote an article about my unique experience with this traditional approach to medicine that was subsequently published in *Sacred*

Web, a journal of tradition and modernity published in Vancouver Canada.[1]

Four years have now passed since my initial visit, but in the back of my mind, I had every intention of returning for the recommended follow up treatment as time and circumstances permitted. In addition to harboring an ancient wisdom of healing that dates back nearly 5,000 years, a wisdom that is the by-product of the traditional knowledge contained within the sacred scriptures of the Vedanta, Ayurveda has preserved a philosophy of medicine that focuses its applications on prevention and longevity in addition to the standard processes of healing and cure. It is in fact the oldest and most holistic medical system still available to modern humanity. What truly makes Ayurveda unique is its professed association with the spiritual and still living tradition of a religion such as Hinduism. The knowledge itself has been transmitted to humanity through divine revelation based the four main books of the Vedas, including *Rik, Sama, Yajur,* and *Atharva.* At later dates, the knowledge of Ayurveda was organized into its own compact system of health as an auxiliary branch of the Vedas called Upaveda or "limb of the Veda" because it dealt with the practical healing aspects within the realm of spirituality.

It was now summertime and I had two full months of leisure spread out before me with no major concerns to speak of and no pressing demands to deal with. Theoretically, there was nothing wrong with me except the usual worries that afflict an individual facing the specter of old age. I had recently turned sixty and have tried to maintain a healthy lifestyle in today's hyper-active world with regular exercise of jogging, rope jumping, tennis, squash and the occasional yoga session to limber up the weary muscles. Yet who doesn't feel the stress and tension of living in today's fast-paced and hectic environment no matter what measures a person takes to

---

1. "The Miracle of Ayurveda: Ancient Treatments for Modern Afflictions," *Sacred Web* #7, Spring, 2001. As a result of that article, a number of readers made the trek East from North America in search of an effective cure for chronic problems that Western medicine was not able to handle successfully, including Ali Lakhani, the publisher and editor of *Sacred Web* himself.

maintain balance in one's routine. According to my Pashtu friend Farmana: "You is healthy as ox, except when you stand up from sitting on floor. Then I see old man in you." Indeed, it was time to return to Kerala, the scene of my earlier success in turning to ancient treatments for today's modern-day afflictions, hoping to live once again in a traditional setting and experience the legendary treatments based on a traditional approach to cure what ails the modern-day body and spirit.

As the old white Ambassador made its way down the main driveway toward the three story modern building that served as the residence for the in-patients, I noted that everything looked smaller and more closely confined that what I remembered. The lush mango tree gracing the lawn now stripped bare of its recently vintaged fruit and the old knobby tamarind tree shading the balconies looked smaller than what I remembered, as did the building itself and the inner courtyard and garden. Dreams and memories have a way of becoming enlarged in the mind when we imagine them or explain them to others. I had written in detail about my experience here and told countless people about it down to every last drop of oil and pressure point, so that in my mind's eye, the place and its natural environs had taken on a grand mythic scale that was difficult to reconcile with the reality of the rain-swept building and what seemed like miniaturized lawns and garden. Even the little swing that I remembered as a charming concession to childhood looked forlorn and out of place as it hung lifelessly from an abiding tree branch. I felt like an adult returning unexpectedly to the dead-end street where I had grown up only to find that the spirit of my memory was somehow betrayed by its present day reality.

As I entered the lobby of the structure and walked toward the reception area, I noted the spotless condition of the surroundings where I had once spent nearly four weeks patiently undergoing the treatments that not only promised but actually delivered a lasting cure. The Vaidyaratnam Nursing Home—for such was its name, Vaidyaratnam being a form of dignified title that was conferred upon the great grandfather of the present-day senior doctor—the ancestral establishment of an old Brahmin family for several centuries. The family of Thaikkattu Mooss, a legend in its own right, has engaged in the practice of Ayurveda for hundreds of years. Ashtavaidyan E.T. Narayaran Mooss is the resident physician and upholder of the ancient tradition and his two sons, Neelakandhan Mooss and Parameswaran Mooss are following in his footsteps and are Ayurvedic doctors in their own right. Under the leadership of their father, whose photo together with his renown father stood in the front lobby abreast the bronze image of the Hindu god of medicine, the establishment has grown to become one of the largest manufacturers of Ayurveda medicines with an extensive network all over Kerala and other parts of India.

In my naiveté, I thought they may not remember me. To my surprise, the receptionist greeted me with a broad smile and immediately called the manager who emerged from the inner offices and embraced me like a long lost brother. "We give you special room," he told me, "because you make us famous throughout world." His hyperbole notwithstanding, I thanked him with humility in my heart, thinking this was my time of retreat and repose, hoping to expel the evil influences within me and lead myself through effort and discipline back on the path of health and well being under the holistic guidance of the Ayurveda treatment. I had set myself a two week time frame to undertake a series of treatments with a view to the elimination of toxicity within the body, reestablishment of balance within the corporeal system, and hopefully achieve an inner equilibrium within my soul that is ultimately the inner reflection of the more outward-bound body, mind, and heart. Perhaps it is evidence of my own particular nature that invites the unusual, the mysterious and the exotic that I should put myself to the test of this rarefied environment that has successfully preserved an ancient philosophy of medicine that is realistic, practical, and above all effective. As such, I am glad that I listened to the call of some distant inner voice that beckoned me to take this leave of absence and sequester myself in the remote regions of South India for a two week retreat and cure for modern ailments that few people living in today's polluted and stressful world can escape.

* * *

That evening, I had my initial interview with the aging Dr. Mooss, the patrician and supreme guide of the Vaidyaratnam Nursing Home. He arrived—carrying his trademark flashlight in case of an unexpected blackout—with an entourage of nurses and a doctor to carefully note down his comments. This initial interview is actually key to the entire proceedings and curiously the timing of the commencement of the cure is of paramount importance, perhaps as a vague residue of ancient times when traditional Vedic astrology[1] and the movement of the stars played a role in the commencement of a successful treatment. Thus I knew from previous experience that I should arrive on either a Monday or a Thursday since treatment of patients only commences on Tuesday or Friday.[2] Dr. Mooss wanted to know the nature and extent of my condition. I told him that I was here for several weeks for prevention and rejuvenation, a concept that he readily understood. I secretly wondered what a Western doctor would have said if I went to his office and asked for treatment under those conditions. Upon questioning, I confessed that I had excessive tension and congestion in the neck and shoulder areas that "carried the weight of not only my head but my overburdened mind." He smiled readily, interrupting the flow of his gruff, no-nonsense manner and added: "We'll fix that for you in a timely manner." After much whispering among his encourage and more note-taking, a course of treatment was arranged that would commence the next morning at 7:30 sharp.

At 6:00 AM, as dawn began to light the world and the birds to sing their sunrise praises to the Divinity, the coffee cart was brought around to the various floors to serve coffee and tea to the patients who eagerly awaited this early morning nectar to commence the new-born day. At 7:30 sharp, an attending masseur knocked on my door to escort me down to the treatment room. Once inside, I was stripped of all worldly garments as naked as the day I was born,

---

1. Needless to say, traditional astrology was a form of ancient knowledge based on revelation that far exceeded the superficial expectations of modern-day astrology.

2. If a patient arrived on a Friday, for example, he or she would have to wait until the following Tuesday to commence the treatment after consulting with Dr. Mooss on Monday night.

except for a piece of cloth tied with a bit of string to cover the private parts, and then carefully laid upon a solid beam of wood hewn from one of the local trees, whence the entire body was drenched in the hot medicated oils that are the trademark of the Ayurveda treatments. The treatment room itself was a study in an altered state of ambiance. As I entered the room, I quickly took in the exotic smells of burning oil and herbs mixed with the scent of earth, while a faint odor of incense lent both mystery and magic to the rarefied setting. In the corner on a shelf a small shrine was on display, with a picture of the god of health and a small candle that flickered tongues of flame into the darkened corner as a remembrance of the higher powers that lay behind the human efforts to heal and restore equilibrium of the body.

This was no ordinary massage I was about to undergo. Two attending masseurs dressed in their sky blue uniforms stood on each side of the treatment plank. At the foot of the platform and off to one side, a third attendant tended a small wok smoking with the heated oils and the poultice bundles stuffed with rice and herbs that would be used in the application of what is called the "bundle massage". This massage consisted of each of the two masseurs gripping two of these poultice bundles after they had been steeped in the hot oils of the wok and then moving them up and down the body, either in a pounding fashion or alternating sometimes with a smooth stroking fashion. The masseurs concentrated first on one part of the body such as the arms, neck, and shoulders on one side, following by a not too subtle pounding on the poultice across the more vulnerable stomach area, then moving down to the legs and feet, with extra concentration on the joints of the knees and ankles. Imagine this happening not on one side, but on both sides of the body simultaneously with two different masseurs, on different parts of the body, using different points of pressure and different rhythms. Whereas one of the masseurs was pounding and stroking my arms, neck and shoulders by holding my arm up askew in mid-air, the other was working on the chest and soft underbelly, creating a weird effect in which the limbs and torso of the body had become merely a "thing", being pushed and pulled and pounded to the delight and good humor of the talkative masseurs, who chatted in Malayalam as if they were running a road race using words as the medium of progress. Once the poultice bundle cooled down slightly from its hot-to-tolerance temperature, it was immediately exchanged for another freshly hot poultice sitting in the smoking oil of the nearby wok, creating a brief lull before the renewed onslaught of the hot-oil poultice across the open field of my supine body.

This barrage of pounding lasted a full hour and belied the sweet promise of relief and relaxation that usually accompanies the term "body massage". The pounding, the hot oil, the deep heat, the herbs, the poultice, the hands, energy, focused mind and good will of the masseur all support the curative process that originates in the soul of the masseur and is transmitted through these artifacts of the alternative medicine back into the shell of the patient's body to generate once again the balance and harmony that should be its natural condition. At the end of the session, I was lifted up and sat momentarily with my legs dangling from the side of the treatment board as though stunned into submission. There the two masseurs—one in front and the other in back—made their final sweeping assault on the body, working out any residues of tension and congestion that may have escaped their attention. Once completed and still dripping with lukewarm oil, I was summarily towel dried from head to foot, whereupon one of the masseurs escorted me back to my room where I was advised to rest for at least a half hour. Needless to say, by the time the session was over, I felt completely exhausted by the ordeal. Only when I was safely returned to my room and seen inside would the attending masseur graciously take his leave with a smile and a bow.

Never in my life have I experienced such an intensive medical treatment to the total frame of the body. The principle behind the treatment lies in the effort to establish a new form of balance within the corporeal frame that stimulates the prime meridians, the flow of energy and the circulation of blood. According to the theories that lie behind the treatment, even a normal body that doesn't suffer from overt complaints has implicit imbalance, latent inflammations, toxicity, and other forms of congestion that inhibit the normal flow of blood, energy, and nerve impulses throughout the body as they go about the business of serving the impulses of the mind and heart.

This bundle massage was done one time only, but over the course of an entire week until the pounding action of the masseurs and the blessing and curative quality of the medicated oils had sufficiently acted upon the muscle and nerve systems to reestablish a kind of order and balance to the body. Remarkably, the first of the subtle changes in my constitution was in the quality of my voice. The sound of the voice was suddenly sharp, crackling and unbelievably clear, free of all cloudiness and any residues of phlegm. Like the unexpected sound of a bullet or the crack of a whip, the voice seemed disembodied with an energy and presence of its own.

In traditional Hindu philosophy, the power and quality of sound has an original primordial significance reflecting a harmony that is embodied in the well known mantra AUM. The voice is not only indicative of a person's character, but is also an expression of the inner spirit. It is not surprising that throughout the various stages of life including infancy, childhood, youth, maturity and finally old age, a change appears in the quality and pitch of a person's voice. The voice is a barometer of one's inner condition, externalized through vibration and sound. According to the yogis, if you want to know the condition of someone's spirit, it is necessary to observe the voice. This renewed sense of power and clarity of voice was a sign to me that the treatment was having a deep effect on my entire disposition. There was some latency of promise, as though a hidden jinnee had been resurrected from the inner well of my being and was made manifest within the sound of the voice.

With massage, internal herbal medicines, hot oils, cooling treatments, diet, life style, a harmonious natural setting, the underlying support of doctrinal principles of a traditional and thus universal knowledge, Ayurveda leaves no stone unturned in coming to terms with the health and well being of a person. With its holistic philosophy of medicine based on traditional sources, Ayurveda uses everything within its means to affect a cure or better to achieve prevention of a disease affecting the body, mind, psyche, heart or soul of the individual. All of these components interact in subtle ways of correspondence so that the disease or health of one aspect of the person necessarily affects some other aspect, for all is interconnected and all draws upon the principle of Supreme Unity that lies at the heart of the traditional doctrine of Hinduism, as well as all of the other orthodox religions of the world. As such, Ayurveda draws upon everything that influences these various components that make up the human person, including massage, medicated oil, internal herbal medicines, heat treatments for certain diseases such as muscle and nerve problems, cooling treatments for arthritic problems and the like. In addition, diet and drinking water play an important role in the overall cure. I immediately went on a vegetarian diet consisting of plain white rice, chapatti or a range of dosas, a kind of wheat pancake; vegetables were seasoned with a wide variety of Indian spices but the use of any kind of cooking oil was forbidden and I had to follow strict guidance about when to eat what. Nor could I eat fresh, uncooked fruits even though it was the mango season, although I did have steamed bananas for breakfast and a mango curry of stewed vegetables for lunch one day that was as tasty as it was unique. One can begin to penetrate the mystique of vegetarianism through such exposure to the traditional Hindu style of cuisine. In addition to the rarefied cuisine, a liter of warm medicated water was delivered to my room every morning and afternoon for drinking purposes, clear rose-colored water with a soothing, healthful taste delivered warm and to be drunk at room temperature.

The room that I was to occupy nearly 24 hours a day for the next 15 days was Spartan, functional, and spotlessly clean. In fact, once a person enters the nursing home for treatment, he or she is not allowed to leave the premises, either to expose the head to the sun or to walk through the mist. It had an ascetic appeal that was not lost on my austere temperament; yet it had all the requirements of a clean and comfortable hotel room. There was a bed on either side of the room, a small table for dining or writing, a corner shelf that held a standard-sized TV equipped with over 50 satellite channels. Off to the side, there were built-in cupboards for clothing and supplies, plus a perfectly adequate bathroom with bathing facilities. In addition, the room had French doors that opened onto a balcony that was a virtual room within a bucolic wonderland of weather and nature that ultimately proved to be one of the key factors in the pursuit of an effective cure for what ails both the body and the spirit.

Beyond the immediate fringe of the premises of gardens and boundary fence lay the expanse of what amounted to a kind of paradisal nature park. What struck me initially was the sheer vividness and variety of the color green. It may sound strange to the detached reader that I had flown into Kerala from the deserts of the United Arab Emirates, whose summer temperatures routinely soar to nearly 50 degrees centigrade and whose expanse of endless sand dunes is virtually mythic. Over the coming days, I sat for hours drinking in the richness of the variations of the color green, the swaying of the stately palm trees, and the cool, misty freshness of the rain. Indeed, the season of the monsoons was in full swing and after a year in the UAE without experiencing a drop of rain, my prayers were answered in the constant deluge of rain that punctuated the routine of my days with its variety of richness, texture and sound.

Day after day, the rains came down and continued to come down and down. The clouds were fast-moving, dark and angry looking, and yet the feeling they created to one starved of the blessing of rain was one of plenitude, variety and richness. The thunder and lightening assaulted the defenseless earth with its show of sound and light in total disregard to consequences, while this display of natural power was mighty indeed and served as a bold testament to the powers that lie beyond our earth-bound consciousness. I knew the rain had begun in earnest when I was awakened from my reverie by a steady drumming on the corrugated roof of the canteen below my window. The waters would roar down the rippled metal roof in almost a solid sheet and showed no signs of ever intending to end. Similarly, the rain drummed on the tin roofs nearby sounding like the deep cords of some celestial organ, as it pelted the broad carpet of the earth and every leaf and branch and blade of grass upon it with its mercy and blessing.

A vast leisure awaited my arrival like a cup to be filled, clear to the horizon of my mind. However, the natural setting of this paradisal nature park provided unlimited interest to my idle imagination as I underwent the rigors of the treatments and conformed to the rules of the establishment. The sights and sounds of nature called to mind a higher consciousness and acted as a soothing balm to the harried mentality that I had brought with me fraught with tension, preoccupation, worry, and psychological knots of every kind bestowed upon me without asking by the frantic world we live in. Looking out at this broad expanse of unpretentious nature so raw and beautiful down to the vivid greens of every blade of grass, who could possibly fret about the cares of the world for here was an ageless world that harbored a sense of eternity and lent generously of its mystique to my weary—and for wont of a better word—modern mind.

Geometric paddy fields drenched in the waters of the rain formed the centerpiece of the scene with a symmetrical architecture of fields awaiting the beneficence of heaven. Encroaching from either side and forming what amounted to the wings of this bucolic setting were extensive palm groves with every manner of swaying palm bowing to the whims of the wind. A number of cows and oxen feasted on the lush grasses of the rain-drenched fields or lumbered through the splashing water of the grasslands with stately elegance; a herd of playful goats caroused their way through the landscape; elegant cranes flew carelessly back and forth or alternatively alighted on the backs of unsuspecting oxen. A flooded streamlet rushed angrily around a number of thatched houses on the fringe of the palm grove and created yet another signature of the Divinity across the landscape. I sat and took it all in, the color, the sights, the sounds, the weather and the energy forces of this natural park as though centuries were passing me by and I had nothing else to wait for but the panorama of the present moment to fill the empty hours of my day. My spirit was stilled and then uplifted by the simple yet august and eternal things in view before me. For once, my vision became cleared of the inessentials that normally occupy our minds and I stared forth wide-eyed at the great simplicities of life.

Of course, people occupied this landscape. Farmers tended their fields; women dressed in colorful saris escorted the oxen morning and evening back and forth to the fields and tied them to the ground so they would not roam afar. Once I noticed a woman carrying beams of wood piled high on her head while a man, her husband presumably, followed behind dutifully carrying his umbrella. She looking stately and elegant in her purple sari as her bare feet paddled their way through water-soaked grasses. And I must not forget the procession of the ducks twice a day rain or shine through the flooded paddy fields. At first, I didn't realize what was happening from the distance of my balcony when I noticed an amorphous living mass of brown color making its meandering way like oozing molasses through the water-soaked landscape until I realized it was a bevy of ducks; there must have been a thousand of them, although an exact number would belie the full impression of the querulous horde that flowed across the field. It was a sight to behold. I say procession because they entered the extensive paddy field from the seclusion of the palm groves like some dance troupe entering from stage right. In procession and *en masse*, they appeared to be a happy lot, preening their feathers, shaking their tails and flapping their wings to the sound of clapping in false flight. The ducks were bunched together and studiously avoiding the grazing cow that looked behind at the petulant horde apprehensively. They were escorted on their early morning stroll by three local Keralites who mothered the group through the watery fields and chased the naughty ducklings back into the pack, stopping occasionally to pick up a straggler by the feet. The commotion they raised with their incessant quacking was enough to awaken the spirits of the fields. Was I being silly in becoming mesmerized by such things or was there some latent insight waiting for the right conditions to emerge like a cloud burst of rain descending from above onto my parched mind. The fact remains that the sight of these unruly animals filled my heart with joy. Perhaps that is insight enough for one hour of the day; but every day they crossed my vision on the way to their routine procession through the wet paddy fields with their inscrutable *joie de vivre.*

In contrast to the color and life of this daytime setting, the night brought with it a blanket of darkness that was as black as a void and as deep as a bottomless well—a darkness that hung like a filmy curtain separating the world of the clinic from the surrounding darkness, forming a true abyss of blackness in front of the eyes. I sat within the security of my little balcony and wondered what it would feel like and what it would mean to be out and about within that vast physical darkness that seemingly harbored a foreboding presence of I knew not what, but was never to find out, for even from the distance there seemed to be a spirit to the darkness of the night that was terrifying to behold to my modern eyes unaccustomed to the absolute blackness of true night uncompromised by the effect of city lights. The only relief to the utter depths of this darkness just beyond the garden wall was the silhouette of those great trees against the muted charcoal gray of that cloud-filled night sky serving as valiant sentinels of the pitch-black night. And I thought: We as modern individuals have insulated ourselves from the natural signs and rhythms of the cosmos; we pretend that the methodologies of a modern-day science will reveal the secrets of the universe through the human instruments of the mind and the senses; we pride ourselves on our technological expertise and our ability to envision a road of progress stretching before us as a result of a profound competence we imagine ourselves to have. Yet the depths of the night leave us helpless and fearful, alien beings in a universe whose true reality escapes us and whose physical manifestation terrorizes us with its mystery and its latent, unknown presence. Thus, a patch of darkness was enough to lead my soul to the very edge of universal mystery.

The late afternoon of my first day of treatment and the following six afternoons became the occasion for two treatments that are said to affect the brain, cranium and central nervous system connecting the brain with the cervical spine, as if the goings-on in this sublime nature park weren't treatment enough for my mind and nervous system. Firstly, around 4:30 in the afternoon, as the incessant rains showered the drenched earth and created a storm of sound that animated the landscape and my mind with the force of every drop, a certain mixture of warm medicated oils was applied to the top of my head, where a cloth drenched in a special mix of oils sat for the next half hour whence I was to remove the cloth and wipe dry the residue of oil from the saturated head with a cotton towel. Under no circumstances was I to wash the head. This was done with strict instructions every three days and only with medicated water. Once this was finished at around 5:30, the doctor and several attendants arrived to perform *nasyam*, alternatively called the dreaded hot-oil nose treatment.

For what was to follow, I had been well prepared by the doctors, so that there wouldn't be any "surprises" and I would know what to do. I was ceremoniously laid upon the bed on my back with a pillow placed behind my neck, thus exposing my face and nose for this rarefied treatment. Then with meticulous care, the doctor poured a number of generous applications of warm medicated oil down first the right nostril, then the left one. After the warm oil made its stinging way at a snail's pace down through the inner labyrinth of the nose and sinuses, the doctor proceeded to massage my forehead and cheeks meticulously, while the attendants vigorously rubbed the extremities of hands and feet to induce circulation and stimulate nerve endings. Needless to say, at this unwelcome invasion, my nose and sinuses reacted with a mild discomforting sensation which was testament enough to the fact that the inner cavities of the skull were congested with unnecessary fluids that had found a home and were reluctant to leave. Soon enough however, I felt called upon not only to spit out the oil that at this point had lodged itself against the shelf of the throat, but to dredge up and expectorate as much as possible the mucus and other residue of fluids that had been lodged within the pockets of the skull.

Between the head oils and the nose oils, this Ayurveda treatment can achieve what Western medicine doesn't dare to think about, namely a kind of washing of the brain and a cleansing of the inner cavities of the skull, thus stimulating and activating all of the inner network of nerves that pass from the brain, down through the skull, into the cervical spine and beyond into the rest of the body. By the end of the first week, my face had lost that puffy, distended appearance that comes with an excess of fluids that tend to gather in the facial area and that become a primary source of much congestion and disease, especially the common cold. Indeed, beyond the physiological benefit lay the heightened awareness to the mind and the consciousness generally, attesting to the close interaction affecting the physical, mental, and spiritual worlds. My mind felt dusted clean of debris, as though a cool wind had blown through and brushed away the autumn leaves of half a century. I liken the experience to having your ears blown of excess wax, when you experience a brilliant renewal and clarity of sound as if you were hearing for the first time. Having swept clean the skull cavities and soothed the nerve endings with warm moist oil, my mind felt refreshed and clear beyond belief, as though I were witnessing the world around me at the dawn of time.

* * *

A person cannot pass two weeks within the confines of a small room without coming to terms with oneself and the infinite leisure—not to mention the creeping solitude—that confronts the weary patient in search of a cure. My mind was sparkling like sunlight on the bay, sending off sparks of clarity and insight into the void of my days; but this was not enough, for the question remained, what would these sparks feed from and where would they land. The problem of how to fill the waking hours of my modern, action-prone mind for the rest of my day demanded some form of credible solution. As I mentioned earlier, it is true that I bathed in the extravagance of the rain and became entranced by the luminous green of the surrounding foliage; but this was not enough to satisfy the ethereal dreams and longings that invade the idle mind bereft of the artifacts and distractions of the modern world. One has to fill the void of the mind with something worthwhile; otherwise the mind will fill the rest of the human spirit with its own random thoughts, at its own frantic pace and with a will of its own.

As part of my professional commitments, I had been asked to select, amass, edit and write an introduction to a compilation of the writings of René Guénon, a French writer who lived in the first half of the 20th century and who had converted to Islam, living much of his later life in Cairo where he died in 1951. Readers of spiritual or traditional literature may well be familiar with his name for he is considered one of the fathers of the so-called traditionalist school of thinking that has flowered into the present era through the writings of such eminent writers of the Traditionalist School as Frithjof Schuon, Ananda Coomaraswamy, Martin Lings, and Titus Burckhardt, all of whom followed in the wake of Guénon's initial insights that were so profound he left his footsteps not in sand but in granite stone, to be followed by those with an appreciation of his prophetic insights into the true condition of the modern world.

While Abd al-Wahid Yahya, as he was known in Islamic circles, had adopted Islam as an orthodox tradition and his formal "way of return" to that sublime Presence that the Sufis refer to as the Supreme Identity, he is perhaps best known and remembered for his incredibly comprehensive and accessible expose of Hinduism[1] as the earliest known and document testament to the primordial tradition to which the religious traditions refer and the metaphysical knowledge of a universal truth that is the cornerstone and essence of that tradition. I considered this a unique opportunity firstly to travel and spend some time in India within a traditional rural setting that could provide the right ambiance for such an endeavor and secondly to pursue a course of reading and study that would relate directly to the healing experience I was attempting to undergo, filling my mind with thoughts of a higher order to be invoked and drawn upon in the pursuit of my cure. During the course of my two week treatment, I had ample time to read my way through the many books of his extensive *oeuvre* at a single blow as it were, without the turmoil and distractions that face the average person living in the modern world. I had at my disposal all the leisure anyone could want to savor, together with the desire to ingest the commanding certitude that radiated through the voice of his writing style and the profound implications of his thoughts.

Two things initially struck me in his writing that relate directly to my experience in pursuit of these traditional treatments that trace their origin and source to the Vedic scriptures. Firstly, he writes in the spirit of a true metaphysician in search of a universal knowledge that is the only absolute in a relative universe, the only truth in a world of contingency, and the only certainty among the seeds of doubt and illusion that we live with every day as earthly beings within the terrestrial setting. Needless to say, if such a metaphysical knowledge that transcends the known world truly exists, then all of the religious traditions from the *ur*-origins of Hinduism to the "seal

---

1. His *Man and His Becoming According to the Vedānta*, (Hillsdale: NY, Sophia Perennis, 2004) is a classic in its own right and a must read for all those interested in coming to terms with Hindu metaphysics and its place in the broad spectrum of religious forms.

of the Prophets" within Islam, religions that have descended into the world of form and contingency through a revelation that contains the essence of this universal knowledge, are instruments that contain the transcendent unity of all principial knowledge cast within the mold of individual forms that suit a particular time period or mentality down through the ages. In this way, even I as a Muslim could unashamedly partake of this ancient philosophy of medicine that has its roots in the supreme identity of a universal principle expressed as Brahma or Allah or God or the Great Spirit of the Red Indians. "For every soul there is a pathway to God," as the traditional saying goes, just as for every people, according to Islam, there is a messenger and a message of the one Truth and the one Divinity.

Secondly, Guénon cast the ethereal principles of an esoteric and metaphysical body of knowledge within an understandable framework for the modern mentality the likes of which had never been done before and perhaps strangely enough had never needed to be done. In other words, he put into perspective for those people in the modern world with the capacity to appreciate what he was trying to convey, the extreme importance of a non-individual, non-formal, otherworldly body of knowledge containing principles of knowledge and a means of spiritual realization and internalization of that knowledge within the human being as a prelude to the fulfillment of the soul and spirit through the realization of the Supreme Identity, which is none other than the Supreme Being. No other person before his time has had the innate ability, the words, the knowledge, or the inspiration to unify into a single universal perspective the broad diversity of religious and spiritual knowledge that has come down to humanity through the ages. Perforce the traditional era knew nothing of what was to come in the modern world with its alien atheism, secularism, and scientistic approaches to the pursuit of knowledge. He set the stage for people to realize the transcendent unity at the heart of all the religious traditions that found its root in a primordial tradition with the power to neutralize time and space within the hub of the cosmic wheel whose spokes then radiated outwards into the world of formal manifestation, that infamous hub being none other than the primordial point where the "unmoved mover" ordains the manifested universe and has the capacity to reabsorb it back unto itself.

The power resulting from the interaction of the branches of a traditional knowledge such as a medicine based on the sacred relationship of body, soul and spirit, or a true cosmology and pure metaphysics such as to be found within the writing of the Vedanta should not be underestimated in terms of the knowledge it conveys, the efficacy it ensures and the certitude it rains down upon the heart and soul. To be ensconced within the timeless, traditional setting of India, adrift within a zone of seemingly primordial nature untouched by the machinations of humankind while graced at the same time by the presence of humans going about their daily routine in humility and peace, all the while partaking of an deep-seated traditional approach to health and well being based on sacred scripture and the oral tradition of practitioners down through the millennia is a rarefied experienced indeed, capturing in practice as well as in essence, the prevailing unity that lies at the heart of all manifestation, rendering transparent and thus transcendent the soul and spirit of all symbolic form.

* * *

The following Thursday night came with all the insistence and timeliness of the present moment. Dr. Mooss arrived with abrupt formality with his entourage of doctors and nurses for further consultation. I was questioned carefully about my responses to the treatments, how I felt, how I slept, how I ate, and whether I had made any improvement. Indeed, I told him that a new level had been achieved and a new leaf had been turned over. There was a buzz of consultation and a second week of treatment was decided upon based on the information I conveyed and Dr. Mooss' judgments concerning my progress. I felt clear-headed, relaxed, and the tension and muscle pain in the neck and shoulders was considerably relieved. The bundle massage was to be replaced with a regular, full body pressure point massage. I was to continue with the hot oil bath to the top of my head in the late afternoon. The highlight of the week, however, was to be the enwrapping of my right hand, arm and shoulder with a bandage packed with mud, herbs and leaves intended to infuse the goodness of the natural plants into my system and draw out its poisons. This bandage was to be applied at 6:00 in the evening, and to be removed 12 hours later at 6:00 AM.

The following morning, Sugatham, my attending masseur, came to fetch me in my room and escort me down to the treatment room. After a full week of treatments, he had come to be warm and friendly, as though I had known him since childhood or had become close with him in the style of those who pass through a difficult experience together. For him, it was his job and I am sure he had to deal with many patients during the course of his day, yet I marveled at his gentle, conciliatory manner and the interest he took in me and my troubles, greeting me with a warm smile and taking me by the hand. There was a sweetness in him that transcended the moment; it was unrequired, unexpected and full of warmth and human spirit. I thought of the importance laid upon the interaction of the masseur and the patient in the philosophy of traditional massage, without which no true cure could ever take place. Within the gift of his treatment lay the blessing of his healing, while within my surrender and trust to his abilities laid the possibility of my cure. What could have been a routine encounter took on the quality of connectedness that hovers over father and son.

The early morning treatment itself, consisting of a full body, hands-on massage with warm medicated oils, consisted of long firm strokes that extended up and down the legs, up and down the arms, first front torso followed by back torso, hands, wrists, knees, ankles and worst of all feet were all given his focused attention. When the masseur uncovered areas of pain or tenderness—for you could not help but whimper and yelp as the hands passed over areas of the body that were congested and sensitive to the pressure-pointing touch of the experienced masseur—he concentrated his attention on those areas with extra strength to work out the congestion and pain. Later, the doctor told me that there are areas of the body that harbor latent inflammations that become inflamed and rise to the surface when given this kind of hands-on treatment. There were areas of the body that I never thought about, such as the tops of the feet, the back of the heels, the base of the neck, that gave way to unrelenting pain that sometimes took days to subside and disappear. After several days of this intensive treatment, I realized that there were parts of my body—in the lower arms and legs for example—that were literally black and blue from the intensity of the treatment that had been uncovered as problem areas of congestion, poor circulation and/or latent inflammation. At the heart of the entire treatment was the desire to restore balance and equilibrium within the corporeal system, with particular reference to the alignment of the nerves, the suppleness of the muscles, and the overall fluid circulation of the blood, in itself a source of refreshment and cure. Indeed, poor circulation in many alternative treatments accounts as the original source of problems when areas of the body begin to atrophy in some way because of the lack of good blood nourishment.

In addition to the various aspects of the total treatment such as the particular treatments already mentioned, one aspect that I haven't touched upon but that remains an important component of this overall, holistic approach to medicine was nutrition and diet. I was given strict instructions about what not to eat and this included surprisingly cold fruits, all meat and fish, including milk and poultry by-products. As a concession, I was granted a boiled banana with breakfast, but this was small consolation to my routine of eating as much fruit as possible, including my beloved apple a day and the myriad fresh dates that are available in the United Arab Emirates, my country of residence. Patients are kept on a strict vegetarian diet and the cooks use every interesting spice under the sun, but no cooking oils of any kind. I was told to have plain white unseasoned rice at noontime, and chapatti in the evening to scoop up my vegetable kormas and curries. It is amazing how prominent one's diet becomes when you are suddenly denied your favorite foods. I consider myself nutrition savvy and steer clear of junk food and any excess of meats; but I sorely missed the occasional coke, cookies, and apple that I considered standard fare at any other time. I don't smoke or drink alcohol, but if I did, these vices certainly wouldn't be permitted during the course of such a cure.

I also systematically drank freshly made herbal medicines twice a day, one in the morning after breakfast and also in the evening after

dinner. These small bottles of warm liquid contained various concoctions of herbs and roots mixed with warm water and oils that
were bitter to the taste and horrible to drink. I confess that taking
these unpleasant medicines was a challenging event that I accepted
faithfully and with determination, realizing that in doing so I would
be benefiting from all the goodness these small bottles contained.
On the final day of my stay at the clinic, I was given special permission to leave the building[1] and walk the 300 hundred meters to the
factory where all the herbs were prepared. The herbs themselves are
farmed and grown in the nearby area by regional farmers who have
contracts with the clinic to provide the required plants for the treatment. I was able to see for myself the complete process from the
rooms where the cut plants and drawn roots were stored, through
the cutting and chopping phase, down to the hot and stuffy room
that must have contained over 15 vats where the wide variety of
roots, plants and herbs were boiled in oils in anticipation of having
the right mix of medicated oils that suited a wide variety of treatments. The dark brew of oils that were frothing and bubbling in
these huge vats resembled melted chocolate, but the sight of these
curative products of nature belied this illusion with their pungent,
earthy smells. This was a golden brown brew that would cure the
chronic ailments of the sick and miserable in keeping with the
Islamic saying that for every disease of mankind there is a cure
found in nature.

All through the second and final week of my two week treatment, I
continued to have the late afternoon brain bath, as I affectionately
called it, when one of the attendants would come into my room
around 4:30 and douse my head—recently shaved for this very
purpose—with a certain prescribed mix of herbs and oils that would
seep into the head and saturate the brain and skull cavity with their
mysterious curative powers. The hallmark of the second week of

---

1. Normally resident patients are not allowed to leave the premises at any time
during their treatment. Clinic officials fear that the patients may pick up unwanted
viruses or bacteria that would seriously interfere with the treatment. They also
want patients to avoid exposure to direct sunlight and the unpredictable effects of
rain and mist.

treatment, however, was the bandage that was to be applied every evening for the rest of my stay. This was no plastic bandage wrapped around a sore finger. This was a full scale cloth wrapping that was to entirely enwrap my hand, arm, and right shoulder. I had complained of a minor sports injury that I had incurred several months earlier when I fell while playing squash. I mentioned that I still experienced some residue of pain from a tendon that had yet to fully heal.

Once again, my friendly attendant and masseur Sugatham trooped down to collect me in my room at the appointed time of 6:00 PM and escort me down to the treatment room once again to apply this cumbersome bandage. At first, he doused the entire hand, arm, and shoulder with medicated oil. As I sat there with the late afternoon sun streaming into the room through the wide open balcony doors and the ethereal sound of Vedic sutras echoed through wall speakers, I noticed another attendant hovering over a piece of cotton cloth over a foot in length and spread what looked like an earthly humus mixture of organic soil and herbs along the cloth as though he were spreading peanut butter on white bread. Once applied, he quickly carried the steaming cloth over and wrapped my entire arm in its warm fetid embrace from my fingertips to shoulder. Thereupon the entire arm to the shoulder was wrapped in the beautiful, large palmate leaves of the caster oil plant[1], known for its curative and restorative properties for such things as inflammation, muscle and tendon problems. The entire bandage was secured by wrapping strands of cloth across my back and under the left arm to ensure that the bandage stayed in place. Once finished, I felt like a trussed up chicken and looked like a half wrapped mummy of ancient Egyptian lore. Once again, Sugatham politely escorted me back to my room; but as I shuffled down the corridor in my slippers under the gaze of patients and visitors standing in the doorway of their room, I felt like Frankenstein in search of my lair.

That night, and every night thereafter until I left the clinic seven days later, I endured this cumbersome cure. Eating dinner with the left hand and scooping up my vegetable curry with broken bits of

---

1. Alternatively known as *Ricinus communis* or Palma Christi (palm of Christ) plant.

chapatti was difficult indeed. I thought sleeping would be a problem, but the evening medicine that I swallowed with a grimace seemed to contain an herb that soon folded me peacefully within the robes of slumber. Promptly at six the next morning, the night attendant came and took me back down to the treatment room to remove the bandage. What relief, indeed what liberation, to be relieved of these mummified wrappings around my arm and shoulder. To my shock and horror, on the second and third morning, I noticed a number of sores on my upper arm and shoulder that seemed to be emitting long dormant poisons; but the attendant quickly treated these eruptions and sores with medicated ghee and assured me that the unsightly sores would soon disappear. Indeed, they did disappear in a matter of days, and by the time I left the clinic, the body has finally expelled a goodly amount of poison through this unorthodox treatment.

* * *

Long standing antagonisms continue to exist between allopathic Western approaches to healing and the alternative, Eastern approaches to medicine based on sacred scripture and ancient practices that date back thousands of years. While the arguments may go on between experts in the field about the efficacy of Ayurveda, acupuncture, homeopathy and other traditional treatments, no one can deny the reality of a truly curative experience. Whether it be the miracle of natural herbs and their mysterious curative powers, whether it be the body itself that responds to certain natural and holistic approaches to health and well being by curing itself, or whether it be the profound interaction of the body, mind, heart and soul of the doctor and the patient abiding by that mysterious relationship that has existed for thousands of years, there can be no denying the true experience of the cure and the restorative powers of the body to balance the clarity of mind and the sense of self consciousness with the presence of an inner spirit that becomes a living reality through the unique interaction of body, mind and soul.

As I walked the corridors of the East and West wings of the building endeavoring to fill the lonely cup of my solitude, I passed by many individuals of all ages, sizes and shapes. Most of the patients were local Keralites or people from the greater subcontinent. A charming Dutch couple had traveled from Holland in anticipation of a traditional cure; the husband, a very friendly and talkative companion to compare notes with as we underwent the treatment, suffered from various ailments including arthritis of the joints; his wife, a very regal and gracious woman had a minor fibrosis of the lungs. Both of them had very progressive attitudes toward this ancient and alien approach to cure. A young teenage girl from Goa had her university studies interrupted because of a several case of rheumatoid arthritis that had mercilessly afflicted her. A Malaysian woman occupied the room across from mine, attended by her devoted husband. She was suffering from obesity and the resultant pain in the joints of the legs. All bore their infirmities with magnanimity and grace; all made the effort to abide by the rigors and demands of the treatment in anticipation of a cure; all displayed the patience and fortitude to see this slow, traditional process through to the end of the treatment, for with these ancient treatments, there are no miracle cures that we modernites have come to expect from synthetic pills.

By the end of my two week stay, I felt physically years younger and refreshed, while feelings of a profound peace filled my soul. A lazy overhead fan stirred the air and the rain came down in sheets and silvery waves, heavy then light then heavy, again punctuated by the roar and whisper of the descending drops as they met the rich earth that lay spread out before me like some sleeping animal. Sounds of the day and night made their presence felt: The ethereal chanting of Vedic sutras emanating from some distant tape recorder, the cacophonous sounds of the night animals, the twittering of birds and the cry of the hawk. The harmonious sound of a harmonica floated periodically throughout the building, roaming through open doors and out onto balconies and rooftops, sharing its melancholy tune with those listening to the echo of its sad refrains. I couldn't locate precisely where the sound was coming from; it seemed to float from both above and below. Whoever played these sonorous notes put their soul in the music they were producing. The simple harmonies and rhythms were full of sentiment and played with love. Sometimes I sat in the hour before sleep staring aimlessly in the dark night beyond the ledge of my balcony, the night hour when secret journeys are made and people probe the inner recesses of their soul by witnessing the twinkling stars, gentle breezes, and little voices of the night. As if in salute to the perennial mystery of dreams, the silhouettes of majestic palm trees stood highlighted against the glow of the Milky Way, itself a pathway leading through the stars of the night sky to some celestial horizon, beyond which lay the field of our outermost dreams.

At the end of my two week stay at the Ayurveda Clinic I had one final consultation with old Dr. Mooss, who brought the consultation process full circle and graciously extended his permission for me to leave with his blessing, wishing me safe return as a person renewed and ready to deal with the contingencies of this world. Arrangements were made for me to take away a month's supply of internal medicines and various combinations of head and body massage oils so that I could continue a month's program of treatment on my own as follow-up to the two week stay at the clinic. The demands of the Ayurveda treatment require commitment and perseverance, but the results to the total person, including body, mind, and heart, are life-long and enduring.

The following morning I took my leave. As I passed beyond the horizon of this bucolic setting back out into the restless world of life and work and the pursuit of happiness, I was already sensing that the peaceful and grateful feeling of health and well being that I had made such effort to achieve was slipping beyond my grasp, making me feel a stranger unto myself as I passed under the grand archway back out into the open world. Behind me, as I took one final look through the rear window of the old white Ambassador, the flowing lawns and placid building lay unsuspecting in some remote and misty peace. Monsoon clouds rolled across the heavens and a suspended stillness hung in the air as though some great sphinx had sighed or held its breath, allowing this moment to feel like the passing of a thousand years. From the distance and with incredible clarity rose single sounds that seemed to chase me away, but that I ended up taking with me as a fond remembrance—the stroke of a distant bell, the lowing of cattle, the patter of rain and finally that soulful harmonica filling the air with its melancholy promise of serenity and repose. In taking these impressions with me, the two infinities of sight and sound accompanied me out of ancient India and became a part of my being as the true expression of the harmony and balance that I had sought and ultimately found somewhere beyond that far distant road in Kerala.

9

AT THE TOMB
OF THE PROPHET

*One prayer in my mosque is better than one thousand prayers in
any other mosque excepting al-Masjid al-Haram.* (Bukhari: 2/
157; chap. 37, 282)

IT IS SOMETIMES DIFFICULT to remember that we are now in the
holy month of Ramadan,[1] a sacred month in the Islamic tradition
when the holy Quran began to descend from the Mind of God to
the mind of the Messenger Muhammad, upon him blessings and
peace, and beyond into the minds and mentality of past, present,
and future generations. However, the events of recent weeks belie
the tradition that says the gates of Hell are shut tight and the gates
of the Paradise are opened wide. Several bombs have gone off in
Istanbul killing numerous innocent civilians and creating wide-
spread damage and havoc among the population. Riyadh, the capital of Saudi Arabia, shook recently with the aftershocks of the
explosions on an apartment complex housing largely expatriate
Arab nationals. The cities of Iraq have become the battleground of
insurgency and counter-insurgency in a surprisingly well-orches-
trated effort to rid the country of an American occupation.

If we listen carefully to the events we hear reported in the mass
media, Ramadan has become a time of heightened terrorism and an

---

1. "Ramadan is the (month) in which was sent down the Quran, as a guide to
mankind, also clear (signs) for guidance and judgment (between right and wrong)"
(2:185).

opportunity for one group or another, either Muslim or non-Muslim, to invoke the holy season of fasting and spiritual vigilance in the name of various suspect causes. Is there anyone left who does not use the name of God or the forces implicit within the context of a given religion for his or her own selfish purposes and ends? Perhaps we are all bounded by the rhetoric of a given time and place and caught in the turmoil of conflicting cultures and worldviews? Is there anyone left who still goes about the business of living in a manner that is in keeping with their ancient and abiding traditions, people who view the reality of their existential situation in the light of enduring principles whose value transcends the time and place of any given moment or region or formal religion even? Are there any people left who still pursue the fine art of living wisely and well?

During the holy month of Ramadan, Muslims flock to the two holy places of Madinah and Makkah because it is a sacred month of raised consciousness of God through the bodily fast and of a heightened spirituality that is the direct result of such a rigorous physical, mental, and spiritual effort. I recently received time off from my duties as a teacher at an engineering university in Abu Dhabi in the United Arab Emirates to join the vast horde who converge on the two holy places of Makkah and Madinah to make the "lesser pilgrimage" called Umrah and to take advantages of the multiple blessings that accompany the blessed month of Ramadan.

The following account highlights certain impressions that resulted from my visit to these two holy cities in Saudi Arabia, impressions that hopefully belie the ignorant and often false notions that now predominate across the globe about Muslims and their beliefs, impressions that may begin to sketch a narrative event of the fast of Ramadan in the holy places of Makkah and Madinah as an expression of faith and spirituality by millions of Muslims the world over in light of their true meaning and significance.

As our chartered Saudia flight, packed with a contingent of pilgrims, circles for a landing on this predawn mid-November morning, I notice in the distance a luminous glow of light reaching vertically into the overcast heavens. The *Masjid al-Nabawi* (The Prophet's Mosque) announces its location at the very center and heart of the city of Madinah in a brilliant display of light. Visible from outer space even, this beacon of light is certainly the most obvious landmark in the darkness of the desert plane. As if in counterpoint to this unexpected radiance, a pale harvest moon descends soberly toward the Eastern horizon, drenching the desert landscape with its silvery incandescent moonbeams. I have returned once again to the City of Light after an interval of 15 years.

The airport itself is small and unpretentious and I pass through customs without much ado. No one seems to notice or care that I am an American Muslim of Boston Irish ancestry, perhaps because I am dressed incognito in the Pathan native cloth consisting of baggy pantaloons tied together with a cloth rope and an overhead shirt that flows down to the knees. I am wearing it because more comfortable attire could not be found that is so well suited to the Islamic prayer rituals and the other demands of the lesser (*Umrah*) pilgrimage. That, together with a white skullcap, allows me the luxury of being anonymous as I blend into the surroundings with the other eager pilgrims. The Saudi Government pilgrim visa stamped across a full page of my passport will gain me entry into the Kingdom even if it may raise some eyebrows and questions later when I return to the US.

The bus ride into town could have been anywhere in the Middle East, the dry and dusty desert landscape by the side of the road, the invading billboard signs advertising things people don't need and shouldn't want, the craggy rocky hills silhouetted against the horizon, the dingy cement houses and cluttered shops huddled together in close proximity as if for protection from some unknown force. We pass a traffic light here, turn a corner there, when suddenly we emerge onto the grand concourse of the sacred mosque of Madinah, called the Prophet's Mosque because the Prophet himself is buried in one corner called the Sacred Chamber in an area that originally comprised the rooms where he lived with his wife 'Aishah. The first mosque of Islam[1] was an extension of the house of the Prophet.

The sight of this magnificent edifice is overwhelming, to say the least, for its mammoth size and stately presence. For sheer bulk and

---

1. The dimensions of the original structure were 2,450 square meters with three doors on the south side, and in the eastern and western wall.

magnitude, this architectural wonder strikes awe in the beholder. The entire structure rests serenely amid an open expanse of plaza that extends perhaps 500 meters on each side of the mosque and whose surface is covered with alabaster and marble.[1] Everything about this broad setting bespeaks of openness, air, and light and provides striking views of the mosque from any angle of approach. This is the very center and heart of the city. Everything beyond the sacred enclosure immediately becomes an afterthought to the necessities of daily life. A grand avenue leads down from the mountains beyond the edge of the small city to the five grand portals that distinguish the front side of the mosque. At a glance as you approach from the grand promenade, the building seems monumental. Like a photo that simply refuses to contain the image you wish to capture, the sight of the mosque simply refuses to be contained in a single glance. You have to span your vision from left to right, right to left, to take it all in, and even then, it seems incomprehensible to fully grasp in all its magnificence.

For all the value of this stately structure, the setting comes alive with the sheer numbers of people that are moving in and out and around the mosque. Much like witnessing the celestial bodies or calculating the astronomical numbers of stars and galaxies, the numbers of people range beyond the scope of clear comprehension and only because you are there with the rest of this vast congregation can you begin to believe what you appear to be experiencing. For the sheer force of its impression, this is like no other moment in time. There seems to be a secret here worth exploring. Indeed the secret lies in the intention of those who have joined me on this pilgrimage, all of whom have a single-minded focus and a purpose that is absolute and beyond any doubt. The sheer numbers of people bring a reality to the situation that might otherwise be lost. It is the supreme example of humanity giving rise to the expression of their deepest yearning and nothing and no one is going to come between them and their aspirations.

---

1. The total plaza area is 235,000 square meters and accommodates 400,000 additional worshippers. The mosque itself may now accommodate approximately one million worshippers during peak times of crowding.

The day is punctuated of course by the five devotional prayers of Islam and at any given moment vast crowds of people are either moving toward or away from the imposing sanctuary of the mosque. As I arrive in the early morning after my night flight to greet the Prophet and extend my "Salaams" as is the Islamic custom, I find myself moving against a sea of humanity who are now exiting the holy mosque after the early morning prayer and the commencement of the fast. The entire concourse is bathed in light amidst the otherwise still darkened night within the city and this light no doubt shines heavenward as a vertical symbol of human aspiration and a love for God like no other love, while grand colonnades bedecked with gilded lamps that are harmoniously dispersed across the concourse illuminate the marble-floored forecourt like silent sentinels watching over the faithful. In the distance in the eastern sky, the promise of dawn begins to emerge over the horizon behind the rocky Madinah hills just outside the city.

Once inside the imposing stone structure of the mosque, the building gives way to endless archways, pillars, and colonnades that extend disbelievingly in every direction and seemingly for miles. The archways receding into the distant areas of the mosque give a feeling of infinity of space while the rows of carpets, and the rows of worshippers standing upon them, give a feeling of an eternity of time, for the ritual prayer captures for the mind of the devotees a moment of eternity within the present moment. The pillars and colonnades, marble bedecked and with glittering brass frames containing shimmering lamps at their crown give a feeling of open expansiveness and light that is breathtaking to behold. The endless rows of carpets left to right, row upon row, extend all the way from back to front of the mosque, which however cannot be seen from the front entrance way.

The faithful have now settled into their routines following the prayer. It is nearing six in the morning and some people have rendered themselves supine in various postures of repose, no doubt through the sheer exhaustion of having spent most of the night in prayer and night vigils within the sanctuary of the mosque as is the custom during the holy month of Ramadan. It is clear that they are either exhausted or accustomed to sleeping on the floor. Some roll up the carpets to use as a pillow. Others have pulled a length of carpet over themselves like a makeshift blanket. They are all in various attires of Islamic dress including *jalabiyas*, kaftans, *thobes*, and the Pakistani *badla* (suit) that I am wearing, complete with shawls, scarves, skullcaps, Gulf-style headdresses, and turbans. Many of them have wrapped themselves in their long shawls or unraveled turbans and resemble shrouds wrapped for burial, recalling sleep as the "lesser death." The mosque in principle is nothing but open, extended space, with no furniture or marking points, containing only floor carpets for the faithful to sit on and the *mihrab* or sacred niche that indicates the direction of Makkah and provides the setting and enclosure for the imam to lead the prayers.

The mosque is a sacred sanctuary as well as the venue for prayer; in Islam it is the sacred architecture *par excellence* and therefore is often considered a work of art. Upon entering the mosque, the Muslim returns to that harmony, order, and inner peace that is the cornerstone of all spirituality. As such, the building gives way to become a primordial symbol of the sacrality associated with a house of worship. Indeed, in the Islamic worldview, the earth itself is a sacred mosque where men and women of all types and generations express their fullest sense of worship through living and working within the sanctions of the Divine Priority, in keeping with the *hadith* which states that "the earth was placed for me as a mosque and purifier."

I intend to make my way through this magnificent place of worship deep into the inner sanctum of the original mosque, which became the extension of the family quarters of the Prophet highlighting the concept of the mosque as the logical extension of the home. It is here along the original southeasterly section of the mosque that the Prophet lies buried, together with his Companions and first Caliphs Abu Bakr al-Saddiq and Omar bin al-Khattaab. It is customary to visit the tomb of the Prophet and greet him with Salaams upon first entering the sacred enclosure of the mosque. I make my way slowly amid the multitude and savor every moment. The mosque is still jam packed with people of every race and nationality. Old and young intermingle; many are lying supine, others are gathered in groups or sitting in circles sharing their impressions.

People are moving about as I am, deferring to the space of others, careful to step over those who are resting on the floor without a care in the world.

As I move deeper into the mosque, I notice that the upper walls and ceiling are embellished with geometric forms, arabesques, Quranic calligraphy, and mini domes hand-carved from wood in remembrance of the traditional era when the handcrafts represented a form of art. Given the size and dimensions of the mosque, it is quite a trek from front to back. Deep within the well of the enclosure, I come upon an inner open courtyard that gives rise to the heavens. It comes upon you unexpectedly and already the dawn light is bathing the inner courtyard in beams of early morning daylight. I take note, however, of a group of huge, light-colored sunshades that have been cleverly designed to open at the push of a remote controlled button and fan out overhead in perfect symmetry to protect the worshippers from the onslaught of the mid-day desert sun that promises to fill the courtyard open to the elements. I am told that the opening of these gigantic mechanical umbrellas is a sight to behold.

I know I am nearing the tomb of the Prophet through two pieces of evidence, the architectural change of the building which has a smaller, more crowded, and less grandiose aspect and dates back many centuries to the time of the Prophet and the early Caliphate era and by the density of the crowds of people all vying for proximity to the resting place of the Prophet. There is a section of the mosque cordoned off and positioned adjacent to the wall of the Prophet's tomb that is referred to and revered as the *al-riyadh al-jannah*, which roughly translates as a "garden" of the Paradise. The Prophet has referred to this part of the mosque by saying: "What is between my house and my *minbar* is a garden from the gardens of Paradise." It is an area that according to the traditions of the Prophet is actually a part of the Paradise that will rise upward and return to its original home on the Day of Judgment, which in Islam is alternatively referred to as the Day of Accounting and the Day of Religion.

Many years ago when I first became Muslim, I remember quietly entering this section of the mosque and ensconcing myself on the light blue carpet distinguished from the red oriental carpets spread through the rest of the mosque. There was indeed not only a special quality of serenity and calm there that one would come to expect in the paradise, but I felt as I sat cross-legged on the carpet as if I had come home at last and that there was nowhere else I needed to go. An otherworldly fragrance seemed to unexpectedly permeate the air and I remember considering what that scent reminded me of until I had to confess that it reminded me of nothing related to this world, that it had an otherworldly quality that seemed exquisite and heavenly.

As I sat in this "garden of Paradise," my mind took on wings and I began to fly. Call it autosuggestion of the tradition if you like, but a dream quality seemed to emerge like dawn mist over the waters of a lake. The strange, otherworldly scent began to raise my level of consciousness from the mundane to the sublime in some unconscious manner, and I felt I was entering another dimension virtually impossible to describe. Then, without warning, I felt a surge of emotion well up inside me from depths I didn't know existed, an emotive feeling so strong and satiating that I could do nothing but surrender to the power of these sacred emotions and I began to sob a storm of hot tears for all I was worth. At first, I did not know why I was crying, except that I realized that the place, the moment, and the overall ambiance were powerful enough to evoke such an unexpected, powerful reaction. The outburst was not convulsive or hectic; it was sheer weeping without an obvious catalyst. It was not the kind of grief caused by the death of a loved one or the loss of a valued treasure; instead it was an emotive collapse without hill or valley, a release from the rigidity that holds us together in life, vast and inconsolable at first as a child's first confrontation with the unknown. The hot tears came as a soothing balm for the trials and tribulations of my life, the frustrations and the shattered hopes, the dreams, the remorse, the failures and perhaps even the successes. I sobbed for the person I had been and the person I might well become. The sobbing slowly died within me throb by throb until a wave as cool as spring water flowed across the shore of my being and an abiding peace streamed through my mind and body. I had received the gift of tears spoken of in the traditions of Islam in which the soul uses the mind and body to free itself of certain complexes of the psyche and psychological knots of the spirit as a form of liberation from the lower self and as a means of purification.

On this occasion fifteen years later, however, I had to forgo scaling the heights of such an elevated spiritual emotion that I experienced on that former occasion—or so I thought—because the section of the mosque called the *riyadh al-jannah* was simply a teeming cauldron of wide-eyed humanity all in contest for a piece in this "paradise" on earth. I therefore joined the more sober, turgid throng making its way down the aisle that passes in front of the three tombs of the Prophet and his beloved companions Abu Bakr and Omar. It was slow going indeed, and except for the occasional shove or elbow in the ribs, perhaps it was a good thing, because as one approaches the front doors of the tombs, with their silver encrusted plating covered with Quranic verses, the realization suddenly dawns with an expectation brimming beyond belief that one is approaching the very presence of the Prophet. Here is where he lived, where he prayed, and where he died. Here lies the man that Allah chose to receive His revelation and to deliver it as the Holy Quran to future generations of humanity. Through his mind passed the very words of God and from him, they passed out into the world of humanity down to the present time. Muslims spend a lifetime attempting to find ways to express their love of God, but their love of the Prophet comes naturally and spontaneously because he is the vehicle and the path through which the love of God is possible.

As I turn a corner and approach the aisle that passes in front of the enclosed rooms containing the various tombs, the dense but still orderly crowd thickens considerably. People with cupped or extended hands in an attitude of prayer are moving slowly forward at the pace of molasses and everyone proceeds deferentially, concerned for the comfort of their Muslim brothers and not wishing to create an undue stir. Then I am there and I send forth my Salaams to the beloved Prophet, upon him blessings and peace. Neither the hectic throng nor the imposing and unexpected presence of military guards at the doors of the tombs can disturb the surging feeling of humility and awe that begins in the pit of my stomach and rises to the tip of my cognitive consciousness lifting me off my feet and beyond the gravity limits of this world. As I shuffle myself along as only one of a surging crowd of worshippers, I feel lost in the wave of a deep and abiding emotion and I think: We remember the Prophet Muhammad every day in our prayers and we invoke his name and sayings as a matter of course, but now I am here at his tomb, visiting his ancient home and place of earthly investiture. I have presented myself here in person to make my holy Salaams to the memory of his sacred person and his exemplary life. Together with all Muslims, I feel a deep and overwhelming love for the Prophet to the extent that the evocation of his memory creates a feeling of melting in the heart and brings tears to the eyes. It is a powerful, indeed an over-whelming moment. In the presence of greatness, I utter my humble prayer as intercession to God through the Prophet as I remember all those in need within the circle of my life, a dying brother on life support, my diabetic friend, and all those who asked me to inter-cede on their behalf.

A moment whose quality will be remembered for years to come has passed me by, just as the slow-moving sea of humanity I am part of has passed by the tomb enclosure. Before I fully realize what has happened, the crowd has deposited me outside the mosque again like a piece of driftwood thrown ashore by the sea. I gaze dis-tractedly and a little disoriented at the luminous glow on the east-ern horizon as the sun announces its arrival and bathes the eastern face of the mosque with its harsh light without any thought or mercy for the faithful.

* * *

Later in the day, after the mid-afternoon prayer whose timing occurs when "the shadow equals the man," I strolled through the open concourse within the forecourt of the Prophet's mosque to witness the late afternoon activities and the preparations taking place for the breaking of the fast, the eagerly anticipated and com-munal occasion that commences precisely at the call of the *adhan* (the call to prayer) just after the descent of the sun beyond the perimeter of the horizon.

The swarm of pilgrims has dispersed somewhat but the place is still teeming with life and activity. The crowds proclaim endless movement in, out, and around the mosque. The *suk* or marketplace at the edge of the concourse begins to come to life with the dying rays of the relentless desert sun that even on this mid-November afternoon has drawn temperatures up to 100 degrees. I hear the grating sound of metal as the shopkeepers open the metal shutters protecting their shops. I espy a small ledge or shelf by a fountain that marks the end of the grand promenade and the beginning of the concourse leading to the five front portals of the mosque. It looks like an opportune place to observe the late afternoon activity around the main square in front of the mosque. Once ensconced on this narrow, uncomfortable shelf, I observe the goings-on.

The grand promenade leading up to the mosque ends here, circling the fountain and returning whence it came. All traffic is blocked, but I notice that certain cars are allowed through the police barriers, especially vehicles that are delivering food to the mosque. It is clear that people have shifted gear from the sluggish ambiance of the hot mid-afternoon. A great number of local people from Madinah are now in full preparation for the breaking of the fast. Across the great expanse of the forecourt, long mats have been laid down row upon row. The rows seem to number in the thousands. Upon this matting is laid a makeshift plastic tablecloth in lengthwise strips. Trucks pull up, trolleys appear out of nowhere, and great cartons of oranges and bananas, large boxes of yogurt and dates, are unloaded by determined and efficient townspeople. Soon thereafter, I notice great vats of briyani[1] being unloaded from various trucks, this being a tasty favorite dish made of meat and rice pungently seasoned with fried tomatoes, onions, and a multitude of spices. The trucks swing in around the fountain, people jump out of the vehicles, and download these great containers onto trolleys, which are rolled away in the direction of the mosque.

Meanwhile, all manner of humanity are making their way somewhere round about the mosque precinct. I notice a group of women moving with stately grace through the swirling masses, several of

---

1. A culinary favorite of Indians, Pakistanis, and Gulf Arabs by way of association, consisting of highly seasoned rice cooked with meat and its juices.

them bearing cartons of goods on their heads, a small rounded cloth separating box from head as a concession to good sense. They look as if they would not be able to walk without them. I see invalids being pushed around in wheelchairs; a man is driving his own motorized chair, an obese person is being pushed around in a makeshift vehicle large enough to accommodate him; there are even one or two people who pass by being carried in overhead litters. Parents with children, husbands and wives, rowdy street urchins who greet me boldly in Arabic with the words "How are you Papa?"

An elderly man with a sculptured beard who was supporting himself heavily on a hand-carved branch of a tree ploddingly makes his way up to me and sits himself down with a tired smile. Our two different worlds meet briefly on this occasion. He greets me with the traditional Islamic greeting that every Muslim understands: *Salaam aleykum* (peace be upon you), and I return his greeting. We exchange smiles and hand gestures in the spirit of communal friendship, brought together here for these few moments in this time and this place in the name of the one God that binds us together. Then, with a sigh, he takes his leave and with the support of the makeshift cane, makes his slow way back into the mosque. My heart goes with him for a few moments in my mind's eye before he disappears from my world once again in the dense crowd.

It is time to give up my treasured shelf by the fountain and prepare myself for the great event of the breaking of the fast and the evening prayer. Interspersed through the great concourse are pavilions with signs indicating that the *hammam* (bathroom facilities) and parking lie below the upper concourse. A set of escalators leads deep into the cavernous underground where there are endless batteries of parking available that can accommodate up to 5,000 vehicles. I observe the curious surreal quality of the sight of various crowds of people serenely availing themselves of these swift moving stairs. On an intermediary level lie the *hammam* areas accessed through a traditional stairway. I proceed there to take care of the necessary natural functions along with a great many other people and once completed proceed to the ablution stations which are well appointed with a stone seat in front of a faucet well placed to accommodate both hands and feet. A small shelf is there for eye glasses, watches, caps, and other paraphernalia that people have with them. The facilities of the *hammam* are marked by convenience and cleanliness and seem very spacious.

It may seem awkward to even mention these things, but to the harried pilgrim, many of whom have no real place to stay, these conveniences make a huge difference in the ease and comfort in which they perform their spiritual duties. To the outsider the ablution may seem like an inconvenience and a test of ritual fastidiousness, but to the Muslim it is a pleasant interlude in addition to having a practical as well as symbolic meaning. I eventually find a free ablution station and sit myself down to perform the Islamic *wudhu*, a ritual cleansing that must precede every prayer and Quranic recitation. Most people have now come to know that it involves the washing of the hands, nose and mouth three times, the arms to the elbow, the head, ears and feet to the ankle. What they may not realize is that after trudging through the dust and heat of this desert clime, the *wudhu* ritual is unexpectedly refreshing and gives pause to the perspicacity of the divine command to undergo this preliminary ritual to wash away not only the sweat and dust and sometimes sleep of the individual, but also on some symbolic level to cleanse the inner human world of the impurities that have crossed the threshold of the mind and heart during the intervals of forgetfulness between the prayers.

When I emerge from the underground *hammam* quarters, the scene has altered considerably. Across the great concourse and forecourt of the Prophet's mosque, a vast crowd now sits politely row upon row that number in the thousands on matting and carpets that extend from east to west across the forecourt. It is a mythical sight that is incredible to behold. The dying sun casts its late afternoon rays across the court, bathing the open plaza and the multitude of pilgrims sitting there in the foreglow of sunset. The expectant people, who have been fasting since the early morning call to prayer, sit cross-legged in front of their simple break-fast fare patiently awaiting the first call of the *adhan* that marks the end of the fast.

There is still a half hour before the call of the sunset prayer and I am determined to brave the crowds within the mosque and find a place in anticipation of breaking the fast and saying the prayer within the mosque enclosure. I make my way toward the great central portal, weaving discreetly through the vast crowd of people either sitting on the ground or moving up and down the aisles that give access to the doors of the mosque.[1] As I take off my sandals[2] and pass through the mighty doorway, I notice a Quranic verse (15:46) chiseled into the stone lintel over the door: "Enter therein, (Paradise) in peace and security."

I am stunned by an insistent echo as I cross the threshold, "Come, come, come, sit here! Tofaddal!" This is the Arabic greeting of invitation to join a repast. Somebody has taken me by the arm and is escorting me through the maze of legs and feet to what seems like the sole remaining place in the otherwise cavernous and body-packed enclosure, roofed with cascading archways in descending order as far as the eye can see. I feel dazed by the sudden good fortune and glad to have a place inside the mosque where I can break the fast and say the prayer. How this was actually going to happen in the next few minutes however was anyone's guess.

As I settled myself onto the carpet in front of my place setting, I see around me that bee hive activity that has made the breaking of the fast possible in the first place. Local citizens of Madinah have commandeered the mosque to create perhaps the largest breakfast place setting in the world. Row upon row of carpets as far as the eye can see and extending across the broad concourse of the inner mosque from east to west have been equipped with food and drink so that the faithful may break their fast. Lengthy strips of cellophane have been laid length-wise. My own place setting represents a microcosm that mirrors perhaps tens of thousands of place settings now existent throughout the mosque. There is an appetizing ring

---

1. The mosque now has 85 doors composed of fine, rare teak spread across 41 wide gates. Covering the surfaces of the doors are brass arabesque medallions that are gold-coated. Inscribed in the center of each are the words "Muhammad, the Messenger of Allah, peace be upon him."

2. Pilgrims take measures to safeguard their footwear. Many people carry a plastic bag with them, and tuck their sandals under their arm when they enter the mosque. There are shelves scattered throughout the mosque where these sandals can be stored and later secured. Losing one's footwear is a practical problem worth taking note of.

loaf of bread, freshly baked and sprinkled with tasty sesame seeds that radiate an odor of wholesome goodness in the style of true bread that one seldom finds today. There are a number of fruits, including an orange and a banana and a handful of Madinah dates at each place setting. There is a full milk cup of yoghurt accompanied by a small tray of freshly ground *zattar* that Arabs favor and like to sprinkle into the yogurt. Every place setting has a small plastic spoon to stir and eat the yoghurt. It is a magnificent if not unbelievable display of planning and forethought. Of course feeding the faithful during Ramadan is incumbent upon the Muslims and brings with it special blessings that are highly favored. Minutes before the call of the *adhan* and the momentous breaking of the fast, *Zamzam* water[1] is poured and passed along the rows from large thermo containers situated along the aisles of the mosque.

In a final gesture of generosity, I am quickly passed a small plastic cup of Arabic coffee pungent with the spice cardamom, which I set down in front of me amid the array of delicacies that await my consumption. Then I hear the piercing cry of the *adhan*. *Allahu Akbar, Allahu Akbar,* followed by the profession of faith that there is no god but the one God and Muhammad is the Messenger of God, magnified tenfold and cutting through the silence like a piercing cry from beyond the known world. The vast congregation consisting of some astronomical number beyond reckoning or comprehension, but certainly approaching perhaps a million Muslims, paused for a brief second as if the loud report of a bullet had unexpectedly sounded, then everyone to the individual invoked the name of God and broke his fast with water and fresh dates in the traditional manner of the Prophet some fourteen hundred years ago.

I break my fast on a date and proceed with my makeshift repast, washing it down with a shot of Arabic coffee and refreshing gulps of the beloved Zamzam water whose purity and crystalline taste cannot be matched from any other well in the world. The thought crosses my mind that saying the prayer amidst this wreckage of food

1. From the Zamzam well at the Grand Mosque in Makkah. The Zamzam water is transported daily to the mosque in special tanker trucks from Makkah, 430 kilometers away.

and drink, orange rinds and plastic cups, could be a problem. I had not accounted, however, for the planning and ingenuity of those responsible for this brief repast. Within minutes, our host for this little section of the mosque and his aids descend upon the rows depositing the leftover bread, dates, and fruit into great plastic bags reserved for the task. Once done, the entire assemblage of waste is carefully gathered up within the folds of the plastic floor cloth, which summarily disappears down the row and out of sight of the worshippers. The entire mosque had been restored to an ordered cleanliness in less than the minute it took me to dislodge my aging bones from the floor and stand together with the other worshippers in well defined rows to offer our sunset prayer.

If the world and all that it contains is woven from the stuff of which shadows are made, and if man is a transient and exile disconnected from his true self—a prodigal in search of his ancestral hearth—then this journey to the holy places that begins sitting cross-legged on a carpet with a million other aspirants and breakfasting together on water and dates becomes transformed into the true journey to that final abode of which the revelation speaks. In partaking of a revealed tradition, one gains entry into a world of vision and light; it is a reality woven of the stuff of which not shadows but threads of light are made. It makes demands on us as in the discipline of the Ramadan fast, but in compensation, its vision and light becomes a part of one's inner world and leads a person beyond the borders of his or her natural shadow self.

I look around at the sea of humanity surrounding me and think to myself: there is power here. The other earthly duties of Islam recall certain qualities and principles unique to each particular duty. The basic testament of faith recalls the serenity that accompanies the knowledge of God. Prayer remembers communication with the Divinity as well as a means of expressing one's innermost thoughts and aspirations. Charity or *zakat* emphasizes the need to remember the poor and needy, while the Hajj or pilgrimage recreates in a formal ritual the journey of a lifetime. The bodily fast, however, in which the physical senses are tamed through the sheer force of a person's will, contains a subtle message of latent potential power that is impossible to ignore. It is a raw and natural power whose force emerges out of its own defining quality. It is the defining power of wind over water, of water against stone, of fire against wood. It is the creative power of the bud to become the bloom or the transformative power of the caterpillar to become the butterfly, a power whose force is to absorb and potentialize everything that runs to meet it and fall under its sway. It is the power of the word to stir the mind, of the voice to move the emotions, of the feathers of a wing to lift the bird. What, then, of the potential power behind the collective whole to bring themselves together and unite under a single unifying truth with a presence of mind and a determination of spirit, with a strength not only to climb but to move mountains?

As I glance across the carpet at the people around me, words simply fail. There is an aura of silence that underscores the general hubbub produced by such a vast congregation that speaks more than words can possibly convey. Facial expressions and body language, friendly eyes and broad open smiles, a nod of the head, a gesture of offering, these become the modes of expression that cut across all language barriers, culture, race, or nationality. I feel an outpouring of warmth and an emotive melting of the heart, a brotherliness and camaraderie that is impossible to explain or describe. A brief vision crosses my mind of New York and Paris and Kuala Lumpur and Sydney, for I am a well-traveled person and familiar with most of the major cities of the world. I have seen New York's Statue of Liberty and Paris' Eiffel Tower. I have climbed the Petronas Towers in Kuala Lumpur and listened to the arias of the Sydney Opera House echo across the Sydney harbor. Nothing, however, can match this staggering spectacle for its sheer magnitude, for the raw projection of a mass of humanity as a single spirit, and the sense of sacred purposefulness that emanates through the broad expanse of the mosque.

Having finished the sunset prayer in congregation with the fellow worshippers, I take my leave of the Prophet's mosque and proceed back out into the grand concourse together with the other streams of humanity who are now set on going about their business at hand. As I disappear back into the vast throng from whence I came, I notice once again the pale and ponderous moon climbing back over the horizon; a full moon, no less, for this is the mid-point of Ramadan, wearily raising its saffron face beyond the broad porch of the horizon to set up vigil once again over the faithful. It is a breezy mid-November evening, one day in the *ayam Allah* (the days of Allah), in the holy month of Ramadan 1424 AH[1] (AD 2003), in Madinah al-Munawwarah, the City of Light

1. The Muslims begin their lunar calendar from the year of the Hegira, when the Prophet Muhammad fled Makkah for Madinah seeking refuge from members of the Quraish Tribe who were his avowed persecutor and enemy.

10

RAMADAN EVENINGS
IN MAKKAH

And when We made the House a pilgrimage for men and a (place of) security, and appoint for yourselves a place of prayer on the station of Abraham. And We enjoined Abraham and Ishmael saying: Purify My House for those who visit (it) and those who abide (in it) for devotion and those who bow down (and) those who prostrate themselves. (2:125)

On a mid-November morning during the holy month of Ramadan in the year of the Hegira 1424 (2003), I made the final leg of my *Umrah* (lesser pilgrimage) journey overland through the black hills of Northern Saudi Arabia. By the time I arrived in Makkah that afternoon, a terrorist bomb had blasted its way through a residential area of Riyadh, destroying an apartment block housing expatriate Arab nationals and killing scores of people including many women and children. Under normal circumstances, if such a concept as normality can be invoked within this context of random terrorism, it is difficult to take in and fully appreciate the enormity of such an atrocity. Under the circumstances of that afternoon as I entered what the Quran refers to as the city of peace and security (3:96) in addition to being the "mother of all cities", it was difficult to reconcile the tragic slaughter and random violence in Riyadh and the prayers and aspirations of those circumambulating the Kaaba, the central focus of the Grand Mosque in Makkah.

In Islam, there are powerful indications concerning what are called in the Islamic Traditions (*Hadith*) the "signs of the hour" (*alamat as-sa'a*), meaning signs of the end of the world as we know it. Surely the image of suicide killers invoking scriptural justifications of a religion for their own diabolic purposes and acting in the name of God by boldly murdering innocent victims for some kind of political or social agenda has got to be a sign of the hour and a warning that the end of a world order as we know it is near, if not already at hand? Interestingly, one of the signs of the very end will be a cessation of the circumambulation around the sacred house in the sanctuary known in Arabic as the *Haram*. One of the *Hadith* forewarns, "Know that the world has come to an end when no one will circumambulate the holy Kaaba."

When my companions and I climbed onto the bus early that Saturday morning to make our way from Madinah to Makkah, a journey that the Prophet himself made with his companions, upon them blessings and peace, when they made their own first pilgrimage toward the end of his life, we had no idea of the devastation that had taken place many miles away in the capital of Saudi Arabia. Most of us had already had a foretaste of trouble, however, in a recent news item in which a shootout had taken place in Makkah where a number of terrorists were killed by the Saudi militia and a large cache of weapons had been discovered. In Makkah no less, the beloved "mother of all cities" of the Muslims and the city referred to as *al-Mukarramah*, "the Generous," security was very tight and 5,000 military personnel had been sent to further protect the pilgrims from any further outrage. It is a far different world now than the world I knew many years ago when I visited the holy places of Islam and first laid virgin eyes on the Grand Mosque and the central issue of the Kaaba. According to a verse of the Quran, "Allah hath appointed the Kaaba, the Sacred House, as a standard for mankind" (5:97).

Just as one greets the Prophet and sends forth one's Salaams as the first gesture of respect on a visit to *al-Masjid al-Nabawi* in Madinah, so also I return to the tomb of the Prophet on the morning of my departure for Makkah, to send forth once again my sincere Salaams together with the final prayers and intercessions on behalf of my close friends and loved ones. It is a melancholy leave-taking indeed. Once again, I make my way through the densely packed mosque after the early morning *fajr* prayer, deep into the inner sanctum of the original mosque that was once the actual living quarters of the Prophet. The visit here in this mosque and at the tomb of the beloved Messenger of Allah has become such a personal encounter that it is difficult to bid farewell without feeling some deep inner melancholy, as if leaving behind a valued treasure or taking leave of someone you know you will never see again, even though Muslims try to carry an awareness of the Prophet in their hearts by actively following his example in their own lives. I feel close to him here as never before and have experienced on this visit a deep inner connection that somehow transcends the normal course of life. It is a nearness and proximity to the Messenger who is the "friend" of God that I hope to take with me and preserve as a treasured remembrance after I leave.

Typically, the start of any journey always involves some kind of separation and loss intermingled with the sweet anticipation of departure and journeying, and this leave-taking is no exception. Back in the hotel, my companions and I don the traditional garment (*ihram*) worm by the pilgrims to Makkah either in the *Hajj* season or at any other time of year when the "lesser pilgrimage" (*Umrah*) is made. The distance between Madinah and Makkah is roughly 430 kilometers, a mere 260 miles by Western standards, but it is an overland journey through rough and harsh terrain. The makeshift plan of our guides organizing the bus trip calls for an early morning departure in order to arrive in Makkah in due time to fulfill the pilgrimage duties before the breaking of the fast and the sunset prayer.

The sense of timing, the pace and the rhythm in the Arab world, however, does not abide by the fixed and firm rigidity of time, place, and movement that one finds in the Western world. Flexibility is the name of the day among Arabs and one learns to flow with the contingencies of the moment and place. As for myself, I had donned the *ihram* garment, a seamless two piece cloth that was towel-like in texture, a kind of makeshift shawl for the upper torso that is thrown over the shoulders, and a kind of wrap-around sarong for the lower torso. Nothing else can or may be worn as one enters the sacred precinct in the pure condition of birth, having of course made the ritual ablution and announced his or her intentions beforehand. For reasons of safety and practicality, a special belt may be worn with secret pockets for money and identity cards that firmly secures the lower portion of the garment against untoward accidents. They say that clothes make the man, but as I sat in the front lobby of the Sheraton Hotel in Madinah early that morning awaiting the other pilgrims to meet the appointed hour of departure, bundled together in my shaggy cloth towels, I felt altogether a man of serenity and repose filling these traditional garments. In some strange sense, it seemed as if the garments themselves, steeped in tradition and symbolic of the neutrality of any kind of fashion, were wearing the man.

The modern overland coach departed around 9:00 AM, several hours after the early morning appointment scheduled for 6:00 AM, but who could possibly care about establishing a fixity in the fluid nature of time? We were together and on our way, sacred wanderers on an ancient pilgrimage taking us back in time to the house that Allah built, not fourteen centuries ago during the time of the Prophet, but several millennia back during the time of Abraham. According to the Quran (2:125), the Kaaba is the house that Abraham himself built, although apocryphal traditions suggest that Adam was the original architect of this "first sanctuary" (3:96) of worship. Here in the heart of a craggy desert wasteland lies the symbolic nucleus of the Islamic religion and the very direction and focal point of all prayer. The sense of direction and place plays an important role in the liturgy of Islam as well as in the human dynamic of its spirituality. The Messenger is the prototype exile as well as the model Muslim and this gives added intensity to the concept that man himself is an exile from his true abode and a transient in search of a final destination. The *mihrab* or sacred niche of every mosque worldwide points in the direction of the Kaaba in the Grand Mosque in Makkah. All prayer makes a symbolic horizontal journey across the globe to the very center of the earth whence the universal aspiration and worship of the Muslims makes an abrupt vertical ascent heavenward, reaching beyond the stars and galaxies toward the celestial horizon of the known universe.

We had hardly left the ragged edges of the city behind and not yet entered the famous hills surrounding Madinah when we made our first stop at the mosque that is traditionally considered the traditional changing ground into the pilgrim's *ihram* cloth. These traditions go back to the time of the Prophet who put on his *ihram* at this stage of the journey. The group I was with dispersed and people made their own way to the mosque to make the ritual of two prostrations in anticipation of the journey ahead. Once this was accomplished, the bus began to make its way into the black hills of Northern Arabia in earnest. It is a stark landscape indeed, uninviting, harsh, and blindingly bright. There is something hypnotic and mesmerizing about the austere setting of the desert. Its arid, uncompromising starkness is set in sharp contrast to the pristine purity and clarity of vision that the bleak landscape affords in compensation. One cannot ignore the sublime signposts and symbols of nature along the way: the infernal bright sun halfway up the heavens already—even the winter sun in the desert makes no compromises and sends its relentless rays of light down onto the open dusty plain without mercy; a dying full moon that was losing its pale early morning edge; the meta-symbolic image of the horizon itself, encircling everything within the envelope of a bi-polar universe of Heaven and earth and containing the message of an inscrutable mystery in what lies "beyond". Across the distinctive and seemingly endless desert landscape, the horizon traces a thin line between Heaven and Earth and marks the defining edge of the known world; beyond lies the mystique of a deep, dark secret.

We have made our intentions to perform the lesser pilgrimage, flown to Saudi Arabia, visited the Prophet's Mosque in Madinah, and journeyed across the heartland of Arabia in remembrance of the journey of the Prophet 1,400 years ago, but nothing truly prepares the mind and heart for the overwhelming sight of the Grand Mosque in Makkah on physical, emotional, and spiritual levels of experience. Makkah itself is an ancient, craggy landscape of jagged, rocky, and uncompromising hills. The road leading into the city feels like a roller coaster ride and the view of cascading hills, houses, and shops precariously lodged along the cliffs is unexpected and disorienting. Then suddenly, the bus crests the top of a craggy knoll and the vision of the gray, white, and pink marbled edifice comes into view like a mirage from some heavenly realm. It is difficult to take in the colossal edifice all at once: its multiple minarets soaring toward the heavens, the massive three-storied structure that has been renovated and enlarged over recent decades in a monumental effort by the Saudi government to accommodate hundreds of millions of pilgrims every year, its incredible bulk wedged uncomfortably within the crowded central valley of Makkah. Surely there is no other physical edifice now existing on earth that can measure up to and compete with this incredible feat of architecture and the symbolic meaning it intends to serve?

A higher reality predominates over the physical reality of the Grand Mosque. Herein lies the very center and heart of the Islamic cosmos. This simple cube of masonry,[1] a form of proto-art that traces its roots through Abraham back to the primordial era of Adam, is the central axis where Heaven meets earth and where the Divine meets the human. Across the globe, the Islamic rites and spiritual practices, in every mosque and in the hearts of every devout Muslim, form a directional pattern that leads directly to the Kaaba in Makkah, which is the earthly reflection of a celestial shrine, which is also reflected within the heart of man. The inherent symbolism of the Kaaba as center of the human being and vertical axis beyond the earthly dimension, creates a feeling of sacred space and sacred time, a coming into the Presence through the sacralization of space. The circumambulation of the Sacred House as a physical reality raises the consciousness of a person to a rarefied spiritual universe as the Kaaba of the human heart meets the central Kaaba of the Divine Reality.

The many-sided circular structure of the Grand Mosque itself gives way to an open-air concourse that is touched by heaven and encircled by the angels, at least so it seems but Allah knows best. The symbolism of the building bespeaks of centrality and the primordial point. At the very center of this sublime nexus rests the Kaaba, while ecstatic pilgrims circumambulate the ancient house like stars circumambulating around the nexus of a galaxy in magis-

---

1. The Kaaba is a small square building made of stones, about 60 feet long, 60 feet wide and 60 feet high. The four corners roughly face the four directions of the compass. The building, made from gray-blue stones from the nearby hills of Makkah, is covered with the Kiswa, a black brocade cloth that has the Islamic testament of faith (shahadah) woven into its fabric and embossed gold-lettered calligraphy as adornment.

terial procession.[1] The house, a simple cube of masonry that is actually a form of proto-art because of its spiritual implications, is the sacred symbolic structure here on the earth that mirrors the empyrean above, with devout pilgrims forever swirling in a steady stream of praise to the one God. To enter this circumambulating vortex of humanity is like no other earthly experience imaginable.

Upon arrival in Makkah, we exit the comfort of the bus and are brusquely thrust into a horde of pilgrims milling outside the mosque. Unexpectedly, we hear the call of the *adhan* pierce through the dull murmur of the crowd like a cosmic cry from heaven signifying the mid-afternoon prayer as we make our way into the mosque through the *Bab al-Salaam*, the portal through which the Prophet traditionally entered the sacred sanctuary. I write "we," not as a literary convention or reference to the group I was with, but as a gesture of conciliation to my faithful companion, Amr, an Egyptian Lab Technician and colleague who had adopted me as his trusted friend on the pilgrimage. Many years living in the Arab world has taught me the wisdom of never doing anything alone, unlike the tendency in the Western world where people maintain a fierce sense of individuality and tend to follow an independent line of action on their own if at all possible. I have learned from Arabs the joys of companionship. They make an emotional commitment once they accept you as one of their own, and I have learned to give of myself in return, something which does not come naturally to me, possibly as a result of my upbringing in the West with its emphasis on independence and self-reliance. While I was the senior in age and rank—and according to the hyperbolic Amr a person who would gain immediate access to the Paradise on the Day of Judgment due to my status as "Muslim convert"—I still deferred to his judgment and common sense, not to mention the kind generosity of self and protective brotherliness that he freely extended to me. I don't think he realized just how reliant a person I really was in this situation, a stranger in a

1. A point of interest: the circumambulation is in an anti-clockwise direction. This is in keeping with a similar pattern found in nature, including the electrons around the nucleus, the movement of the earth around the sun, and the movement of the stars around the central core of the galaxy.

strange land, and dependent on his good will and friendship to help me through the challenging rituals before us.

As we entered the mosque and made our way toward the magnetic draw of the rhythmic mass of people circumambulating the Kaaba, I was becoming increasingly alarmed. The crowds were overwhelming and I was beginning to wonder, as I wrestled with my unfamiliar and ill-fitting garments, whether we would be able to find a place, indeed some special place in the shadow of the Kaaba, where we could say the afternoon prayer with serenity before performing the *Umrah*. Various aisles were still open to people moving in and around the sanctuary and Amr suggested that we position ourselves right there in the aisle in view of the Kaaba when in a matter of minutes all motion would stop and the prayer would commence. In fact, the mosque was jam-packed with not a free space to be found. The heat even in November can be oppressive and I thought of those in the open courtyard under the intensity of the late afternoon desert sun. There in the shade, as I made my prostrations during the prayer (*salat al-asr*), I was sweating profusely and my heart began to beat erratically. I had been fasting since predawn with no food or water and felt a little dehydrated, dizzy, and concerned about my ability to fulfill the requirements of the rites; but the motions of the ritual prayer and the intensity of the situation, together with the presence of my friend nearby, guided me through the difficulties of the moment.

Amr's broad, respectful, village-boy smile greeted me upon the completion of the prayer. We were now to perform the sacred rituals of the "lesser pilgrimage" that date back to the time of the Prophet fourteen hundred years ago. It is interesting to note that the rituals themselves transcend the time of the Islamic Messenger and refer in their essence and symbolism to the Abrahamic era, shifting the focus of the rites beyond the inception of the religion of Islam proper to a more universal setting and significance with the patriarch Abraham as the symbolic father of the prophets.[1] Essentially

---

1. Indeed, it is a sad legacy that the Jews and the Muslims, who trace their Semitic line back to the great patriarch Abraham through his two sons Ishmael and Isaac and whose symbolic value still conveys a profound meaning to the world's population, are such bitter enemies in today's world.

there are three main duties to be performed according to the dictates of the lesser pilgrimage and these include the circumambulation seven times around the Kaaba in an anti-clockwise direction with the Kaaba on the left, followed by prayer at the Station (*maqam*) of Abraham,[1] and finally the *Saiy* which consists in running seven times between the hills of Safa and Marwa. We hoped to negotiate our way through these rituals together with the vast congregation of *Umrah* pilgrims and complete the *Umrah* before the sunset prayer and breaking of the fast.

With affection and open eagerness, Amr took my arm and led me through the confusion of the crowd toward the swirling orbit of people moving about the Kaaba in a steady stream of worship and spiritual rapture. "We need to get as close to the Kaaba as possible," he whispered urgently in my ear. No sacramental dictate required us to get as close as possible to the Kaaba, yet custom and tradition suggested proximity to the structure if possible. I also knew that Amr harbored a secret desire to kiss the black stone, said to be a meteorite fallen from Heaven that is lodged in a silver encasement in the east corner of the cubic structure which marks the place of commencement of the *tawaf* or circumambulation.

No Muslim who has made *Hajj* or *Umrah* will deny that the circumambulation is a physical experience that takes stamina and will power. When you view the scene from the roof of the Grand Mosque or witness the event through TV cameras hoisted on high, it gives every appearance of being a rhythmic stream of humanity flowing in sublime unison around the central axis of the world. However, the reality of being amid this throbbing, densely packed mob is tumultuous and unpredictable and yet all the while nobody seems to care about the tumult around them or complain about the crush of people. Upon entering the throng, you lose your sense of personal identity and personal space and become one with the teeming horde moving about the symbolic vision of the ancient

---

1. Inside the Station of Abraham is kept a stone bearing the prints of two human feet. The Prophet Abraham is said to have stood on this stone when building the Kaaba and the marks of his feet are miraculously preserved.

edifice and focusing all your hopes and aspirations on the reality of the Divine Being in a state of ecstatic rapture.

Entering the ritual practice of circumambulation is like entering into the "once upon a time" of myths and folktales, *in illo tempore*. The pilgrim enters into sacred time that is actually the "real" time of the "vertical" or eternal dimension, as opposed to the horizontal, linear, and progressive time that we experience here on earth as a relentless, forward-moving machine. I fell immediate victim to this sublime transcendent state of mind as if by some remote control of heaven and felt at one with the rotating vortex of the crowd. I no longer seemed to matter as an individual entity for I had been swept away in this "first sanctuary" to a primordial time of perfection and heightened consciousness when the truth is there to behold, there to witness, and there to be known as nothing else can be known. As I circumambulate the sacred Kaaba, I make my entreaties, I send my greetings, I pray to Allah and worship the Divinity. Soon enough, beyond all reckoning of time, I am truly swept away by a flood of emotion and higher sentiment as I become one with the wave of worshippers. Indeed, I feel myself giving up and surrendering to this moment of eternity in time and this central place that makes possible the ascent of man beyond the horizon of the rational mind and beyond the dictates of the lower self.

Amr has managed to seize a seven beaded cord resting on the wall by the Station of Ishmael along one side of the Kaaba with which to keep track of the seven circumambulations that are required of the *tawaf* ritual, although how he has managed this feat is anyone's guess as he grins sheepishly at me with the beaded cord. Our arms are locked together for security as we make our way round and round within the circumference of the sacred precinct. I am happy to have this fellow with me as we make the circumambulation in communion with the Spirit of God that overshadows the environment. It feels as though I have known him for a thousand years.

Perhaps it is the writer and natural-born observer in my nature, but I unconsciously take the time to notice the behavior and movement of the people around me. Everyone seems solicitous of the other's safety and comfort, although admittedly the movement around the Kaaba is far from harmonious at ground zero. It takes effort just to keep standing and one is literally carried forward on tiptoes by the mob pressing in on every side. Still, no one exaggerates the hectic quality of the procession and everyone seems to be trying to defer to the person nearby. Of course, there is every size, shape, and color of person to be imagined in this vast horde of humanity. I see the elderly and the young, husbands and wives, fathers, sons, and daughters. There are groups of women clinging together for safely and surprisingly strong as they race past me. There are groups of men, from Iran, from Ethiopia, from Malaysia, from China, arms linked together in a chain for support. People of all races and nationalities are praying aloud, uttering in Arabic the Quranic epithets and litanies that are appropriately noted for the occasion, entreaties to Allah for health, for blessing, for provision, for the *hasanat* or good things of this and the next world. The elderly and the crippled are being carried in litters overhead on the hands of husky black Africans; others are being moved along in wheelchairs by family members or friends. In one shocking instance, I felt a rustle at my feet and upon looking down toward the marble floor of the enclosure, I see to my horror amid the disorder of moving legs a crippled woman crawling along in circumambulation on all fours with a look of determination and joy on her face.

I cling to my Egyptian friend Amr for stamina and support, approaching an age when I can call myself elderly and fearful of falling down and being overrun by this juggernaut of moving humanity. On the sixth round, a way close to the wall of the house suddenly opens, seemingly miraculously, for both Amr and I noticed that the agitated waters of humanity we were among have unexpectedly opened a path to give free passage to the vicinity of the *Hajar al-Aswad* or the beloved black stone, known as a sacred meteorite fallen down from Heaven during the primordial era. I think to myself that Amr and I are of one accord.

Under normal circumstances, it is well-nigh impossible to get anywhere near this sacred artifact for the crowds that are clambering to touch and kiss the holy object. Amr suddenly sees the opportunity and makes his move, veering toward the black stone and dragging me alongside with him. We are immediately engulfed once again by the teeming throng of people surrounding the stone and only footsteps away from touching the sacred object. I look up and see Amr standing by the silver frame of the black stone grinning broadly with satisfaction. I knew that he has achieved his goal and has touched the stone. I try to lean forward and extend my arm as far as possible in the direction of the blessed object, but I simply cannot move another inch forward. I am about to give up the effort and blend back into the wave when I feel a hand seize my wrist and move it down into the framed enclosure wherein resides the *Hajar al-Aswad*. It is the swift movement of Amr's powerful grip that has made this possible. For a second, I feel the cool, electric presence of the stone run up through my arm and down into my soul and I smell the unearthly fragrance of the Paradise evoking a memory of some primal purity and perfection amid the chaos of the moment. Then, we are both summarily thrown beyond the area of the building containing the black stone by the crowd surging forward around the corner, whence we raise our right hands to greet the Divinity one last time before commencing the final *tawaf* around the Kaaba.

Once this sacred ritual is completed, we ease our way out from the surging mass and make our way over to the Station of Abraham where we find a small area to make the traditional two prostrations. After that, the traditions allude to the ritual of drinking and refreshing oneself with the Zamzam water, spring water that dates back to the time of Abraham. According to the Islamic traditions, Hajar, one of the wives of Abraham, was searching within the area of the Kaaba for water for her son Ishmael. In her desperation, she ran seven times between the two hills of Safa and Marwa[1] adjacent to the precinct of the Kaaba. She eventually discovered the waters of Zamzam flowing from under a rock and began to drink. In commemoration of this hardship, the pilgrims run seven times between the hills of Safa and Marwa[2] and refresh themselves with the

---

1. The distance between the two hills is about 500 yards.
2. "Behold! Safa and Marwa are among the symbols of Allah. So if those who visit the House in the season or at other times should compass them round, it is no sin in them. And if any one obeyeth his own impulse to good, be sure that Allah is He Who recognizeth and knoweth" (2:158).

Zamzam waters. Indeed, after the ordeal of the *tawaf*, which we undertook in the afternoon under the blazing glare of the relentless desert sun,[1] the waters of Zamzam were unbelievably refreshing—not to drink of course because we were still fasting, but to pour over our heads and faces.

The final ritual calls for the pilgrims to run seven times between the Makkah hills of Safa and Marwa in remembrance of the ordeal of Hajar and the infant Ishmael. To that end, the Saudi government has constructed an enclosure between the two hills in the form of a two-storied hallway adjacent to the Grand Mosque proper. It is a magnificent setting of a two-way hallway enclosure with two tracks running down the middle to accommodate wheelchairs and litters. As Amr and I undertake this final ritual of the lesser pilgrimage, we enter once again the vast crowd of pilgrims similarly recommemorating the ordeal of Hajar and her son. It is difficult to recreate within this magisterial setting adjacent to the Kaaba the dry, dusty terrain amid two now famous hills in which the wife of the patriarch experienced her desperation, although anyone who has lived in Saudi Arabia knows just how hot it can get in that country. Even now, several millennia later, it is not an easy task even in this sublime setting. After running a number of times through the concourse of these two hills, both Amr and I are feeling hot and tired and thirsty. Perhaps it was appropriate that we were still fasting and had been fasting from food and drink since before dawn because it added to the rigor and poignancy of the moment. We finally completed the tiring trek back and forth seven times in keeping with the tradition which considers seven a sacred number in the science of numerology associated with the Islamic traditions.

The final act of the pilgrimage upon completion of the *Saiy* is the cutting of the hair. The Prophet advised either shaving the head or cutting a part of the hair and to that end there are multiple barbershops ready with straight-edged razors to service the pilgrim community. Both Amr and I decide to trim each other's hair, however, for the sake of convenience. We have both had our heads shaved on

---

1. Most notably, the marble floor of the precinct contains special cooling metals to prevent the soles of the feet from being scorched by the intense heat of the sun.

the former occasion of the greater *Hajj* a number of years ago. Hot, tired, and feeling emotionally drained after the effort of the sacred rites, which have taken us nearly two hours, we obligingly snip off various locks of hair from each side of the head including the crown. We then depart the mosque enclosure in silence and climb the stairs leading up the side of the mountain encroaching upon the back side of the Grand Mosque to make our way to a nearby hotel.

* * *

Upon completion of the lesser pilgrimage, the rest of the visit seemed to flow in the wake of its afterglow. Exhausted but exhilarated though we were, Amr and I still had a busy schedule ahead of us. We had only a few minutes until the call of the *adhan* for the sunset prayer (*salat al-maghreb*) and the breaking of the fast and we needed to check into the hotel, change out of the pilgrim cloth (*ihram*), wash and present ourselves at the Grand Mosque once again. Later that evening, after the fifth and final prayer—which occurs at the point of total darkness after the sunset—there occurs the traditional Ramadan prayers called *al-tarawiyah*. At best, many non-Muslims think that the holy month of Ramadan calls for the Muslims to fast from dawn to dusk. What they may not realize is that in addition to the fast, the month involves added austerities including special prayers and night vigils that have been enjoined by the Prophet. The *al-tarawiyah* prayers call for twenty *rakaa'* or prostrations during which a full *juz* or part of the Quran is recited.[1] During the last ten days of Ramadan, additional night vigils take place in the early morning hours before dawn, which are witnessed by the angels.[2]

1. There are 30 *juz* in the Quran. Each of them is of equal length comprising 20 pages of text in a standard publication. Reciting a *juz* each night during the *al-tarawiyah* ensures that the entire Quran will be recited by the faithful during Ramadan. In addition, many Muslims read a part of the Quran per day on their own as part of their spiritual efforts and to earn the blessings that are associated with Quran recitation during the holy month of Ramadan.

2. The Night of Power (*al-Laylat al-Qadr*) takes place on one of the nights during the last ten days of Ramadan. It is a night, according to the Quran, that is "better

After a hurried breaking of the fast and a few moments to refresh in the hotel, we made our way back into the Grand Mosque for the night prayers. Lest the reader need reminding, movement in and out of the mosque at any time requires negotiation through vast crowds of people. At the prayer times, it is advised to be well ensconced somewhere within the inside enclosure and inner concourse of the mosque in front of the Kaaba, otherwise it is just about impossible to get inside the mosque itself. Amr and I decide to attend the evening prayers on the roof of the mosque. I have been told that at any one time, the mosque itself can hold over a million people by rough estimates. The mosque enclosure includes the ground floor area of building and open courtyard within, a second floor, and a roof with a capacity for hundreds of thousands of worshippers.

We make our way along the roof of the hallways that connect the hills of Safa and Marwa where we earlier had performed one of the rites of the pilgrimage. As we move forward along the roof through a narrow passageway together with a steady stream of pilgrims with the same intentions that we have, I notice row upon row of people already positioned on carpets laid down on the roof for purposes of the prayer. Amr and I hope to reach a point on the roof close to the open concourse with the vision of the Kaaba in front of us as we recite our prayers. Alas, we find a place close to the edge of the roof where we can say these special prayers—which take nearly two hours—in comfort, but we do not have a direct view of the Kaaba. Instead, from this vantage point on the roof, we have a panoramic view of the entire Grand Mosque, including the rest of the roof, the second and ground floor, and the open plaza in the middle of this ensemble containing the Kaaba and the orbiting mass of humanity that continues day and night with its circumambulation. There must have been a million or more worshippers gathered together at that moment to offer their *tarawiyah* prayers.

than a thousand months" when the angels and the Spirit of God descend to earth with Allah's permission. The Prophet was not specific about when precisely the blessed night occurs, alluding in his sayings (*hadith*) to an odd numbered day and hinting at possibly the twenty-seventh night of Ramadan. Consequently, the last ten days of Ramadan are traditionally held in reserve for supererogatory prayers and spiritual disciplines.

The imam of the Grand Mosque leads the prayer and recites the appropriate Quranic verses. At the Quranic injunctions that occur during the movement of bowing and prostration, there is the voice of the imam followed by the voice of a human echo, in keeping with an early tradition before the era of microphones that had a second voice mid-way in the mosque echo the calls of the imam in distant areas of the mosque where the imam could not be heard.

We took our places, heard the call to prayer, and began the ceremony of prayer as the evening passed into night. During this night vigil time itself fades away, together with the individual, just as day eventually fades away into night. You stand, you bow, you prostrate yourself with forehead touching the ground—considered in Islam the position of most profound humility and the moment when a person is closest to Allah—and you no longer understand yourself as you know yourself to be in normal times. As time goes on, there is a stripping away of all the cares of the world, the mind becomes free of the psychological complexes and knots that unceasingly worry it during the course of the day, and the soul takes on the wings of the dove as it soars above the cares of the self and the world. A feeling of attachment develops that springs from the deep well of desire in which everything matters because it reminds you of God, followed by a profound feeling of detachment that enters the higher consciousness of mind like a wind moving through fields of wheat, a detachment in which nothing matters except God.

I look out onto the world momentarily during this spiritual reverie to witness the scene around me. The rugged Makkan hills are clearly visible all around the mosque enclosure. Various hotels and palaces loom from the distance over the sanctuary. I see the bowed heads of a million strong people in front of, in back, indeed all around me, who have come together as one community with one aspiration and one goal. The voice of the imam cuts through the layers of the night like the sound of a reverberating bell, cold and clear and full of latent power. It rocks the surrounding area in a wave of amplification that reverberates outward into the night sky aglitter with distant stars. The imam intones the sacred words of the Quran, what the Muslims believe to be the actual Words of Allah, throughout the mosque enclosure, and their amplification moves through the congregation standing in rows with hands folded and heads bowed, through the rooftops of the city and out into the surrounding hills of this "mother" of cities. An intense, electrifying light floods the mosque and open concourse of the interior. As I look toward this primordial point which houses the Kaaba from my vantage point on the roof, it seems as though an unearthly illumination moves vertically heavenward from this center of the earth, a monumental beacon of light reaching to touch the heavens as a symbolic visual representation of the aspirations of the worshippers.

Through sound and light, there seems to be a visionary outpouring toward the heavens that is matched perhaps only by the psychic and spiritual outpouring of the minds and hearts of the worshippers. This sound and light experience electrifies the worshippers—perhaps I should speak for myself alone—with a feeling of devotional rapture, heightened by the onslaught of the words of revelation that not only echo through the night sky but that reverberate their tonal vibrations down into the very texture and fabric of the human body. Many people may not realize the importance that Quranic recitation has during the prayer ritual. The essence of the prayer is praise and worship of the Divinity and the essence of the worship is the recitation of the sacred sound of the Quran because of its ability to transport the listener through the psalmody of the chanter into another dimension of reality altogether.

The chanted Quran is the prototype of all sacred sound. It is a kind of divine music that overlays a person's soul with a knowledge of origins and provides the guidance that will lead him in the right direction on his way of return to God. "The first words of the Sacred Text revealed by Gabriel surrounded the Prophet like an ocean of sound as the archangel himself filled the whole of the sky. The sound of the Quran penetrates the Muslim's body and soul even before it appeals to his mind. The sacred quality of the psalmody of the Quran can cause spiritual rapture even in a person who knows no Arabic."[1] The Quran contains a majesty, a harmony, and a rhythm that pours out from the sound of the sacred text and cannot

1. S. H. Nasr (ed.), *Islamic Spirituality*, p 4.

be translated without seriously altering the nature of the profound sacredness that emanates from the letters and sounds. There is a majestic projection of sound that is primordial, central, and eternal; primordial in that the sound and meaning resorts back to its original source in the Divine Mind; central because it brings man immediately back from the periphery of his earthly existence to the very center of his being; eternal because it lifts a person out of earthly and horizontal time to the vertical dimension of the eternal now, the sacred present, that neutralizes and ultimately transcends the temporal march of time with its window to eternity.

By the end of the special *al-tarawiyah* prayers several hours later and after this visionary outpouring of sound and light, the inner heart, that inner sanctuary that is the spiritual counterpart to the physical cardiac heart, feels expanded, open, and full to bursting. All of the sacred symbolic images that the traditional literature uses in speaking about the capacity of the heart to contain the Divinity come to mind to describe the feeling upon completion of the *tarawiyah* prayers. If the heart is a cup, it is now filled to brimming; if it is a hidden cave, it is now filled with light; if it is a sacred crypt, its secret is now revealed; if it is the seal of the intelligence, it now sees with a clear certainty; if it is a holy niche, it is now cast in the glow of some higher emotion impossible to describe.

As Amr and I gathered up our individual prayer carpets and as the bulk of the dense crowd was beginning to thin out and leave, I suggested that we make our way now to the edge of the roof so that we could look down upon the inner plaza of the Grand Mosque. As we leaned over the railing and gazed down reflectively upon the scene below, I felt a great filling of soul and spirit. I remember the tradition that the sight of the Kaaba is a form of worship; I remind myself by saying the words; I hear Amr telling me the same and the mind registers the fact and concedes its truth. Yet the reality of the experience cannot be contained by words, cannot be fully comprehended by the mind, cannot be actively taken into the soul by the will. It simply happens without cognition or force. The two of us stand there as if hypnotized. We take in the sight; we behold the vision of the Kaaba *in situ*; we meet it face-to-face and in person. And a small miracle happens. We do not enter the house, not literally and not figuratively, instead the Kaaba enters us to become the Kaaba of the mind and heart, a spontaneous outpouring of pure emotion from the human to the Divine, the final emotion if you will from the human soul to the Spirit of God.

* * *

It may seem odd to report that I was counting the hours to my departure in the style of those who do not want something to end, this being perhaps a kind of prefiguration of the desire to experience eternity. In fact, there was very little time left in the holy places. My group had arrived in Makkah on Saturday afternoon after having spent two blessed days in Madinah. The *Umrah* rituals on Saturday were now complete; I had the full day of Sunday to spend in the Grand Mosque and I was scheduled to leave on Monday after the noon prayer to return to Abu Dhabi in the United Arab Emirates and take up my duties once again as a professor of academic writing. After the early morning prayer on Monday, I took advantage of a lull in the crowd and the protracted dawn, before the onslaught of the harsh desert sun, to make my "farewell" circumambulation (*tawaf*) around the Kaaba, this time alone among the vast multitude without the aid and support of my Egyptian friend Amr. To facilitate freer movement and because I had the leisure of time, I kept to the outer fringes of the circle this time, creating a longer circuit for myself, but far less tumult than the mayhem in the center closer in proximity to the house.

I will not repeat my experience of the *tawaf* again; only to say that it was as intense and personal as before, perhaps more so, now that I was on my own. This time, however, I kept to the periphery of the circular orbit rather than experience once again the tumult at the center of the populous storm of people. I experienced the same heightened awareness and the elevated "God consciousness." I witnessed once again the fervid devotion of the worshippers and the intense configuration of multi-national and multi-racial peoples. I noticed a heightened "military" and security presence inside the Grand Mosque and most notably in and around the Kaaba itself.

Standing on the wall of Ishmael[1] were three unarmed officers surveying the crowd. In Makkah, the city of peace and security, so identified in the Quran itself, I would have felt this presence incongruous if it weren't for the shattered reality of a very real threat of terrorism in the world today from which no place seems immune, not even the city of peace.

Because of commitments back in Abu Dhabi, about 14 members of our group had scheduled to return "early." Our Saudia flight was to leave on Monday evening at 6:00 PM. The rest of the 60 odd members of the group were to return the following Wednesday. One would not expect to make a commentary about the weather in Makkah, except perhaps to mention the intense heat experienced there for much of the year. On this mild mid-November Monday, however, the weather was notably "strange." According to Arabs in this part of the world, cloudy weather is "good" weather, while rain is considered a blessing. The sky was overcast with an eerie saffron glow and while there were bundles of angry-looking clouds moving quickly across the heavens, they looked as dry as ashes. The air was blustery and full of dust. As I sat in the mosque most of that morning reading the Quran, feeling transfixed by the presence of the Kaaba in my line of sight and melancholy at the thought of leaving the physical presence of the beloved Kaaba behind in a few hours, I could hear the force of the wind blowing through the vestibules and hallways of the Grand Mosque, shattering the serenity of the place with echoes of slamming doorways and rattling windows. I could see eddies of dust swirling like ghosts through the worshippers; but I did not care. Nothing mattered but the heightened feelings of spirituality I was experiencing at the moment. I would have time enough after the noontime prayer to come back down to earth and negotiate my way back into the ways of the world.

Indeed, the prayer came and went in a flash; its memory lingered and continues to linger in the mind as a sacred remembrance of the timeless and the eternal. I returned at once to the hotel, making my way out the back and up the stairs carved into the hill to the hotel

---

1. The graves of Ishmael and his mother Hajar are purportedly within this semi-circular wall.

overlooking the sacred enclosure. I needed to get my things and return immediately to the lobby to board the bus arranged for me and my companions scheduled to make our way on the hour's journey to the Jeddah airport in time enough to escape the worst of the weather and meet the heightened security and airport formalities in time enough for our 6:00 PM flight. I quickly gathered up my belongings and gifts: a few bottles of musk oil, a fragrance mentioned specifically in the Quran as a scent of the paradise and beloved by the Muslims especially at prayer time; a few prayer carpets, possibly made in China, but bought here in the holy city of Makkah and thus highly valued by my Muslim friends and colleagues, and some white skull caps, again highly treasured for their "Makkan" quality, for want of a better term.

When I returned to the lobby around 1:30 that afternoon, there was a great hubbub at the entrance of the hotel. Upon closer inspection, I discovered an unbelievable sight: The day had suddenly and paradoxically turned into night. I looked up at the sky disbelievingly, up and down the street, at the well-lit shops across the street, and the same sight greeted me in the form of an uncanny darkness. People were looking up at the sky wondering where the day had gone. It had the feeling of a total eclipse, for suddenly everyone behaved as if the person next to them were a long lost friend. Portentous events such as this have a mysterious way of making brothers out of perfect strangers. Within minutes, all speculation about the peculiar darkness was resolved when the heavens opened their floodgates. It began to rain sheets of streaming water, the lightning shattering the pitch-blackness of the daytime night, and the thunder rolling across the heavens in competition to the resounding roar of the falling rain on the metal rooftops of nearby shops. This was a storm to behold anywhere, not to mention in Makkah, where it nearly never rains and certainly never quite like this.

Porters ran through the rain toward the massive bus awaiting our passage to the Jeddah airport and unceremoniously threw the luggage stuffed with our precious Makkan gifts into the carriage hold. Grateful in this instance to be dressed simply and wearing plastic sandals, I gathered up my Pakistani pantaloons and ran for the security of the bus that promised to provide the perfect vantage point to view the spectacle of the storm. The other Emiratees of my group followed suit, including the *harem* (the women). Within minutes the doors of the bus were sealed shut and we were on our way. The inside of the bus was aglow with excitement; rain in these places is a rarity and the mood within the bus gave testimony to this unexpected downpour.

The querulous Saudi driver ground the massive touring bus into gear and with a lurch forward we began to make our way deeper into the thickening storm. The excitement inside the bus soon died down with the growing realization that we were heading into trouble. The women were sitting together in the back, the rest of us were interspersed randomly throughout the bus, while I was sitting alone with my thoughts. Undoubtedly, everyone was watching the incredible spectacle of the storm through the bay windows of the bus. Makkah is no easy town to negotiate through even under normal conditions. It is hilly with narrow, difficult-to-navigate streets that link up to main arteries leading out of the city. We eventually made our way through the rain up and down the side streets abreast of the Grand Mosque, all the while noticing the flash flood conditions quickly developing along the side streets and alleyways adjacent to the vicinity of the mosque, itself situated in the central valley of the city. We were making our way around the mosque and heading west to Jeddah, the port city situated on the Red Sea. The gathering floodwaters presumably also had the same idea presumably and were following the dictates of the topography of the land in which flowing waters find their natural course to the sea. In this instance, the gathering flood showed no mercy and made no concession to man, animal, or object as it followed its own natural tendencies and the dictates of its own violence. Within its turgid forces, the flood gathered unto itself everything in its path. I watched spellbound through the window of the bus as the cascading floodwaters gathered strength and rushed through the narrow byways and alleyways along the crevices of the hilly terrain down into the center of town.

As we advanced beyond the fringe of the mosque quarter, the cars alongside were coming into increasing difficulty. The main road was unwittingly receiving the floodwaters and becoming itself a raging torrent. I soon realized that this was going to get worse before it got better. I had visions of watching stories of flash floods on CNN in places like Bangladesh or the flood plains of the Amazon; but this was happening to me, now, here in the desert, in the middle of an arid zone, in Makkah of all places! Was I to be swept away a second time in this beloved city, this time literally? I was beginning to wonder as I sat on the edge of my seat looking out and clouding the window with my hot breath as floodwaters crept higher up the side of the bus.

I saw that the cars on the slip road and the side roads perpendicular to the main road were in trouble. Several on the hill above had been compromised and had washed aside into the gutter like abandoned toys. People were milling about on higher ground, standing in doorways with water up to their waists and looking out from second story windows at the cars below inundated with water. The bus itself made a brave attempt to forge its way through the amassing river, unnatural and diabolical as it all seemed. The cars adjacent to the bus, both on the road and off to the side, were becoming inundated by the floodwaters. The flow down from the Makkan hills was simply too much too soon, and the landscape simply could not accommodate the raging waters. This was quickly becoming a flash flood of monumental proportions.

Through it all, the massive bus, like a great ship at sea, coursed its way through the wild current and cresting waves that came crashing down against the side of the bus from the sidelong rush of water running down the cliffs. First one car, then a second, surged perpendicular to the curb out of their normal direction, the one slamming into the other as the torrential current of the waters crashed into the side door and window of the cars. Another came crashing by and stacked itself up against the gathering build up. The people inside were terrorized; it had all happened so quickly, and with no experience with such matters, they had suddenly become trapped. They couldn't very likely stay where they were and survive and they certainly couldn't leave the car at that point, for they would be swept away in the blink of an eye. I have no notion what happened to them. The huge bus passed them by, and the instant became an immediate memory of how destiny and the forces of nature can invade the serenity of the day.

One describes all this as if this flash flood happened in but a momentary flash. On the contrary, several hours had now passed by; we were still on the bus in the thick of the flood; we had only advanced perhaps a kilometer or two west of the Grand Mosque; torrential rains continued to inundate the area, and it seemed at that point that we could as well have been in no-man's land awash in a sea of swelling tide and not still in the heartland of Makkah in the shadow of the Kaaba. Traffic was stalled everywhere and many cars were fully compromised, even the four-wheel drives. At one point, as we slowly made our way forward along a main artery heading out of town, I noticed several police vehicles by the side of the road where a mini avalanche had occurred. Gallons of water had poured into the gap inundating a number of cars to the extent that you could only see the roofs of the cars surfacing above the waves. The subdued faces of those standing around the police car seemed to convey a sad message.

Only the scenic cruiser we were in continued without fail to advance through the encroaching deluge. The bus driver was having none of this trouble. He cursed heaven and earth, in addition to a multitude of drivers and cars that managed to get in the way of his forward movement. If he could not advance the bus, he turned left or right down a side street to find a way through the morass. When that did not work, he simply revved up the engine and careened across the central strip, almost losing an exhaust in the process. When all else failed, he simply drove down the wrong side of the road waving aside whatever vehicles were still left mobile along the way. The water at this point had reached well over the luggage area and was alarmingly approaching mid-way point, not far from the windows. Still, the driver cursed the weather and swore at the drivers in his way. His crude manner bordered on the humorous, while his insolence toward the weather and the road conditions gave the rest of us courage that we would get through this in one piece. Meanwhile, the engines continue to purr like a kitten; the indomitable bus and its spirited driver still continued to make way through the abandoned cars, the sludge, and the debris, not to mention the still raging waters of the flood.

After three more hours of persistent anxiety, the bus finally escaped from the inner confines of the city and made its way toward the outskirts of the town. The foreboding among the group of us inside the bus had died down, together with the floodwaters, and I noticed a developing party atmosphere along the sides of the road, where people were milling about splashing each other with water and dunking themselves. We were approaching the time of the sunset. We had been fasting throughout the entire ordeal and were still attempting to reach the airport in Jeddah, even though the plane was scheduled to leave in another 15 minutes time.

At the call to prayer, we were still marooned on the bus with nothing to eat. People on the roadside however realized our predicament and sprang into action. The door of the bus and several windows were opened and people threw small cartons of juice, bottles of mineral water, and little cartons stuffed with Makkan dates with which to break the fast. This spontaneous display of quick thinking and perception conveyed to me an intense feeling of camaraderie and brotherhood; to think that people by the side of the road had understood our predicament and come to the aid of a passing bus to feed its passengers, an experience comparable to the breaking of the fast in the Prophet's Mosque in Madinah in terms of power and impact.

At 7:30 that night, an hour and a half after the flight departure time, as we slowed down for security checks on the outskirts of the airport, a message came through on one of the cell phones of an Emiratee who I noticed had been making frantic calls to unknown places that the plane was being held for us, yet another example of the fluid nature that events can often take in the Arab world. An airline representative met us with a walkie-talkie in contact with the plane. Porters were on hand to receive the luggage, which was pulled from the hold of the bus along with the water and sludge that had been deposited by the floodwaters. We were rushed through the airport, our passports were unceremoniously stamped, and we were sent on our way without further delay. As I passed through security, a Saudi guard stopped me and asked where I was from. In the rush of it all, I was a little surprised. "America", I hesitatingly replied, unwilling to come out of my incognito status even for a friendly inquiry, for this is an era when the politics of a person's country can get them into trouble. The man surveyed my Pakistani cloth and roped-tired pantaloons and laughed aloud. "If you're American," he replied in Arabic, "then I'm from the other side of China." On that note, he waved me on with an expression of good-humored disbelief spreading generously across his face, and with the words *salam alaykum* (peace be with you), I was gone.

I wish I could report that from the plane I saw the great beacon of light emanating from the hallowed precinct of the Grand Mosque, rising heavenward as a visionary seal of my Makkan experience as I did when I first arrived in Madinah; but that was not meant to be. In compensation, I felt within my mind a translucent clarity after five days in the two cities of light and peace, while within my heart the smoldering embers continued to burn of this intense, spiritual sojourn that hopefully will linger a while to illuminate the shadows of my life within the latticework of passing time. This account has been written in remembrance of a unique and memorable visit to the two holy places of Islam, when the body, soul, and spirit of a man made a sacred journey to the very center of the earth, were swept away, and came back again to tell the tale.

www.ingramcontent.com/pod-product-compliance
Lightning Source LLC
Chambersburg PA
CBHW022016090426

42739CB00006BA/159